Culture, Power, and the State

Rural North China, 1900-1942

CULTURE, POWER, AND THE STATE

Rural North China, 1900-1942

Prasenjit Duara

Stanford University Press
Stanford, California

Stanford University Press
Stanford, California
© 1988 by the Board of Trustees of the
Leland Stanford Junior University
Printed in the United States of America
Original printing 1988
Last figure below indicates year of this printing:

00   99   98   97   96   95   94   93   92   91

CIP data appear at the end of the book

Published with the assistance of
China Publication Subventions

To the Memory of Judy Strauch

Acknowledgments

It is a pleasure for me to acknowledge the many people who have helped at various stages of this study. My intellectual debt to my teacher Philip Kuhn is far greater than that suggested by the abundant references to his published work in the study. Cynthia Brokaw, Paul Cohen, Al Dien, Philip Huang, Huang Chin-hsing, Lillian Li, Esther Morrison, Ramon Myers, Susan Naquin, Mary Rankin, Benjamin Schwartz, Judy Strauch, and Lyman Van Slyke gave of their time generously or with a minimum of arm-twisting. Harold Kahn, Elizabeth Perry, and Susan Mann suffered through repeated readings of the manuscript and came up with many helpful comments each time. John Ziemer has been an invaluable copy-editor.

Abroad, years ago, friends and teachers in Delhi firmly established the intellectual directions from which this study has emerged. The distances we have traveled since have always enriched our subsequent encounters. In Japan, Saeki Yuichi and Hamashita Takeshi made my affiliation with the Tōyō Bunka Kenkyūjo of Tokyo University very productive. Uchiyama Masao and the Mantetsu group in Tokyo, with whom I met regularly, pointed me to ways of using the Mantetsu materials with caution and profit; there was a sense of fulfillment when we met again four years later in Sand Well—one of the villages we had studied. My meetings with Ishida Hiroshi and the Mantetsu group in Kyoto were also fruitful.

Some of the material in this volume has appeared in my article "State-Involution: A Study of Local Finances in North China,

1911–1935," *Comparative Studies in Society and History* 29, no. 1 (1987), copyright © 1987 the Society for the Comparative Study of Society and History. I am grateful to Cambridge University Press for permission to reuse this material.

Various institutions have helped support the study. The Social Science Research Council funded my year in Japan and Taiwan. A Whiting fellowship allowed me to write the dissertation without distractions. A stint with the Center for Chinese Studies at the University of California, Berkeley, helped me begin revising the dissertation, and a two-year Mellon fellowship at Stanford University helped me complete the book. In the summer of 1986, a fellowship from George Mason University enabled me to visit some of the villages I was writing about in North China. The directors and staff of the Harvard-Yenching library, the East Asia Collection of the Hoover Institution, and the Library of Congress made their resources readily accessible to me. I am grateful for all of this support.

My family in Assam, who have had to patiently explain my arcane preoccupations in America to friends and relatives, now have the option of showing them the fruit of these ten long years. I hope the book can serve as an adequate measure of my deeply felt gratitude to them. And, finally, I owe much to Juliette, whose appearance in the last year of writing seemed to make its completion wonderfully easy.

P.D.

Contents

Maps and Figures

Tables

Culture, Power, and the State

Rural North China, 1900-1942

Introduction

[handwritten: how does he demonstrate state strengthening?]

Two broad historical processes distinguished the first half of the twentieth century from earlier times in rural China. The first was the series of economic changes stemming from the impact of the West. The second represented the efforts of the state to deepen and strengthen its command over rural society. This study focuses on the second process: the impact of state strengthening on the organization of power in rural North China.

Economic changes in the hinterland were felt only in the twentieth century when extensive railway construction facilitated closer economic integration than had heretofore been possible. Studies of the North China plain in the 1920s and 1930s have established the significance of this impact, particularly on areas where cash crops had traditionally been grown or had recently been introduced.[1] Yet if only because of the limited penetration of the world economy, this economic transformation was restricted in scale. The two most important works on the farm economy of North China, those of Ramon Myers and Philip Huang, both indicate that this economic penetration did not basically alter the small peasant economy characteristic of this region.[2]

In most of this area, however, state strengthening, which had also been taking place since the turn of the century, had, by the 1940s, greatly transformed local society—indeed, it had changed the links between politics, culture, and society in rural North China. The efforts of the Chinese state to penetrate local society more deeply began with the late Qing reforms (*xinzheng*) in the early 1900s. The subsequent, seemingly irreversible course of develop-

[handwritten: how does he define state?]

ment of this state resembled the process in early modern Europe that Charles Tilly and others have called "state making."[3] The similarities include the impulse toward bureaucratization and rationalization, the drive to increase revenues for both military and civilian purposes, the often violent resistance of local communities to this process of intrusion and extraction, and the effort by the state to form alliances with new elites to consolidate its power.

Tilly and his colleagues have carefully distinguished the phenomenon of state making from that of nation building. State making in eighteenth-century Europe was characterized by bureaucratization, penetration, differentiation, and consolidation of control; nation building refers to the creation of an identification of the citizen with the nation-state and an increase in his participation, commitment, and loyalty to it. They argue that in Europe the two processes were historically separate, with nation building generally occurring after the formation of strong nation-states.[4]

In this respect, the process of state making in 20th-century China may be distinguished from the earlier European process. In China, state making was proclaimed within the framework of nationalism and related ideas of modernization. Mary Wright was the first to observe how the dramatic outburst of anti-imperialist nationalist sentiment throughout China at the turn of the century propelled the imperial Qing state (1644–1911) on a course of state strengthening and modernization for the sake of national survival.[5] Ironically, the pressure to modernize also came more directly from imperialism. We see this pressure behind the late Qing reforms that introduced modern-style schools, fiscal innovations, new police and military organizations, administrative units, and local self-government institutions at all levels of society during the first decade of the 20th century. In part, the reforms resulted from the desire of influential foreign powers to see a modernizing government in China after the Boxer Rebellion. In part, they resulted from the Boxer indemnities levied by these powers on the bankrupt Qing government, which then had to strengthen its abilities to generate these funds from within the empire.[6] All historical forces seemed to converge on the necessity of building a modern state.

The Chinese pattern of state strengthening—closely interwoven with modernizing and nation-building goals—itself foreshadowed a process that would become increasingly common in the newly emergent states of the developing world in the twentieth century. Unlike the eighteenth-century European states, over time the responsibility for the progressive growth of national power, wealth, and modernity would become the responsibility of the new states. Studies of national constitutions from 1870 to 1970 show an expansion of claimed state authority over many sectors of social and economic life, as well as an expansion of the rights and duties of citizenship—all proclaimed within the ideology of the modern nation-state.[7] Furthermore, the effort to expand the power of the state in the developing world (measured, for instance, in terms of government revenue as a percentage of GNP) continued despite the frequent rapidity of changes in particular regimes.[8]*

In the early 20th century, regimes changed with amazing rapidity in the political landscape of China as well, at both the central and the regional levels. But in North China, one of the most important aspects of state strengthening—the ability to penetrate and absorb the resources of local society—continued more or less uninterrupted during the entire period. All regimes, whether central or regional, appeared to respect the administrative extensions of state power in local society because, whatever their goals, they assumed that these new administrative arrangements were the most convenient means of reaching rural communities.

The impact on rural communities of these new administrative arrangements was felt most sharply in the realm of village leadership and finances. Under the late Qing reforms, the village was required to develop a fiscal system to finance modern schools, administrative units, and defense organizations. Moreover, the state began increasingly to demand new taxes to finance indemnity payments and, later, the wars that characterized the first half of the 20th century. All the new taxes that the village had to pay, known collectively as *tankuan*, quickly began to outstrip the land tax severalfold. These taxes differed fundamentally from the land tax and other past taxes because they were levied by the state not on the individual or private property directly but on the village. The village, which was left to devise its own means of allocating these taxes, thus developed taxing rights and a budget. Additionally, its

---

*This is, incidentally, one reason why the Wallersteinian notion of weak states in peripheral regions is not really tenable in the postcolonial era.

importance was considerably enhanced as formal leadership structures, entrusted with the task of supervising such modernizing enterprises as schools and public works, as well as with the allocation and collection of tankuan, were formed at the village level. The historical and sociological concerns of this study converge in considerable measure on the changing status of this leadership during the first half of the 20th century.

The importance of local leadership at this time is readily apparent. The simultaneous demands of modernization, nation building, and state making presented enormous challenges to the emerging Chinese state. Moreover, these were superimposed conditions: they had not emerged organically from historical developments in Chinese society, as they had in Europe. All the more reason, then, that this state needed to develop a cadre of local leaders committed to achieving state goals. And it needed to develop this cadre faster than the rate at which its modernizing policies destroyed traditional forms of authority in society—if it was to avert a social crisis and a crisis of legitimacy.*

The purpose of this study is to probe this dynamic of state-society relations in China. In what ways were the power and authority of the old imperial state felt in rural society? How were they linked to the organization and representation of local authority? In what ways did state penetration transform the bases of local authority as it sought to create new forms of leadership and implement new policies? It is evident from these questions that we need to analyze the organization of power and authority in local society before we can understand the transformations wrought on it by the growth of state power.

The concept of power used here is unabashedly an eclectic one.[9] I use it to denote the ability of persons, groups, and institutions to obtain compliance through a variety of means. These include violence, coercion, persuasion, and the acceptance of their authority or legitimate power. Although the scope of this definition is rather catholic, the fact is that the relations of power are a component element, often invisible, of most social interactions. These

---

*Although I frequently use the language of modernization, I use it to refer to modernization as the ideology of the modern state—as an object of study, not as a tool of analysis.

relations of power exist in all domains of social life such as religion, politics, economics, kinship, and even friendship.

Scholars have tended to study what they intuitively sense to be the most significant of these "power-ful" domains in society, say property relations or politics. Rather than prejudge this issue, I examine the relations of power in all the major domains of rural social life. I try to show how the relations of power in these domains, for example, of religion or patronage, affected the exercise of public power in the countryside: the power that defined rights and obligations and regulated the distribution of resources in this society. Operationally, I examine the relations of power through institutions and networks that range from those that were subvillage in scope to those that enmeshed several rural settlements, all assimilated into a morphology of power I call the "cultural nexus of power."

This nexus was composed of hierarchical organizations and networks of informal relations that constantly intersected and interacted with one another. Hierarchical institutions, such as those of the market, kinship, religion, and water control, and networks, such as those between patrons and clients or among affines, provided a framework within which power and authority were exercised. The term "culture" in "cultural nexus" refers to the symbols and norms embedded in organizations that were meaningful to their members. These norms encoded religious beliefs, sentiments of reciprocity, kinship bonds, and the like, which were transmitted and sustained by the institutions and networks of the nexus. The affiliation of symbolic values to these organizations lent the nexus an authority, which enabled it to serve as an arena for the expression of legitimate leadership aspirations in local society. In other words, considerations of status, prestige, honor, and social responsibility, quite apart from the desire for material profit with which they may have been intertwined, were important motives for leadership within the nexus.

I elaborate on the idea of the cultural nexus in the first chapter. In it, and through the chapters on brokerage, lineages, religion, and patronage, I argue that not only local power structures but the imperial state itself had relied significantly on the cultural nexus to establish their authority among the rural communities of North China through at least the end of the 19th century. The fateful efforts of the 20th-century state to penetrate rural society through means outside the cultural nexus and to destroy parts of it would ultimately undermine this state itself.

The Sources

The core of my village-level research is drawn from the six-volume investigation of the North China plain conducted by the research bureau of the South Manchurian Railway Company (commonly abbreviated as Mantetsu) from 1940 to 1942. These volumes, which are mostly in Japanese, are called *Chūgoku nōson kankō chōsa* (Investigation of customs in Chinese villages; hereafter referred to as *CN*). Although these surveys contain information on many counties in Hebei and Shandong, the bulk of the materials deals with six villages in six different counties of the two provinces. These materials were also an important source of data for the two most significant works on the peasant economy of North China: Ramon Myers's *Chinese Peasant Economy: Agricultural Development in Hopei and Shantung, 1890–1949*, and Philip C. C. Huang's *Peasant Economy and Social Change in North China*. Huang, in particular, has dwelt at length on the problems of using these surveys and methods to overcome them. I refer readers especially interested in this issue to Chapter 2 of his book.

A major portion of the *CN* materials are interviews with peasant informants, who sometimes gave contradictory and unreliable testimony. As Mantetsu investigators Hatada Takashi and Konuma Tadashi informed me, this was partly because, as part of the colonizing government, the interviewers were not trusted in some places, and partly because of the eccentricities of individual informants (personal interviews, Tokyo 1981–82). Both Konuma and Hatada suggest that the best way to use these interview materials is extensively and intensively, rather than to scan them for occasional information.

In reading the six volumes, I devised certain methods to establish the accuracy of the information. Most of the interviews were conducted with a certain number of villagers, and the Japanese interviewers asked many of the same questions of the different people they interviewed. Consequently, by using the interview material extensively, I was able to cross-check the data with information from other informants. Close familiarity with the important informants through intensive reading, on the other hand, gave me an idea of the reliability of a particular informant. Furthermore, in some volumes as much as a third of the information is in the form of primary written sources. These include stele inscriptions, contracts, and records from the village level up to the county level. I have used these Chinese sources not only to reconstruct historical events but also to verify interview testimony. Using these tests allowed me to sift the information to gain an accurate picture of what was happening in the villages.

I have supplemented the *CN* materials with other surveys conducted by the South Manchurian Railway Company, studies by other Japanese scholars, and the ethnographies of rural North China written by such contemporaries as Sidney Gamble and Martin Yang.

For the study of the state, I have primarily used Chinese sources. These include government reports, compendiums of laws, and local gazetteers, as well as the writings of many contemporary observers, especially on the fiscal situation. By far the most valuable sources in this category have been the investigations of the scholars affiliated with the Economic Research Institute (Jingji yanjiusuo) at Nankai University, Tianjin, conducted in the 1920s and 1930s. Under the leadership of Fang Xianding, the institute produced a number of talented researchers, such as Feng Huade and Li Ling, who carried out researches in North China. I have found most useful their intensive investigations of the records and financial practices of the county and other lower-level units in Hebei. Judging from my exchanges with agricultural economists at the institute in the summer of 1986, it is clear that Nankai retains its status as a leading center of agricultural research in contemporary China.

Villages of the North China Plain

The known history of present-day rural communities of the North China plain goes back to the Yuan-Ming transition, in the late fourteenth century. Many of these villages were settled during the reign of the first Ming emperor, which brought to a close a dark era of warfare and depopulation in the region. After expelling the

Mongols, the Hongwu administration (1368–98) undertook massive land reclamation and resettlement efforts.[10] Temple stelae, gravestones, and genealogical fragments evidence the importance of the Yongle reign (1403–24) as a second period of resettlement. The origins of many villages can be traced to this second effort, which took place soon after the Yongle emperor, then the Prince of Yan, seized the throne from his nephew in Nanjing. At the conclusion of the civil war, which echoed the earlier devastation of North China by the Mongols, the Yongle emperor is said to have resettled the area with immigrants when he moved the capital to Beijing.[11] Based on the earliest founding dates of village temples, Yamagata Kanki's survey of 44 villages in 31 counties in Hebei and Shandong confirms that an overwhelming number of villages in the sample were established during these two reign periods.[12] Evidence from the *CN* villages also bears out this conclusion.[13]

As Arthur Smith wrote at the turn of the century, "Tradition reports that vast masses of people were collected in the city of Hung-tung Hsien in southern Shan-hsi, and thence distributed over the uncultivated wastes made by war. Certain it is that throughout great regions of the plain of northern China, the inhabitants have no other knowledge of their origin than that they came from that city."[14] Yamamoto Bin, a sometime *CN* investigator who conducted much independent ethnographic research in North China during the 1930s, also noticed that an overwhelming majority of Hebei villagers from all over the province claimed that their ancestors had hailed from Hongdong county in southern Shanxi. Fascinated by the legendary qualities of their claim and the reverence in which they held this alleged ancestral native place, Yamamoto undertook a special project to investigate the origins of the villages. His investigations led him to believe that the claim was not without some truth. From the records of Hongdong county, he verified that officials had mobilized large numbers of people in this area during the Yongle campaigns to resettle the various depopulated parts of North China. Later research indicates that during this period, the bulk of the resettled population was in fact brought in from the southern Shanxi prefectures of Zezhou and Lu'an.[15]

There was another phase of settlement during the early Qing, although it was considerably less important than that of the early Ming.[16] According to Yamagata, the Ming-Qing transition saw not so much the founding of new settlements but a general shake-up of the community composition of the villages. He traced the appearance of multi-surname villages in North China to this transition.[17] Be that as it may, the two periods of settlement represent the beginnings of an ascendant phase in the two Beijing-based developmental cycles of what G. William Skinner calls the North China macroregion. This phase saw the development of a complex and integrated regional economy, with a corresponding growth in population, and was followed by a declining phase marked by famine, epidemics, invasion, rebellion, and depopulation. As Skinner points out, the temporal rhythms of these cycles in the North China macroregion were closely associated with the rhythms of the dynastic cycle. Not only was this because imperial policies were most effective in the metropolitan macroregion, but because "North and Northwest China were far more vulnerable to foreign invasion than others, and . . . the devastation associated with interdynastic warfare over the dragon throne was invariably great in the metropolitan macroregion."[18]

This historical sketch of the area serves to highlight the manner in which the rise and decline of rural settlements in North China was closely linked to the fate of the imperial state. It would be fascinating to follow this link through the subsequent history of these villages, but that formidable project is outside the scope of this book. When we pick up the story again at the end of the imperial era, we see once more how the most vital areas of village life become deeply enmeshed in the ordering efforts of an intrusive state.

The six *CN* villages and other areas referred to in this work lie in Hebei (known as Zhili before the Nationalist takeover in 1928) and the parts of Shandong that lie in the North China plain (see Map 1). The pattern of agriculture and the institutional arrangements that were developed to exploit the soil to some extent reflected the economic geography of the region. The soil of the North China plain is a mixture of river-laid alluvium and wind-deposited loess. The average precipitation is dangerously low (21 inches a year) and droughts are common in May and June. Summer temperatures are high, rising to 100 degrees F; in winter temperatures frequently fall below 0 degrees F, with bitter cold winds.[19]

Because of the cold weather and low rainfall, little cultivation was possible during the winter months. In the early 20th century,

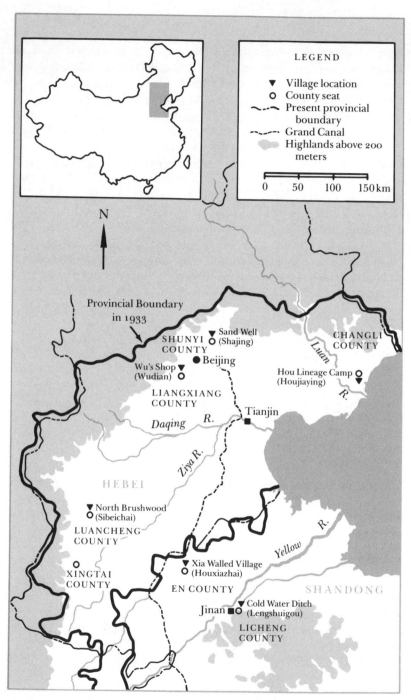

N

Provincial Boundary
in 1933

SHUNYI ○ ▼ Sand Well
COUNTY   (Shajing)

Wu's Shop ▼   ● Beijing
(Wudian) ○

LIANGXIANG
COUNTY

CHANGLI
COUNTY

Luan

Hou Lineage Camp ○
(Houjiaying)   ▼

R.

Daqing *R.*   ■ Tianjin

Ziya R.

HEBEI

▼ North Brushwood
○ (Sibeichai)

LUANCHENG
COUNTY

R.

○
XINGTAI
COUNTY

▼ Xia Walled Village
○ (Houxiazhai)

EN COUNTY

Yellow

SHANDONG

Jinan ■○
▼ Cold Water Ditch
   (Lengshuigou)

LICHENG
COUNTY

Map 1.   The Six *CN* Villages on the North China Plain. Adapted from P. Huang 1985: 36.

winter wheat was cultivated in southern Shandong, but in Hebei agriculture was limited to one crop a year or three harvests in two years. The leading spring-planted crop was sorghum, followed by millet. Cotton cultivation was found throughout, although there was a slight concentration in central and southern Hebei. In the summer, corn, sorghum, millet, soybeans, sweet potatoes, and peanuts were cultivated.[20]

One estimate of cultivated land for the entire North China plain put the average at 27 *mou* (4.5 acres) per farm family in the 1930s. The average figure for Hebei, Shandong, and Henan was 22 *mou* per farm household.[21] Both Myers and Huang accept the proportion of land cultivated by tenant farmers as only about 15 percent of all village land.[22] Thus in most but by no means all of Hebei and Shandong, landlord-tenant relations did not form the basis for village social arrangements. This is not to deny the existence of stratification within the village but simply to forewarn the reader that the relations of power in this society differ from those found in South and Central China, or in many other agrarian societies where tenancy forms the principal relation of production in the countryside.

The materials that I discuss are organized thematically, and at no point is all the information on each of the six principal *CN* villages presented in a single place. Since the reader may find it difficult to keep track of each village, I briefly introduce the six of them here. In the summer of 1986, I had the opportunity to visit two of these villages: Sand Well and Cold Water Ditch. Sand Well (Shajing) village is located in Shunyi county, approximately 30 kilometers north of Beijing and within a 15-minute walk of the county capital. Although I was treated with warm hospitality each time I visited Sand Well, I was struck by the absence of visible community life in the village, compared for instance, with the hustle and bustle of a village I visited in South China. Perhaps this is because large numbers of Sand Well's inhabitants worked in the nearby county capital. At any rate, Sand Well once had a flourishing community life, which we will see through the activities of its crop-watching and religious associations. Indeed, even as late as the 1940s, village leaders had fought determinedly to regain control over community temple lands. There is a story in the *CN* volumes that was retold to me by both *CN* interviewer Hatada

Takashi and by the octogenarian Zhang Rui, assistant headman of the village at the time of the *CN* survey (it is analyzed in Chapter 5 below and was also discussed by Philip Huang). Retelling it might help the reader identify Sand Well as a village with an active community life and a resourceful leadership. When Fan Baoshan, a local bully from neighboring Shimen village, conspired with the priest of the City God temple in the county seat to take over the village temple lands, village leaders initially felt powerless to challenge them. Then, in a moment of inspiration, they turned to their interviewer Hatada Takashi to plead their case for them. He did so, and they regained their lands. To this day, the older folk at Sand Well remember Hatada with fondness and gratitude.

Cold Water Ditch (Lengshuigou) is located in Licheng county in Shandong, not far from the provincial capital of Jinan. Now, as in the 1940s, it is an enormous and prosperous village. Before the end of the war, it had a population of 370 households—far greater than the average North China village of approximately 100 households. Until the early Republic, Cold Water Ditch had a flourishing religious life, eloquently testified to by the 25 or so temple stelae from the Qing period. Sadly for the historian, not one of these invaluable village "records" survives in the village today. Indeed, it is my impression that few such traditional materials survived the Cultural Revolution in the villages of North China.

A third village located close to a metropolitan center is Wu's Shop Village (Wudiancun) in Liangxiang county, south of Beijing. Lying in the path of armies on the way to the capital, it was constantly subjected to the depradations of wars that ravaged this area in the first half of the century—to the extent that Philip Huang calls this a "shell-shocked village." What little community life existed in this hapless and impoverished village at the beginning of the century centered mostly around temple festivals. But as if the terrors of war were not enough, religious authority in Wu's Shop Village held the promise of terrors beyond: a temple plaque recorded the stark words, written afresh every year, "So you, too, have come" (*Ni ye laile*). The villagers believed that the words suggested the inescapability of retribution since they would all have to confront the gods at the end of their alloted span.

Hou Lineage Camp (Houjiaying) in Changli county, northeast Hebei, is close to the Manchurian border. It benefited considerably from this proximity from the opening of Manchuria to Chinese sojourners and settlers until the 1930s, when the Japanese occupation prevented Chinese from traveling and conducting business in Manchuria. As its name suggests, the village was dominated by the Hou lineage and its several segments. The numerical preponderance of the Hous did not, however, ensure their continuing control of the village. As successful members of minority lineages returned from Manchuria and invested their wealth in the village, they increasingly came to challenge the hold of the founders of Hou Lineage Camp.

Houxiazhai in En county is in northwest Shandong. The Chinese names of this and the following village do not translate easily into English. Nor is there only one possible translation for either name. Rather than burden the reader with a complicated explanation, I have chosen to translate Houxiazhai as "the walled village (*zhai*) of the Xia family at the back" and abbreviate it as Xia Walled Village. En county is just north of the Yellow River, and the area has historically been subject to flooding, which has made its soil sandy and infertile. Xia Walled Village was certainly among the three poorer villages of the six *CN* villages. The fact that it was once a walled village suggests that historically it probably had to protect itself from bandits and other predators. We do know that in the 1920s it joined the militant Red Spear sectarians in the area to protect itself against widespread banditry. However, it is not religious associations but lineage organizations and rivalries that provide the clue to understanding the political dynamics of this village.

These factors also explain the polity of another poor village in the cotton-growing region of south-central Hebei—North Brushwood (Sibeichai; literally, "brushwood to the north of the temple") in Luancheng county. Lineage ideology was reportedly so strong here that during its banquets, the lineage was seated according to a distinct hierarchical pattern exemplifying the principles of patrilineal descent. The eldest of the most senior generation, or the lineage head, occupied the seat at the northern head of the table. Thereafter, each succeeding generation followed the other, and within the generation, each individual followed the other in decreasing order of age until the southern end of the table, which was occupied by the youngest member of the most junior generation.

From these sketches, we can isolate some characteristics along which the villages may be grouped (see Fig. 1). They may be

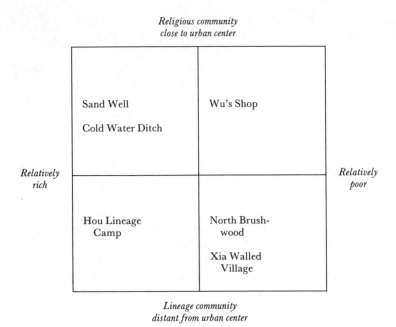

Fig. 1. The *CN* Villages

grouped (1) according to whether they were relatively well-off or poor; (2) according to whether religious or lineage principles formed the more important organizing principle of society; and (3) according to their relative distance from a major urban center. The last two characteristics are correlated: the religious-community villages are located near large urban centers, whereas the lineage-community villages are farther from such centers.

For ease of reference, the English and Chinese names of the six villages and the county in which each is located are presented below:

English translation	Chinese name	County
Sand Well	Shajing	Shunyi
Cold Water Ditch	Lengshuigou	Licheng
Wu's Shop Village	Wudiancun	Liangxiang
Hou Lineage Camp	Houjiaying	Changli
Xia Walled Village	Houxiazhai	En
North Brushwood	Sibeichai	Luancheng

One

The Cultural Nexus of Power

In *Rebellion and Its Enemies in Late Imperial China*, Philip Kuhn probed ways of distinguishing dynastic decline from the fall of a civilization in 19th-century China.[1] He concluded that although the imperial administration was disintegrating, the power of the local gentry, an important foundation of the old order, had by no means been undermined. In its time, this was a novel and powerful argument, not least because it rooted the analysis of the polity in the social order. The notion of the "cultural nexus of power" seeks to widen the framework for understanding the polity of a civilization still further—to encompass the realm of culture, especially popular culture. In so doing, I go beyond such obviously important but partial concepts as gentry society and Confucian ideology.

The cultural nexus formulation enables us to understand the imperial state, the gentry, and other social classes in late imperial China within a common frame of reference. It achieves this by grounding the analysis of culture and legitimacy within the organizational context in which power is wielded. In its organizational aspect, the cultural nexus serves as the framework that structures access to power and resources in local society. It also serves as the arena in which politics is contested and leadership developed in this society. Since its other roles rest on this organizational foundation, I consider this foundation first.

The cultural nexus integrates a variety of organizational systems and principles that shape the exercise of power in rural society. These include hierarchies of a segmentary or nested type, found, for instance, in the organization of lineages and markets. Hierarchies may be composed of territorial groupings whose membership is based on an ascriptive right, as in certain temple organizations; or they may be formed by voluntary associations, such as water-control or merchant associations. Also part of the nexus are informal networks of interpersonal relationships found, for example, between affines, patrons and clients, or religious teachers and disciples. Organizations may be inclusive or exclusive, single-purpose or multipurpose, and so on.

The point is that these principles cannot exhaustively be understood by a single overarching system, such as the marketing system or any other *system*. Rather, together they form an intersecting, seamless nexus stretching across the many particular boundaries of settlements and organizations. Thus, from an objective point of view, the nexus appears not to be a very useful construct. But its coherence lies within a subject-centered universe of power. Persons and groups who pursue public goals do so within it, and it is their reach within this nexus, and not a geographical zone or a particular hierarchical system, that defines the parameters of local politics and the perimeters of local society.

Organizations in North China were rarely fully isomorphic with each other. That is to say, it is hard to find both identical centers of coordination and identical spheres of jurisdiction among them. Rather, they were interlocked in various ways, including personal relationships in informal networks that acted as the weft linking key points in these organizations. Power in local society tended to be concentrated at the densest points of interaction—the nodes of greatest coordination within the nexus.

From a historical point of view, these nodes of coordination constantly shifted over time, moving from within the village to outside of it, or gathered density, sometimes concentrating at one point, such as the village or market town, and sometimes becoming much more widely diffused. I believe that the changes of the 20th century reshuffled the points of coordination. One important result of this reshuffling was the rise, for the first time in the recent history of China, and the subsequent decline of the village as a nodal unit of great significance. Below, I examine how these developments were in no small measure bound up with the fiscal and political imperatives of state penetration.

The Cultural Nexus and the Marketing System

One can scarcely venture far into the study of local society without encountering the magisterial work of G. William Skinner on marketing systems. At first sight, the idea of the cultural nexus appears to represent a step backward in our understanding of this society. If local social systems can be explained by the principles governing the marketing system, as Skinner initially claimed, then why encumber an elegant model with complications? In fact, however, as Skinner himself later acknowledged, there is no isomorphism between the marketing system and the social system. In *The City in Late Imperial China*, he wrote:

Local organization above the village is a vastly complex subject. It is clear from work published in the last decade that the internal structure of the standard marketing system was more variegated and interesting than my 1964 article began to suggest. Extravillage local systems below the level of the standard marketing community were variously structured by higher-order lineages, irrigation societies, crop-watching societies, politico-ritual societies . . . and the jurisdictions of particular deities and temples; many if not most were multipurpose sodalities manifesting more than one organizing principle.[2]

My purpose, therefore, is not to flog a dead horse. Instead, I hope to salvage the most valuable insights of the marketing system model and rework them into the cultural nexus formulation. In the analysis of marriage networks and irrigation associations in this chapter, I demonstrate two different ways in which the marketing system was assimilated within the cultural nexus; and throughout the book, I indicate ways in which this system was articulated with other organizational systems in the nexus. I begin by looking briefly at the role of markets in the villages of the *CN* survey, particularly in the 1930s and 1940s.

Most of the *CN* villages were located near the county capital, which also served as their market town. Consequently, they were oriented to a larger marketing center—usually an intermediate market, rather than the standard markets. A notable exception to this was Hou Lineage Camp, in Changli county, Hebei, whose principal market was Nijing, a standard market that also became the headquarters of the administrative village in 1940–41. Villagers mostly frequented this market, which operated on a five-day cycle, but they also participated in the market of the county capital located about 10 kilometers away (1 km = 2 *li*).[3] Xia Walled Village in En county, Shandong, was also oriented to a standard market town before the Japanese invasion of 1937. Subsequently, its market was shifted to the county capital,[4] as part of an effort by the Japanese to acquire greater control over markets by limiting their numbers to larger centers.

County capitals often corresponded to intermediate or central marketing centers commanding an area with a radius of 7 to 10 kilometers. This included as many as 10,000 people from 30 or 40 villages. These centers also functioned as standard markets on certain days when villagers participated from a more restricted area of about 2.5 kilometers.[5] Unlike the standard marketing area studied by Skinner in Sichuan, the standard marketing areas in North China varied considerably in size. In Luancheng county, Hebei, marketing areas were said to comprise as few as 3 and as many as 20 or more villages.[6]

Markets were most important for villagers as places to buy and sell products and to acquire credit. Since the data from the *CN* villages do not make it possible to quantify the actual amounts of peasant produce marketed, I limit my comments to a few impressionistic statements on the marketing process. Although there had been a discernible increase in the number of families growing commercial crops and in the acreage devoted to commercial crops since the late Qing, notably of cotton,[7] agriculture was still basically subsistence oriented. In the case of cotton, evidence from North Brushwood and Wu's Shop Village in Hebei suggests that peasants marketed their surplus cotton only after satisfying their domestic needs for clothes and shoes.[8] In the case of food grains, only high-value crops such as wheat and rice, grown mostly in small quantities, were sold in the markets. As with cotton, they were sold only after a certain amount had been set aside for domestic consumption, chiefly for use during the New Year festivities. Sorghum and corn were consumed at home, but for most families in the villages the amounts available for consumption were insufficient. They often bought food grains with the proceeds from the sale of high-value crops or took loans to tide themselves over the year.[9] Even in one of the most prosperous villages of the survey, Hou Lineage Camp in Hebei, where most of the crops produced were consumed at home, only six of the 114 families did not buy food in the market in any year.[10] Thus, for the most part, the subsistence orientation of villagers was modified by having to turn to the market during periods of shortage.

Aside from periodic purchases of food grains, villagers also bought oil, agricultural implements, and, occasionally, cloth. But these were not always bought at the market towns. Some villages, like Xia Walled Village and Cold Water Ditch in Shandong, had stores in the village where the residents bought many of their daily necessities. Villagers also bought these goods from itinerant peddlers who made the rounds of the villages. Moreover, items like agricultural implements and cattle were bought at temple fairs, sometimes held in distant parts of the county.[11]

Because of the greater availability of capital at the marketing center, it was an important source of credit. This was especially so for poorer villages like North Brushwood, where the financial grip of the moneylending landlords living in the market increased through the 20th century (see Chapter 6). In Sand Well, too, it was claimed that in any year, eight or nine of the 70 families borrowed from the market, and four or five borrowed from families within the village.[12] However, in others like Xia Walled Village and Cold Water Ditch, a greater portion of the credit was generated from within the village itself.[13] In Wu's Shop Village, few people received any credit since they were so impoverished. Informants stated that in the late Qing eight or ten households had received loans from the market, but that hardly any did so by the 1930s. Since a great deal of land had been sold outright to outsiders, credit was not easily available because villagers could not provide collateral.[14]

Thus the market was not the only important source of credit. Furthermore, in many cases even when villagers received credit from the market town, the store supplying the loan was managed by a resident of the village. This was the case in Sand Well and Cold Water Ditch.[15] Other services provided in the market also suggest the continuing importance of village ties, so strongly emphasized by Philip Huang. Village contacts were important as middlemen in the acquisition of credit and in the market for land and land use.[16] In selling their produce, villagers were expected to use the services of a licensed middleman (*yahang* or *jingji*), who charged a commis sion for his mediation. In some villages like Wu's Shop and North

Brushwood, villagers approached only those middlemen from their own village.[17] It appears that the relations of the villager to the market did not develop at the expense of his ties within the village but may even have reinforced these ties as he used them to improve his position in the market.

I have attempted to establish that the market alone did not dominate the commercial life of rural folk; village ties were important in the provision of some services, as well as in facilitating actual transactions in the market. From the perspective of the cultural nexus, it was the interplay between market relationships and village ties that shaped rural economic transactions. But the nexus formulation goes still further; it shows that even together the village and market were unable to secure all the social and economic needs of the villager. Below, I look at a range of extra-village ties; none is fully subsumed by the marketing system, but neither can any be understood apart from its interactions with the marketing hierarchy.

A Case Study: Marriage Networks

In an effort to demonstrate that the marketing system also formed a social system, Skinner showed that the standard marketing area tended to be endogamous in Sichuan. Daughters-in-law were usually taken from within the standard marketing community. He demonstrated this by showing how marriage brokers operated from the market town.[18] Data on marriage networks from two *CN* villages reveal that the marketing system model is only partially able to explain these materials. We have to look as well to other kinds of relationships in the cultural nexus to appreciate the full significance of marriage networks.

There are two sets of marriage data for Wu's Shop Village in Liangxiang county, Hebei, near Beijing. One set is derived from two informants who provided the names of villages from which their lineages had received brides. This sample includes 12 villages supplying 19 brides.[19] The second sample is a list of affines contributing money to a funeral.[20] Together the two sets consist of a total of 24 villages housing 75 affinal families. Two villages housing four affines could not be found on the map and were thus excluded from the analysis.

Another set of data is from North Brushwood in Luancheng county in Hebei.[21] In this village, 17 from a sample of 180 brides were taken from the village itself. However, since we are interested in extra-village marriage networks, only the remaining 163 brides, drawn from 49 villages and towns within the county, are considered below. These brides were distributed among grooms from four lineages in North Brushwood, but an overwhelming number were married to the largest lineage, the Hao.

From the data on the distances of the villages to the market town, it appears that the bulk of the villages supplying brides were located within a five-kilometer radius of the market town. Thus, it is entirely possible that these villages were located within the marketing area and the relationship between the two was mediated through the marketing center. However, both North Brushwood and Wu's Shop are relatively close to their market towns, being 2.0 and 1.5 kilometers distant, respectively. Moreover, most brides were expected to come from villages within walking distance of those they married into. Thus the evidence can also be interpreted to suggest that the bride-giving village may have belonged to a sphere of the bride-receiving village organized independently of the marketing system, based, for instance, on the time needed to walk to these villages or on the existence of prior affinal relations.

One test to determine the sphere to which the villages belonged involves looking at bride-giving villages outside the marketing area. Were the bride-receiving villages obtaining large numbers of brides from villages outside their marketing area? A piece of evidence supporting the hypothesis that the villages were located in the market system is that in Luancheng county, only one of the 13 villages that sent out more than five brides (this group sent a total of 94 out of 163 brides to North Brushwood) was outside the five-kilometer range of the market.[22]

A stronger test is to see whether most of the bride-giving villages were closer to the bride-receiving villages or to the market town. If a substantially larger proportion of the bride-giving villages were located in areas closer to the receiving village than to the marketing center, then we can hypothesize that the market was not of central importance to this network and that distances between villages formed the crucial variable. In Fig. 2, I plot the distance of bride-giving villages to the bride-receiving village, as well as to the

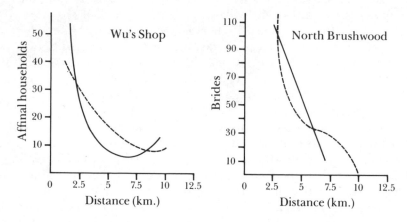

Fig.2. Marriage Networks in Wu's Shop and North Brushwood. Distances are the distance of the bride-giving village from (a) Wu's Shop and North Brushwood (solid line) and (b) the marketing center of the bride-receiving village (dashed line).

marketing center of the bride-receiving village in the two counties.

The data presented in Fig. 2 show that differences in distances did exist but were not so great as to prove one point or the other. In Liangxiang county, where Wu's Shop is located, 55 villages with affinal relatives were within a five-kilometer radius of the market, whereas 60 such villages were within a five-kilometer radius of the village.[23] In Luancheng county, 141 brides were drawn from a five-kilometer radius of Luancheng market, and 157 were drawn from within a five-kilometer radius of North Brushwood. A similar picture emerges when the radius is reduced in the latter case: 106 brides were drawn from a 2.5-kilometer radius of the market town and 100 from within the same radius of North Brushwood.[24] Consequently, although the data do not give definite answers, they certainly do not disprove the claim made by Skinner that the marketing area tended to be endogamous.

However, even if it is true that marriage networks were contained within the marketing *area*, there is reason to believe that the marketing *center* was not necessarily, or even often, the place where the marriage match was determined. Affines and friends located in the two villages of the parties seeking marriage partners were most often the people who effected the match. Village informants repeatedly claimed that their affines or relatives of their friends played the role of go-between by finding a bride in the village in which they resided. Ishida Hiroshi, who has also interpreted the Luancheng data, has compiled 20 cases in which the relationship of the go-between to the marriage partners is recorded. In 13 of these cases, the go-between was an affinal relative of one of the parties, and in only one of these cases was the match effected through a connection in the marketing center. The remaining 7 go-betweens were either friends, relatives of fellow villagers, or other acquaintances who linked the two villages directly.[25] Moreover, in Hou Lineage Camp, Changli county, informants claimed that villagers received many of their brides from the village of Xinjinbao because they had many affines there among the Xing and Ju lineages.[26]

Thus, the theoretical model of the marketing system is only partially relevant to an understanding of marriage networks. The marketing area was important in delimiting the boundaries of marriage networks and the accompanying social links, but the actual layout of these networks was quite autonomous of the functioning of the marketing center. This kind of relationship between a network and the marketing area represents one way in which organizations were linked in the nexus—by the partial or complete overlap of the spheres of jurisdiction of organizations. Irrigation communities exhibit another type of linkage: organizations share a common coordinating center, but not common jurisdictions (see below).

What role did affinal networks play in the cultural nexus? In North China, affinal networks worked in modest ways to secure the everyday livelihood of rural people. The role of middlemen in customary law illustrates the importance of affines in securing contracts, whether for loans or land tenure or the sale of land (see Chapter 6). Moreover, the affine was someone to whose village one could move when crisis struck. Generally, these relationships facilitated access to resources in rural society, often by linking ordinary families to more formal and powerful organizations such as lineages and administrative hierarchies. In so doing, these networks joined different types of organizations through interpersonal relationships and thus forged yet another means of integrating the nexus.

As ties that functioned relatively autonomously from the market, affinal and other similar networks broaden our understanding of how rural people functioned during periods of disruption when village-market relations weakened. The enduring quality of these networks, which bypassed the market, was especially crucial during such periods when resources within the village were insufficient to support life. Just as commercial relations with the market reinforced several bonds within the village, so, too, direct relations between villages, which may initially have been formed in the marketing center, assumed a life of their own and had a significance that our present understanding of marketing relations may not let us appreciate.

Culture, Legitimacy, and the Late Qing State

As mentioned above, the term "culture" in "cultural nexus" refers to the symbols and norms embedded in networks and organizations. These norms and symbols encode religious beliefs, feelings of reciprocity, kinship bonds, and similar sentiments that are often deeply held by, and often deeply hold, the people participating in the organizations. These symbolic values lend the nexus an authority and respectability that in turn motivate those concerned with social responsibilities, status, and prestige—as distinct from the material gains with which these concerns may be intertwined—to seek leadership within the nexus.

Thus leadership in local society was articulated through an institutional framework suffused with shared symbolic values. But the overtly consensual character of these cultural values masked how they were produced and used in society. This subtle and complex process continuously involved competition, accommodation, and adjustment of perceptions and interests among different social groups, including the state. Thus, it was not only because the nexus structured access to resources, but because affective symbols embedded in it worked to legitimate authority in local society, that it became an arena of intense competition—a competition over the use of consensual, authoritative values to serve particular needs and interests.

How, one might ask, if these symbols were used to advance sectional or individual interests, could they still generate consensus about legitimacy? Much of the discussion of the cultural nexus is designed to address this question, but from the outset, it is clear that much of the answer lies in the medium itself. Unlike material resources, symbolic ones are plastic, capable of being molded and manipulated even for opposing goals, while still retaining their conative power—the power to motivate, inspire, and impel. Throughout this book, I focus on the specific conditions and circumstances accompanying such multiple uses of symbols. The discussion of ritual hierarchies among irrigation communities in this chapter illustrates how the authority of the Dragon God, Longwang, worked to maintain the overall stability of the system even as it permitted the pursuit of various sectional interests.

The competition over the symbols of legitimate authority took place not only among contenders within local society but also with outsiders such as the imperial state. In this way, the nexus became a channel through which rural settlements came to be linked to the outside world and a means through which agencies such as the state reached into rural society. By utilizing these channels, the imperial state sought to partake of the nimbus of authority that surrounded them. As shown in later chapters, this state did not always find it easy to direct the normative materials in the nexus toward its own interests and often had to struggle to inscribe its own hegemony on popular symbols.

The reason for this is that not all organizations and symbols in the nexus worked to legitimate the orthodox order. Many, though illegitimate in the eyes of orthodoxy, were perfectly legitimate to the heterodox. The nexus thus enables us to understand the creation of legitimately acknowledged, though not necessarily legally or formally authorized, leadership. Nonetheless, I believe that the Qing state was moderately successful in converting much of the nexus into a sprawling infrastructure of popular orthodoxy that legitimated the imperial order until the end of the 19th century. No doubt, it was able to do this with the help of upwardly mobile rural elites for whom this conversion process reinforced the role of the nexus in legitimating their leadership.

This way of looking at state-society relations acknowledges the centrality of culture in this relationship. When we consider culture, it is simply not enough to look at Confucianism, the gentry, or gentry-dominated institutions. The state used various channels, such as corporate merchant groups, temple communities, myths, and other symbolic resources embedded in popular culture to reach into local communities. The cultural nexus of power seeks to highlight this multiplicity of modes through which the state dealt with these communities.

Case Study: Irrigation Communities in Xingtai Prefecture, Hebei

The following study of irrigation communities in the 19th century is designed to illustrate how the cultural nexus brought the imperial state and local communities together within a common framework of authority. These communities were located in Xingtai prefecture at the foothills of the Taihang mountains in southern Hebei. The total irrigated area of Hebei during this time did not exceed 15 percent of the cultivable acreage, and so the particular institutional complex to be found here was certainly not typical. But many of the same organizational forms are encountered throughout this study, and everywhere in China: functional, ritual, political, and economic hierarchies, gentry networks and the imperial administration, all constantly acting on each other to shape the drama of local politics. The extraordinarily rich *CN* materials from Xingtai are so focused on local politics—of water control in this case—that when combined with the gazetteer information on the wider society, they provide an ideal opportunity to see the cultural nexus in motion.[27]

The rivers that irrigated the eastern part of Xingtai county and the neighboring counties of Ren, Nanhe, Pingxiang, and Shahe are called Oxtail (Niuwei) and Hundred Springs (Baiquan) (see Map 2). Several groundwater springs fed into these rivers, the most important of which was the Hundred Springs (Baiquan), which is to be distinguished from the river of the same name. Peasants built dikes and sluices from these rivers and springs to irrigate their fields for the cultivation of rice and other crops. Most of these irrigation canals were established in the 16th century or during a second phase of rebuilding in the Yongzheng period in the 1720s and 1730s.[28]

The most conspicuous unit of the irrigation system in Xingtai was the *zha*—a metonym for the association of water users derived from the word for sluice gate. These groupings, which I call "gate associations," incorporated members from two to ten villages and controlled the distribution of water shares in the system. But these were not the only units in the irrigation system that managed and manipulated water resources. Rather, there was a hierarchy of organizational levels, all the way from the family to small groups to gate associations to alliances of gate associations and finally to the drainage basin of the river—the maximal unit. Water-using families responded to the varying circumstances of scarcity and the need for cooperation by segmenting or combining at these different levels or, in other words, by a constant process of fission and fusion along the hierarchy.

The hierarchy of irrigation communities was superimposed on a hierarchy of village and market settlements. The two hierarchies, however, were not identical. Gate associations were not coextensive with the village because the associations were larger than the village. Moreover, not all village residents were members of the association. Nonetheless, there were certain important structural connections between the gate association and the settlements. The managers of the association (*xiaojia*) were often representatives of a specific village. For instance, a manager of the Universal Salvation (Puji) Association always came from Zhang Village.[29] In other words, although the village as a whole was not often a recognizable unit in the irrigation hierarchy (except perhaps in the Hundred Springs Association), nonetheless representation of fellow villagers in an association meant that the political resources of the village could be mobilized within the association.

This is particularly observable in the case of certain villages within the association that were more influential than others. Sometimes a locational advantage may have initially caused these villages to become dominant, but once dominant, they invariably used their organizational resources to preserve this dominance over other villages. In the southeast section of the fifth ward of Xingtai county, there were nine villages of the loosely organized Hundred Springs Association. One of these villages, Kong Bridge (Kongqiao), was located at the fork of three canals, which gave it a position of great strategic importance vis-à-vis the villages dependent on these canals further downstream. In 1851, under the pretext that water rights had become extremely confused, Kong

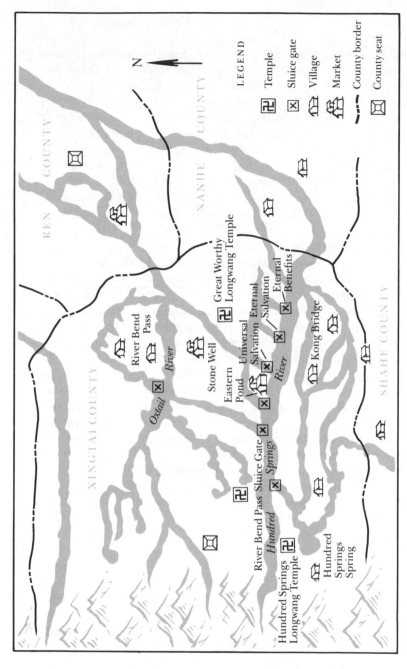

Map 2. Irrigated Regions in Xingtai and Neighboring Counties. Redrawn from *Xingtai xianzhi* 1905: 1.12.

Bridge set up a more or less independent organization, the He-koushe (literally, River Mouth Society), which became a property-owning body and engaged in land transactions. It also had an elaborate structure consisting of 17 officials, many of whom were village leaders. The frequent references in the records and plaques to conflicts between Kong Bridge and other villages suggest that Kong Bridge developed the organization to strengthen its position over its less happily located neighbors.[30]

By and large, however, few villages developed their own water-controlling units. Few villages in North China had all the organizational resources to dominate even a single association. The kind of settlement that did possess the economic and political resources to play this role was the market town. By identifying themselves with the organizational core of the association, the leaders of these towns were able to exercise a dominating influence on the association. Two examples are the two market towns of the region, Eastern Pond (Dongwang) in the Eastern Pond Association and Stone Well (Shijing) in the Universal Salvation Association. In Eastern Pond, the headman of the gate association was appointed by the market headman.[31] By the 20th century, the relatively powerful governments of both market towns played an important role in the finances of their respective associations. In Eastern Pond, when the association ran a deficit, the town government made it up and levied a tax on the residents. In Stone Well, members of the association paid their dues through the town government.[32]

Market towns and strong villages were able to bring to bear the organizational resources of their communities to dominate the associations. In this way, the leadership structure of the irrigation communities was able to exercise a fairly tight control to ensure internal stability and external protection. In fact, this kind of sharing of a common coordinating center—between the market and the gate association—was a widespread way of linking different hierarchical systems in the nexus. But, as could be expected of the nexus, even though the market town exercised an important influence on the power structure of the association, the irrigation hierarchy was not subsumed by the marketing system. The marketing area and the principles of the marketing system were not particularly relevant to the interactions of gate associations.

For purposes of water utilization, the relevant territorial system was not the marketing system, but the systems defined by the three drainage basins of the rivers supplying the sluices. These systems determined or delimited the spread of alliances among water-control organizations in the region. The first system used the waters emerging from the groundwater spring called Hundred Springs, which ultimately fed the Hundred Springs River. The second system was located north of the Hundred Springs River and used the water of this river. The third system was a little more complicated. It was called the River Bend Pass (Guanwan) Association and was composed of one large gate association in Xingtai county. Whereas most of its villages were located north of Oxtail River and used the water from this river, one of its sluice gates was located on Hundred Springs River several kilometers south of the villages and east of Eastern Pond Association in the second system. Thus it was part of the drainage basins of two rivers, though most of its water came from Oxtail River to the north.

Naturally, the drainage basins of the three river systems not only did not follow the boundaries of the marketing area, they also did not follow the boundaries of the county's administrative system. The drainage basin of the Oxtail River included a number of gate associations in Ren county; that of Hundred Springs included those in Nanhe county; and the groundwater spring of Hundred Springs fed canals that irrigated lands in Shahe county. Although this fact does not really deny the significance of the political boundary, it does suggest that as far as water control was concerned, the drainage basin was the self-sufficient region.

Conflicts, coalitions, and cooperation typically occurred within the drainage basin. The sources mention only one instance of conflict between groups of two different river systems. This concerned the particular canal in the River Bend Pass Association that shared the drainage basin of the Hundred Springs River, the second system. The case had to be resolved by the county magistrate. The stele recording the incident states that it was a dispute between the River Bend Pass Association and the seven associations of the Hundred Springs River drainage basin, which included two associations from Nanhe county—thus referring to the two drainage systems as the parties to the dispute.[33]

Examples of cooperation within the drainage basin come readily from the Hundred Springs River system. All the gate associations here got together once a year in order to dredge the Hundred Springs River and repair its dikes and bridges. The gate associations of both counties that shared the waters contributed equal amounts of labor and money irrespective of the actual volume of water they used. A conference discussing these matters was held in the third month at Eastern Pond market, which was attended by leaders from as far as the People's Salvation (Jimin) Association in Nanhe country.[34]

Running roughly parallel to the irrigation hierarchy was a ritual hierarchy of temples to the Dragon God of rivers and rain, Longwang. Not only did each village have a Longwang temple but each gate association also had a Longwang temple or its own Longwang deity in a Longwang temple. On several occasions—for example, the fifteenth day of the second lunar month when the new leadership of the association was selected, the birthday of Longwang, the end of the year, or during periods of drought—the leaders of the association worshiped the deity. They provided offerings, burned incense, and subsequently, feasted together.[35]

This religious dimension of irrigation communities is perhaps one of their most nearly universal features in China. I have come across temples to tutelary gods of irrigation communities in studying such associations in Chahar, Inner Mongolia, Shaanxi, Henan, Taiwan, and the New Territories.[36] The following exchange, reported from Changli county, is a simple cosmological statement about the powers of Longwang:

Q: How was heaven created?
A: I am not sure, but they say it was created by the Jade Emperor.
Q: What about earth and man?
A: I do not know.
Q: Why does man live?
A: Because he eats.
Q: But then why does he die when he gets old?
A: The years of a man's life are predetermined by the Jade Emperor. One cannot live beyond that.
Q: What about plants?
A: They exist because of earth and rainwater.
Q: How so?
A: Because they can borrow their power.
Q: Does rainwater have power?

A: Yes.

Q: Who gives it power?

A: Rain is created by the Jade Emperor's subordinate, Longwang. The rain contains Longwang's power.

Q: Why does Longwang make it rain?

A: Rain is the source of the ten thousand things. Without it man cannot live. In the end, he creates rain to save humanity.

Q: When rainwater has not yet touched the earth, who does it belong to?

A: Even though it was created at the command of the Jade Emperor, since it was actually made by Longwang, it belongs to him.

Q: Does it still belong to Longwang once it touches the earth?

A: Earth and water are public resources [*weigong*].[37]

The ceremonies and rituals that sacralized the gate association constituted it as a moral community in a particularly powerful way. This is because a single act of disobedience, expressed, for instance, in the sale of individual water rights, threatened the entire apparatus of coordination and control essential to the system in a more radical way than it did other communities. It is thus hardly surprising to find awesome representations of "huge coiled dragons" in Longwang temples in Chahar (now in Hebei) "tearing to pieces the bodies of evil doers"[38] and to observe in other irrigation communities, the practice of offenders' atoning for their crimes by making offerings to the Dragon God.[39] The Longwang temple was not only a locus of identity, but of authority as well.

But just as the meaning of a ritual is transformed by changes in its historical context, so too the dynamic process of fusion and fission altered the function of the temple ceremony in Xingtai at different levels in the hierarchy. Since the ritual order paralleled the hierarchy of irrigation communities, ceremonies not only fulfilled a communitarian ideal but also facilitated the pursuit of competitive urges, thereby giving the system an ingenious flexibility.

In the Hundred Springs Association, probably the most loosely formed of the gate associations, water users from the nine villages made their offerings at the Longwang temple of the association. This temple was located by the Hundred Springs Spring, which was said to house Longwang's mother. All nine villages of this association met together on the day of Longwang's birthday but performed their ceremonies in units of two and three villages. Later, when the leaders feasted, they separated by village.[40] The ceremony expressed the flexible nature of the organization with its nested identities of village, the subgroup, and the association. Although the entire association was a unit of cooperation in managing water, historically all three levels had been operative in the competition for water: single villages had fought with their neighbors, small groups with other small groups, and associations with associations. The temple and the ceremony thus embodied the principles of cooperation, as well as segmentation and recombination—the strategies employed in the competition for water.

The same feature was found at higher levels. For instance, there was a large temple to Longwang at Great Worthy (Daxian) village. On the fifteenth day of the second lunar month, the leaders of the three gate associations in the neighborhood, Eternal Benefits (Yongli), Eternal Salvation (Yongji), and Universal Salvation conferred about their work and performed their ritual duties at the temple. Subsequently, the leaders of each association ate separately. Earlier, when the associations had just been formed, there had been endless conflicts between them and their common enemy, Eastern Pond, further upstream.[41] The powerful Eastern Pond Association was centered in a market town and claimed superior rights to these waters because it had been formed before any of the others.[42] It did not perform its regular ceremonies at the Great Worthy Longwang Temple. An informant from Eastern Pond said that this was because the "Great Worthy Longwang's jurisdiction extends over the waters of the gate associations in the downstream area. Even if one of our villages were to worship there, it would do no good. Moreover, this village has no connection with their Longwang." Incidentally, the Eastern Pond Association, which also shared the waters of another system, patronized two Longwang temples other than its own and sent the image of its deity for periodic reconsecration at the ceremony of one of them.[43]

Thus the ceremony of the three associations in the Great Worthy Longwang Temple, I believe, symbolized both their autonomy as individual units as well as the coalition formed to combat their superior competitors, such as the Eastern Pond Association. The close relationship of these three associations was evident even in the 20th century. And inevitably, they also fought on several occasions with each other.[44]

The Great Worthy Longwang Temple served as the ritual center not only for the three gate associations but, on another occasion, for a much larger area encompassing the drainage basin of the Hundred Springs River. On the first day of the seventh lunar month, the leaders of the eight associations in the two counties that shared the drainage basin and cooperated in dredging the river got together and made offerings at the Longwang temple at Great Worthy village. In 1853 contributions for the repair of the temple came from a wide area, including Nanhe and Shahe counties.[45] In such cases, the temple serving as the ceremonial center of the gate associations over such a wide area cannot be understood as a focal point of coalition strategies. Rather, it functioned to bring together potentially competitive groups to cooperate for their collective survival.

The nested hierarchy of ceremonial centers thus ritually defined the territorial jurisdiction of each unit, as well as each level of the system where fission and fusion could potentially take place. A similar hierarchy of irrigation association temples has been observed by John Brim in the New Territories.[46] The ritual hierarchy was, of course, a familiar Chinese idiom establishing authority beyond the formal administration of the imperial state, reminiscent of the supernatural bureaucracy in popular religion, which mirrored the imperial bureaucracy. It was as if, by co-opting the hierarchical symbolism of the supernatural, the imperial state extended its authority through the ritual medium into village society.[47]

The fluid hierarchy of Longwang temples in Xingtai indicated a more complex phenomenon that incorporated and went beyond the functions of the celestial bureaucracy in the villages. C. K. Yang and Arthur Wolf saw the celestial bureaucracy as essentially symbolic instruments of control for the imperial state. There is no doubt that the worship of the Dragon God became increasingly prominent in the state cult during the Qing. By the late 19th century, large numbers of imperial edicts bestowed honors and titles to the Dragon God. An edict from 1869, for instance, granted him an honorific title, recording that in that and the previous year the Dragon God had prevented the dikes of the swollen Yellow River from bursting by his sudden appearance along these dikes.[48] It is not important whether the cult of Longwang developed originally from local or state worship. The fact is that it participated in a system of authority sanctioned by the state, and for this reason was, like the cult of the Earth God, uniquely suited to define the territorial jurisdictions of communities. In this sense, the ritual hierarchy represented the preservation of what C. K. Yang has called "the ethico-political order" in local society—one of the functions of the cultural nexus.

Unlike the celestial bureaucrats, however, the hierarchy of the Dragon God temples represented a creative manipulation of the symbolism of ritual centers by the irrigation communities themselves. The gate associations constantly needed to segment and recombine in order to maximize their interests as competitors and their effectiveness as cooperators. What the ritual hierarchy of Longwang temples provided was a stable framework of authority within which the flux of shifting alliances could take place. As a device demarcating authoritative jurisdictions, the Longwang temples were a remarkable community institution that not only reduced the necessity of state intervention but also gave the system enormous flexibility.

The relationship of the ritual hierarchy to the irrigation associations points to a key feature of the cultural nexus: authority in local society was a product neither of some Confucian ideal conferred from a higher culture nor of an idealized solidary community. Rather, the local representation of authority emerged from the partial overlap and interplay of sectional, communal, and imperial definitions of popular symbols. As the discussion of the Guandi cult in Chapter 5 makes clear, the pursuit of these particular symbols by various groups enabled these symbols to provide a common framework of authority. More important, it did so even while very different, and sometimes conflicting, interests continued to be pursued.

There were, of course, times when competition could not be contained within the framework of ritual authority, when the rules for building alliances and segmenting no longer applied, when competition gave way to open conflict. During these times, the relevant arena in the cultural nexus had to be widened, and the imperial state as administration, rather than as symbolic representation, came into contact with irrigation communities. This widening also necessitated the involvement of powerful networks linking the resources of several organizational systems, particularly when such disputes led to litigation.

Ordinary disputes within and between gate associations were mediated by conferences of the association leaders—which may or may not have included the gentry in their midst—and did not involve litigation and the state.[49] Litigation became inevitable either during major conflicts between alliances of gate associations or when conflicts occurred across county borders. Both situations were inevitably accompanied by the mobilization of networks of the gentry. It is in this kind of networking that we see a principal force behind the formation of coalition strategies. These strategies were designed to maximize the political resources of any organization, especially if it needed to deal with the state. In most cases, this meant garnering as much gentry support as possible, not only because the gentry had influence with the local authorities, but also because they were crucial when litigation began.

It is easy enough to understand that conflicts between major alliances involving the resources of higher-level centers such as market towns—for instance, when the three associations of the Great Worthy Longwang Temple fought Eastern Pond, and when all seven associations of the Hundred Springs River basin combined their resources against the River Bend Pass Association— would generate gentry networks and entail litigation. But even when the parties to a conflict were small, a conflict across county boundaries inevitably triggered litigation and gentry involvement.

Conflicts across county boundaries were not uncommon because disputes occurred within drainage basins and drainage basins cut across political boundaries. An 1875 case illustrates the political implications of such a conflict. A quarrel took place over the provision of labor services on the river and canals within the Eternal Benefits gate association. This association was composed of one dominating village from Xingtai county, Jingjiatun, and five villages from neighboring Nanhe county. Although the issue was a minor one and the scale of the conflict was limited only to the association, it became a huge affair because the gentry of both counties began litigation and the case went up to the prefectural authorities. After protracted negotiations, the two sides were brought together, and an agreement was hammered out.[50] This case is particularly apposite because it shows how a small conflict could assume a much greater dimension because of political boundaries.

The same pattern emerges in all cases of conflicts involving units belonging to two different counties: the conflict occurred within the drainage basin and always involved the administration and the gentry.[51] For example, a stele from the Wanli period (1573–1620) of the Ming dynasty records that after several canals had been established in the area of the Hundred Springs Association, the people of Shahe county became interested in using the waters of the Hundred Springs Spring. They approached the Xingtai county magistrate, but he refused permission. Subsequently, the prefect reversed the decision and permitted them to construct a canal. During the construction, they blocked off the flow of water to one of the oldest canals in Xingtai, diverting it to their own use. Enraged, the people of the Hundred Springs Association began litigation. The case reached the prefect, and finally the Shahe associations were forced to restore the waters to the Xingtai canal. The stele recorded the names of one higher-degree holder (*jinshi*) and seven lower-degree holders. Once again, the fact that the conflict crossed administrative boundaries forced the attention of the administration and mobilized gentry support.[52]

These cases demonstrate that although administrative boundaries did not constitute an obstacle to forming cooperative arrangements across them, their existence could have wide ramifications. Precisely because the gate associations belonged to two different administrative units and the county magistrate was more likely to pursue a case in the interest of his own county rather than one that divided it and because networks of gentry power grew around the hierarchy of political centers, a small dispute could grow, triggering the mobilization of political networks and prefectural intervention. Thus the intersection of the drainage basin by the administrative hierarchy had the effect of specifying a constituent area and strengthening it over other areas by making available greater political resources than it would otherwise have had.

The irrigation communites of Xingtai reveal several features of the cultural nexus. First, they illustrate the interconnectedness of the nexus and the manner in which the various organizations were linked—the manner in which the administrative hierarchy intersected with the drainage basin, the market center interlocked with the irrigation association, and the ritual hierarchy interacted with different levels of the irrigation community. They also show the mix of power resources that each type of organizational connection brought with it, depending, for instance, on whether the market town, the gentry, or the administration were or were not involved. Finally, in demonstrating how religious belief in Longwang was tied in with the various different organizational requirements of the communities, they also enable us to glimpse how the interplay of different interests formed the representation of authority in local society.

Conclusion

Beginning with Marx and Weber, a succession of paradigms has dominated the historiography of state-society relations in China. Philip Kuhn and Susan Mann have observed that these writers and the first generation of Western historians, impressed by the immensity of the imperial Chinese state, viewed the forms of local society and local elites largely as outgrowths of this overwhelming state structure. The authority structures of local communities seemed to be entirely controlled by the imperial state through the examination system, the bureaucracy, and official ideology.[53]

This paradigm was superseded in the 1960s by the "gentry society" paradigm, which saw the literati as mediators between state and society, possessing a dual identity as state servants on the one hand and local magnates on the other hand. Historically sophisticated, this paradigm saw the gentry playing an equilibrating role, balancing the interests of state and society during periods of dynastic strength, but noted the dominance of gentry and local interests during periods of dynastic decline. Nonetheless, as local studies mushroomed during the next decade and a half, even the broader explanatory power of this paradigm appeared to fall short in many respects.

The critique of the "gentry society" paradigm came from those who studied the gentry and saw it as a highly segmented entity with differentiated links to the state. There were even suggestions that long-term, secular developments among the gentry defied the balancing and cyclical character of state-gentry relations.[54] However, a systematic critique has yet to be made that incorporates not only the myriad channels outside gentry control through which the imperial state reached into local society but also the symbolic and dynamic representation of this state in popular culture.

Even at the lowest levels of rural society, the imperial state did not exist only in its cultural form. In the next chapter, I discuss in some detail the manner in which the imperial bureaucracy and the sub-bureaucracy intervened in rural society. But it is clearly important to identify the state as a collection of normative and symbolic representations, interlaced with Confucian ideals, though by no means exhausted by them. In this manifestation, the state functioned first and foremost as a series of legitimation strategies: controlling the distribution of rank and honors, performing paradigmatic rituals, and inscribing its hegemony on popular symbols. For the rural folk, these were the ways in which the state was represented in the cultural nexus of power.

The discussion of irrigation communities in the cultural nexus brought together local communities, the gentry, and the imperial state within this common framework of understanding. By concentrating on cultural constructions such as the Dragon God as significant media linking the imperial state with local communities (which included the gentry), the analysis shifted the focus away from Confucianism and the gentry as the sole means of understanding state-society relations. At the same time, by drawing attention to the point at which the gentry mobilized its special resources in local politics, this analysis located their role in the cultural nexus as a whole. In the next chapter, I discuss "protective brokerage," another way in which the gentry was incorporated into state-society relations within the cultural nexus.

The importance of the cultural nexus for irrigation communities was tied significantly to the paternalistic state's overwhelming reliance on symbolic representations to secure local order. In turn, this made possible the conception of a framework of legitimate authority in rural society that fused state and local needs. I hope to demonstrate that this proposition is broadly true for rural communities in North China until at least the end of the 19th century. The fateful efforts of the 20th-century state to renounce and even destroy parts of the nexus, while simultaneously faltering in its endeavors to create viable alternatives to reach into rural society, would ultimately undermine the state itself. In the cultural perspective, then, a critical turning point in state-society relations begins at the turn of this century.

From a structural perspective, the cultural nexus proclaims the analytical priority of the study of organizations over settlements. The nexus is modeled after Skinner's insight that it is most important to identify the wider scheme—in his case, the marketing system—in which villages are located in order to understand developments in the village itself. It is evident that a range of organizations, from those that were subvillage to those that reached beyond the market, affected the lives of village inhabitants. Indeed, it is not at all clear what constituted a village in the first half of the 20th century since the direct and indirect effects of state policy continued to transform village boundaries. At the same time, the activities of these organizations were not necessarily coordinated at the marketing center or necessarily circumscribed by the marketing area, as the study of marriage networks and irrigation coalitions has shown. But they were often constrained or enriched by the ways in which they interacted with the marketing hierarchy. Instead of focusing exclusively on the marketing system, I suggest that it is the repertoire of organizational forms and their interconnections that must be identified before we can understand the importance of a particular settlement.

The cultural nexus derives its strength from its rooting of the analysis of culture and legitimacy within the organizational context in which power is exercised. The nexus was not simply the arena in which power was contested; nor was it only the framework that structured access to resources; it was also the *matrix* within which legitimacy and authority were produced, represented, and reproduced. We have glimpsed how the production of symbolic values was related to the functional requirements of organizations. More important, we saw, and will see further, how the interplay of different social interests was involved in representing these values as authoritative. If the state wanted to create viable new forms of authority, it would have to found them on organizations that responded to the changing needs of local society.

The cultural nexus notion is not intended as a model. To be sure, it is a category that describes the general and the generalizable, but it has limited predictive abilities. Although it permits us to see the pattern of historical change, we will also see inconsistencies in this pattern—where the state transforms certain institutions and practices and not others that it might well have (and, according to a model, should have). This same historical complexity also does not permit the bald generalization that the state operated only through the cultural nexus before the 20th century and only outside of it after this time. However, I will assert that over this period the state gradually relinquished and destroyed certain important channels of communication within this nexus without being able to create working alternatives. Much of the middle chapters of the book elucidate this assertion. The final chapters examine the consequences of this failure.

Two

Brokering Rural Administration in the Late Qing

The most ambitious administrative means by which the Qing sought to control society during its vigorous early years were the artificial decimal systems of the *baojia* system of self-surveillance and the *lijia* systems of financial responsibility. Research in this area is still too meager to determine whether the Qing ever began during these early years to approach its ideal of a society thoroughly controlled by bureaucratic devices. It is clear that by the late 19th century, even where they existed in the villages of North China, these devices were forms without function—or, more precisely, without the function intended by their makers.

The administrative functions of the imperial state in the countryside included the maintenance of public services, such as granaries, waterworks, and law and order, and the securing of its fiscal interests. Although the ultimate survival of the state depended on coordinating all these functions, in the late Qing at least, fiscal interests represented an inner zone of interest that dominated administrative activities in rural society. It was the zone in which it was least likely to tolerate competitors from among the elite.[1] It was also the interest that implicated it most deeply in the material lives of the people.

By the late nineteenth century, the Qing secured its fiscal interests and conducted much of its administrative business through a system of dual brokerage. A broker is one who acts as an agent for others in a transaction, usually for a fee. Much of late Qing administration in rural society was in fact, though not in theory, carried out by such fee-charging agents. This kind of "state

brokerage" was one I shall call entrepreneurial brokerage, and it is
to be contrasted with another type—protective brokerage. Typically, in the latter, community organizations collectively and
voluntarily undertook to fulfill tax and other state demands precisely in order to avoid dealing with entrepreneurial brokers, who
were frequently viewed by the peasants as predatory. The purpose
of this chapter is to develop this dual-brokerage model in the
context of the fiscal needs of the late imperial state and study its
relationship to the cultural nexus.

The expansion of revenues became critical to the survival of the
Chinese state in the late 19th and early 20th centuries as it became
increasingly bankrupted by internal rebellion and external defeats.
It became even more critical when the state launched a program of
state strengthening and nation building at the turn of the century.
But the problem of ensuring and stabilizing its fiscal base in
agriculture was scarcely new to the Qing. The Qing state inherited
two intimately related problems of land tax administration from
the Ming. Both stemmed from the larger demographic and economic changes of the Ming-Qing transition and the monetization
of taxation known as the Single Whip reform, and both would
continue to preoccupy the state through the Republic and the
communist transition. The first concerned the problem of evasion
by taxpayers; the second, the problem of engrossment by tax-
collection agencies.

The commercialization of the agrarian economy had led to the
emergence of a highly fluid market in land. Keeping track of who
owned which piece of land for tax purposes posed enormous organizational challenges to the state. The Qing originally based tax
assessments on two types of complementary records: the fish-scale
registers (*yulince*) and the yellow registers (*huangce*), most recently
recompiled during the Wanli cadastral surveys of the Ming. The
fish-scale registers were basically records of taxable land against
which information on the taxpayer was periodically entered. The
yellow registers were records of households against which the
taxable land that they owned was entered. These registers were
supposed to be updated every year. Under ideal circumstances, the
two types of registers provided a means of controlling tax information. Moreover, the completeness of the information eliminated the
need for intermediaries between the taxpayer and the state—the

other important desideratum for a well-functioning tax system. However, the organizational capacity of the Qing state was unable to keep up with the freewheeling market in land, and even by the early Qing, these registers were no longer considered reliable.[2]

Jerry Dennerline has shown how fiscal reformers of the Ming and early Qing attempted to implement various plans to deal with tax evasion. One such plan was to create registers that listed both the name of the household and the particulars of the property, items that had previously been listed in the two separate registers. This would have enabled bureaucrats to fix tax liability on the basis of a single record. Reforms such as this, however, were doomed to failure because powerful households managed to avoid registering themselves.[3] By the time of the great rebellions of the mid-19th century, none of these reforms had taken root, and what remained of the fish-scale and yellow registers was mostly lost or destroyed. There was an attempt to reconstitute the fish-scale registers during the Tongzhi Restoration in the mid-1860s, but with little apparent success.[4]

By the latter half of the 19th century, the imperial state began to rely heavily on the records of county functionaries, who were the only people capable of creating tax registers with a bare resemblance to the actual tax-paying capacity of the land. The registers of these tax clerks (*sheshu, lishu*) in North China were records of households like the yellow registers, but unlike the yellow registers they were not compiled anew every year. Indeed, for all their indispensability, these, too, were notoriously unreliable since they were based on the clerk's personal ability to uncover, and inclination to report, the actual amount of land a household owned.[5] Following a Japanese land investigation of the Jidong region of northeastern Hebei in the early 1940s, for instance, the taxpaying acreage doubled.[6] Thus the state was unable to overcome the problem of tax evasion. What is more, reliance on these registers compromised an implicit, if mostly unrealized, principle of the imperial state: establishing a direct, unmediated relationship with the taxpayer.

Tax engrossment by the agencies of collection and transmittance was probably as old as the Chinese bureaucracy itself. Indeed, Max Weber saw it as a structural characteristic of the patrimonial bureaucracy in China, where officeholding, especially at the county level, was essentially prebendal.[7] The formal salary of the county magistrate was nominal, and his real income derived from a tacit right conferred on him to retain the surplus from his jurisdiction remaining after submitting the stipulated taxes to higher authorities. In other words, the absence of a practical distinction between private and public funding in government tempted local administrators to levy taxes and use "public" monies as they pleased.

Madeleine Zelin has lucidly analyzed the difficulties created by this system. The financial pressures placed on county-level governments by (prebendary) provincial officials left county administrators no recourse other than imposing illegal surcharges on the populace and demanding "gifts" from their unofficial subordinates. The heroic, if short-lived, reforms of the Yongzheng emperor (1723–36) were designed precisely to rationalize public office and open up the channels of revenue transmittance. This was done by formalizing the surcharges, having them sent directly to the province, and reallocating them as official salaries and funds for public purposes. The emperor thus sought to eliminate "corruption" and strengthen the institutions of bureaucratic rule by setting limits on an official's access to funds, while simultaneously providing him with sufficient funds to obviate the need to levy surcharges.[8]

The failure of the Yongzheng reforms draws attention to an aspect of the system that deserves more emphasis than Zelin has given it. The reforms sought to rationalize only the official bureaucracy—the channels of transmittance—and not the actual administration of tax levying and collection. This was in the hands of a host of subordinate, local functionaries whom Weber recognized as being the real power behind a transient magistrate.[9] Even in the early Qing, great numbers of clerks and runners, although cut off from administrative office, proliferated in entrenched subadministrations, representing local interests.[10] These subordinates effectively ran the administration because bureaucratic control over them was extremely weak. To be sure, there was no dearth of regulations attempting to define their conduct, but these regulations applied only to the fraction of clerks and runners who had a statutory existence. Moreover, the enforcement of these regulations depended on the magistrate, who was held responsible for any malfeasance on their part. In turn, however, the magistrate was so utterly helpless without them that Ch'u T'ung-tsu notes that "government regulations for dealing with the clerks, though comprehensive and greatly detailed, remained ineffective."[11]

An even weightier reason behind the inability of the formal bureaucracy to control subadministrative personnel was that it had no control over their incomes. These subordinates were either unsalaried or paid far less than a living wage. In effect, the bureaucracy expected them to survive on customary fees from the people every time they had some dealings with them. In this sense, the subadministrative personnel resembled the tax farmer, who, in return for performing a certain service—collecting taxes—acquired a right to gather amounts above the tax quota as his personal income. There were, in some cases, regulations governing the fees that could be collected. But the regulation of customary fees (*lougui*) was left to the county authorities, and the magistrate was in no position to supervise what they took. To quote Ch'u again, "Obviously, the situation was beyond the control of a magistrate unless he was willing and able to pay the various expenses out of his own pocket."[12] Few magistrates were willing or able to do so.

Thus, practically speaking, the representative of the imperial state, the magistrate, was able to administer a jurisdiction of roughly 300,000 people only by "contracting" out many administrative functions to local individuals and groups with the experience to run the business of government. In return for their services, they were tacitly granted the power to make collections from the populace that were not subject to strict supervision. In fact, the whole pattern of customary fees among magistrates and higher-level officials—the prebendary system—was a replication on higher levels of practices among these personnel. By the 19th century, provincial supervision of the customary fees demanded by the magistrate had become a nominal affair, like the magistrate's supervision of subordinate personnel.[13] Unlike these personnel, however, the magistrate was a part of the bureaucracy, located on its career path and subject to its "status sentiments." Moreover, several other aspects of his role in office were subject to minute bureaucratic regulation. Lower personnel were not restrained by any of these conditions and conducted their operations in a relatively open field. Indeed, the disinclination of the Yongzheng reformers to bureaucratize this class of personnel prevented them from fully realizing their goal of rationalizing fiscal administration. This method of utilizing subadministrative personnel was a form of state brokerage. As in other arrangements of the same class, found across cultures, such as revenue farming and mercenary armies, the principal motive driving state brokers to undertake these often onerous and low-status jobs was an entrepreneurial one. Their aim was to maximize the returns from their positions and bailiwicks. The familiar litany of evils associated with clerks and runners should therefore not be seen as acts of corruption but understood in terms of the state-brokerage model. In a bureaucratic organization, corruption is associated with the violation of public laws by officeholders. In late imperial China, the norms and customs regulating the sources of income and the activities of the state brokers varied locally and provided an extremely vague basis for enforcing compliance. In the brokerage model, clerkly tyranny becomes a feature of the system itself.*

Clerks and runners played the same role in North China in late imperial times as they did elsewhere. They came into regular contact with the people in the litigation process and, most extensively, in the administration of various taxes: making registers, issuing notices and receipts, urging payment, and making arrests. Large numbers of them were unsalaried. It was reported that in parts of Hebei, only about a tenth of the runners in a county received any salaries.[14] The amount of taxes that they were able to skim off is suggested by an investigation in 1736 that disclosed that of the three million taels of overdue land tax, 80,000 taels had been embezzled by clerks and runners.[15]

County clerks and runners were not the only agents that brought the state to the rural populace. There was also a structure of subcounty government that was, however, extremely ill-defined. Administrative nomenclature varied greatly from county to county. The following list presents this structure in the late 19th century

*I use the term "entrepreneurial state brokers" to describe this group of functionaries used by state power, but who had no legitimate means of deriving an income in an increasingly commercialized society. Although I occasionally also use the phrases "venal brokers" or "predatory brokers" in order to highlight the arbitrary or oppressive nature of their activities, these terms are too loaded to work as definitions. They apply a moral judgment before they address the peculiar structural characteristics of this group.

rather schematically from information in *CN* and from the gazetteers of the six counties in *CN*:[16]

	Shandong, county:			Hebei, county:		
Unit	En	Licheng	Changli	Luancheng	Liangxiang	Shunyi
Level 1	xiang	xiang	ban/bao	xiangbao	?	bao
Level 2	li/tu	li/she/tu	she/pai	she	li	lu
Level 3		difang	difang		difang	difang
Village	difang			difang		

In most counties, the highest level was known as the *xiang* or the *bao*. Regrettably, it is also the level for which we have the least information from North China. Saeki Tomi believes that the xiang could have anywhere between 40 and 100 villages.[17] The number of units at this level per county seems to conform to the numbers in the nation as a whole—from four to six. According to Hsiao Kung-ch'uan, there were four xiang in most counties, "each one outside the four gates of the walled city."[18] Hsiao regards it as a unit containing a number of villages, rural markets, and perhaps one or more towns. According to him, it was originally a Song administrative division made up of a number of *li*, but by Qing times it had ceased to be an official division. Nonetheless, "it had semi-official recognition and occupied a definite place in the pattern of rural life." It seemed to play a role in the tax-collection process because there are references to people "who took charge of money and grain" there.[19]

In all identifiable cases, the seat of the xiang or the bao was located in a market town.[20] Might the marketing hierarchy have been congruent with the administrative hierarchy below the county level? Although the administrative seat was located in the marketing center, we cannot assume that the marketing area was coterminous with the area of the xiang because the xiang was usually located in an intermediate market, and villages were often oriented to more than one intermediate market. But the powerful gentry at this level were probably the preeminent political actors in the countryside. Evidence from Changli county suggests that the state may have tried to establish quasi-governmental arrangements at this level in order to use these markets as nodes of local power structures. A report mentions that the gentry publicized the orders of the county government and collected money for various projects.[21]

Even so, many of the functions at this level were related to fiscal administration. As the Hebei *Explanation of Financial Administration* noted, in "previous times there was a subcounty tax-collecting office, the xiang."[22] Indeed, a striking feature of this entire structure, in the late Qing at least, is the overwhelming dominance of functions and personnel related to fiscal administration.

Most of the units at level two—the *tu*, *she*, and *li*—were made up of approximately 20 to 40 villages and had come to be exclusively associated with the tax-collecting process. The li was a unit of the lijia, or decimal-unit system of tax payment, and was the highest unit of that system. Throughout the 18th and the 19th centuries, as this system began to break down, the li came to be a territorial unit under the xiang, a representative of which urged tax payment, and even collected taxes.[23] At its inception, the tu was a subdivision of the li, but in many parts of Shandong and Hebei, it gradually came to occupy a position comparable in scale and function to the li.[24] The she was originally a small unit organized to promote agriculture. Zhang Yufa suggests that it was a cooperative unit that managed granaries and other activities. By the late Qing, it, too, had become a tax-gathering or tax-urging division in parts of North China.[25]

Philip Kuhn has observed that these tax divisions became redundant once the tax registers began to be compiled on the basis of the settlement in which the taxpayer resided (the *shunzhuang* system) rather than on the division in which the land was located.[26] However, the tax divisions continued to play a functional role as the units that delimited, not the taxable land of the area, but the villages and settlements in which the taxpaying household resided. In each tax division, the state engaged a clerk (sheshu, lishu), mentioned earlier, who periodically entered all the taxable land that the taxpayer owned, no matter in which division the land was located. The manner in which the clerks verified the holdings that a taxpayer in his division held elsewhere is discussed at length in Chapter 8. Relevant here is the fact that in many places, the registration clerk not only updated the registers but also urged and even collected taxes. Since he received no salary, he was expected to survive on fees and commissions charged for the services he rendered.[27] The registration clerk was a state broker who in certain situations could come to resemble a tax farmer.

At level two, we also find another type of subadministrative structure whose provenance was distinct from that of the tax division and its personnel, but to which it came to bear some functional resemblance by the late 19th century. Examples of this type are the *lu* and the *pai* in Shunyi and Changli; the personnel here were called *baozheng* and *difang* respectively. The baozheng appears somewhat anomalous at this level. The office seemed to be related to the baojia system of population registration and surveillance and served as the communication link between the county and the village, or sometimes with level 3. The baozheng headman of the lu in Shunyi county in the period before 1903 controlled a small force of three or four policemen who arrested bandits, and he also acted as tax prompter.[28] This kind of figure was quite unusual, however, and his presence in Shunyi may be explained by the fact that its proximity to Beijing made for rather tighter policing arrangements there.

It is well-known that by the mid-18th century, the baojia personnel had assumed many tax-urging and tax-collecting functions, thus blurring the functional distinction between the baojia and lijia.[29] Similarly, the baozheng, the difang, and similar personnel at level 2 undertook tax-urging and, sometimes, tax-collecting functions. Thus, in certain respects, they came to resemble their counterparts at the same level—the clerks in the tax division, who, as mentioned above, often urged and even collected taxes. In Liangxiang county, for instance, the elders (*laoren*) at this level performed both policing and tax-related functions.[30]

The jurisdiction of the difang, or rural agent (also known as *dibao* and *xiangbao*), more commonly covered level three, rather than level two, of the subcounty governmental structure and comprised half a dozen to twenty villages. It is at this level that the most intriguing questions regarding the relations between state and society and the brokerage model are posed. Before proceeding, however, I would like to accent a particular feature of late Qing local administration in North China: the relative paucity of entrepreneurial brokers *below* the county level. Writers like Weng Zhiyong believed that with the proliferation of transit taxes (*lijin*) in the late Qing, entrepreneurial opportunities for state brokers opened up below the county level and their numbers increased rapidly. He also felt that they were now drawn from a wider catchment area, had become extremely mobile, and were thus much less susceptible to restraint by local ties to the community. My own reading of the evidence from North China, backed by Susan Mann's demonstration that the bulk of transit tax revenues came from outside the northern provinces, suggests that entrepreneurial brokers were not yet so prevalent at the subcounty level in North China and that their profusion at lower levels of the system would have to wait until the Republic.[31]

The role of the rural agent in state-society relations has been the subject of a small controversy in the literature. Most scholars agree that although the institution was old, the agent became important only with the breakdown of the baojia system. His role was originally independent of this system but came to supplement it and, in some places, virtually supplanted it. The agent's functions were to urge tax payments, maintain population registers, and report murders, robberies, fires, and property disputes. He provided witnesses for inquests, sometimes collected delinquent taxes, and, on rare occasions, levied special taxes as well. It is also universally agreed that the rural agent's status was low; no doubt one reason for that was his having to deal with the demeaning clerks and runners. Characterizations of his social background range from poor to middle peasant.[32]

The disagreements center around his role as a link between the state and local community. Whereas an earlier generation of scholars like Hsiao Kung-ch'uan saw him as a representative of the community, later writers like John Watt believe that he was decidedly not a representative of a rural community or a protector of its interests. They believe he was an important subcounty agent who was appointed by, and responsible to, the magistrate.[33] Saeki Tomi sees the agent playing both roles: a representative of a community (though not its leader) and a link-man for the government. He performed many community tasks such as repairing dikes and cooperated in the relief of communities hit by such disasters as locusts and fires. At the same time, he served as the lowest-level functionary of the government and was particularly well-equipped to do so since he was a representative of the community. In other words, Saeki does not perceive any necessary contradiction between the two roles.[34]

I believe that Saeki's characterization of the rural agent is essentially correct, even though I argue the point somewhat differently. The state utilized the services of the rural agent without remunerating him or attempting to incorporate him into the bureaucratic apparatus. As a state broker, his ability to monopolize the channels of information between the village and the state conferred on him a certain measure of power. The sources reveal several instances of rural agents' using this power to their own advantage and even terrifying villagers.[35] Yet if the common image of the rural agent did not always fit that of the entrepreneurial state broker, it was not only because he did not belong to the organized sub-bureaucracy of clerks and runners. It was mainly because, as a low-status member of the community to which he belonged, he would not find it easy to challenge or disregard the sentiments of its powerful and influential leaders. Moreover, many communities developed intervillage cooperative arrangements (particularly at level three) precisely in order to control people like the rural agent. It is to these arrangements that I now turn.

This class of cooperative arrangements is best understood within the framework of the brokerage model of state-society relations. A number of villages came together (or perhaps were brought together by the state) either to fulfill a service that would have otherwise been performed by an entrepreneurial state broker such as a clerk or tax farmer or to deal more effectively with the state and its agents as a collective body. The organization itself often undertook the role of the broker, but here the motive was not entrepreneurial but to protect community interests. Instances of this type are the late Qing cooperative or voluntarist *tu* (*xietu, yitu*) and the voluntarist markets (*yiji*) discussed by Philip Kuhn, Susan Mann, and others.[36] Such organizations sought to circumvent the predatory activities of tax farmers and state brokers by collectively choosing a representative of their own to deal with the task at hand.*

Philip Huang's description of how the villages of Baodi county in Hebei joined together to select their own rural agent suggests that their organization falls into the same category. Representatives from some twenty villages chose the rural agent (xiangbao) and

---

*Of course, this kind of organization may not necessarily have protected everybody in the community equally. Powerful community figures may have benefited more from them than did others.

submitted his name to the county authorities for approval.[37] Further afield, Mark Allee's study of the state and rural organizations in 19th-century northern Taiwan reveals a remarkably similar picture where both gentry and nongentry leaders were involved in these protective organizations.[38] In the *CN* villages, the best example of this kind of self-protective community arrangement comes from Changli county in northeastern Hebei. In this county, there were four levels between the county and the village. The highest was the *ban*, of which there were three. Below them were six *bao*, located in the larger market towns. The subcounty administrative offices established there are discussed above. Below the bao were the tax divisions, the *she* (see Chapter 8). At the same level, there was also a unit composed of over twenty villages called the *pai*. There were six or seven pai per bao and a total of 46 pai in the entire county. There was, however, no functionary attached to the pai; nor did it have any clearly recognizable function in the late 19th century. Functionally, the more significant unit was the half-pai, composed of about a dozen villages.

The half-pai was said to have been started so that the villages would not have to deal individually with the rural agent. The constituent villages contributed money for all his needs when he was engaged on official business between the village and the state. For instance, they paid for his stay at an inn and other expenses in the county seat and for all the costs of investigating and reporting a murder, including the expense of a coffin. The recurrent references to his expenses probably refer to the bribes and "fees" that he must have had to pay the subadministration in the county yamen. Finally, the villages in the half-pai contributed money to pay his twice-yearly "salary."[39]

Although the system of the half-pai found its raison d'être within the framework of subcounty administration, it sometimes transcended its original purpose and became a locus of cooperation for other activities as well. It was the basis on which intervillage self-defense forces were formed. On several occasions, crop watching was also organized around it, but these efforts could not be sustained because a dozen villages were too numerous to be properly coordinated. Be that as it may, the half-pai is most accurately seen as local society's organized defense of its own interests against predatory power brokers and the state. The group contributed money to bail out innocent villagers arrested by yamen runners, and during floods it petitioned the authorities for tax reductions.[40]

An interesting expression of its role as an instrument of the community's self-defense against revenue farmers is recorded in a stele in Nijing market dated 1895. Nijing had become a periodic market only recently, and because it was still small, it did not participate in the Confucian ceremonies held in the 12 officially recognized market towns in the six bao.As a result, the butchers of Nijing had never supplied meat for these ceremonies. However, some years previous to 1895, the magistrate dispatched the butcher–tax farmers to collect the meat levy from Nijing. The butchers of Nijing resisted, and a prolonged conflict ensued between the tax farmers and the butchers. When meat disappeared completely from the market, the gentry of the area became involved in the case. Finally, a settlement was negotiated; the butchers were to pay a tax, but it was explicitly stated that the collection was to be undertaken not by the licensed tax farmers but by the rural agent as a way of avoiding having to deal with the hated tax farmers.[41] The half-pai employing the rural agent thus worked much like the voluntarist market (yiji) discussed by Susan Mann where the marketing community took over the management of its own tax dues. In this case, the rural agent was considered more trustworthy than the tax farmer, probably because his ties to the community were believed to be stronger.

The system of the half-pai also provided the format for alliances and intervention in the political process at a higher level. A stele from Mogebao, a bao and an intermediate market town, records that the dues collected by the ban functionaries allegedly to provision the military were five and even ten times in excess of the original demand. The pressure had become so unbearable that all the leaders of the pai within the bao discussed the matter and publicly elected 8 representatives. These representatives submitted a petition to the military authorities, who ordered an investigation, and in 1904, an order was issued stipulating the precise sum to be collected, never to be increased or decreased. The stele was signed by representatives from each of the half-pai in the bao.[42] The aggregation of the politically active cells of the half-pai along the hierarchy of subcounty administration was thus a creative means developed by communities to expand their power in local society.

Similar intervillage sodalities responding to political or administrative demands can be found in several of the other *CN* counties.[43]

Protective brokerage arrangements, exemplified by the half-pai system in Changli, were an important part of the cultural nexus of power in local society. Organizationally, the half-pai's aggregative character—or seen from the top-down, its segmentary character—made it a powerful community instrument enabling intervention at various levels of the system. Another relevant organizational feature was the interlocking but nonisomorphic relationship with other organizational systems, most notably the marketing system. For instance, although the coordinating nodes of the half-pai were located in the intermediate markets, the actual number of villages in a half-pai was numerically regular and incommensurate with those in a market town. Thus the organizing principle of protective brokerage responded more to the hierarchy of administrative places than to that of markets. At the same time, however, its culmination at a marketing center, as well as the accretion of other functions in the half-pai, lent this form of brokerage the power and prestige that enabled it to become a vehicle for the expression of legitimate leadership in the nexus. And, no doubt for these reasons, the imperial state found this form of brokerage superior to entrepreneurial brokerage as a channel to reach into the rural interior.

Yet, even though protective brokerage was used extensively in the 19th century, it was by no means an unequivocal solution to the problems of the state, particularly those of tax evasion and engrossment. One reason for this was that the distinction between the two types of brokerage, entrepreneurial and protective, though analytically valid, was practically and potentially an ambiguous one. This is particularly evident in what was considered one of the most notorious forms of brokerage in Qing times: *baolan*, or tax engrossment by the local gentry. In this form of unauthorized tax farming, the gentry assumed the prerogative of collecting the taxes of commoners for a commission. It was clearly a profit-making enterprise because of the commissions that they charged. At the same time, gentry involvement in tax payments for others was also protective because it was often a response to the excessive levies of clerks and other entrepreneurial brokers. These levies could drive small, weak households to seek the protection of large, influential ones because by paying the taxes through the elite, the poor could avoid many of the illegal surcharges. Baolan expressed both aspects of state brokerage and the ambiguous relationship between the two within the community.[44]

Domination by the elite thus made it hard for the state to be fully comfortable with protective brokerage as a form of revenue collection. But there were other reasons as well for the imperial state's suspiciousness. Protective brokerage could not solve the basic problem of tax evasion, not only because the elite were involved but also because the actual landholdings of a settlement were a jealously guarded community secret. Moreover, although this kind of brokerage might protect communities, it could not necessarily prevent engrossment by entrepreneurial brokers as long as they were engaged in the procedures of levying and collection. Indeed, where entrepreneurial brokerage expanded its role, as it did in many parts of North China in the 20th century, it inevitably made inroads into protective brokerage, which began to languish or become subverted.

In fiscal and administrative matters, the late Qing state dealt with rural communities principally through the dual-brokerage scheme described above. Once again, the "brokerage model" is superior to the "gentry-society" model as a way of characterizing relations between the imperial state and rural society. The two types of state brokerage help us to understand how a single representative of the imperial state governed the population of an entire county, without at the same time forcing us to accept an artificial cohesion among a segmented gentry. Nor need we accept an equally artificial distinction between gentry and nongentry elites. Gentry and commoner leaders alike were to be found in the protective brokerage schemes of all the examples cited—Changli, Baodi, and northern Taiwan.[45] And, as can be seen from the examples of baolan, there was no shortage of lower-gentry involvement in entrepreneurial brokerage.

To the extent that entrepreneurial state brokers saw their jobs solely in terms of their own profit, their networks cannot be considered part of the *cultural* nexus, which functioned to generate legitimate authority. Protective-brokerage organizations, on the other hand, were eminently a part of the nexus. But their real significance lay in the way their potentially ambiguous status affected the nexus. Although organized by community leaders and imbued with community values, these organizations were always susceptible to domination by entrepreneurial interests. In this sense, protective-brokerage organizations were among the most sensitive elements in the cultural nexus, registering the changing balance between the legitimizing effects of symbolic values and the delegitimizing effects of entrepreneurial brokers. Thus they also play an important role in the rhetorical structure of this essay as the analytical hinge that joins its two wings: the cultural and the administrative. Their growing subversion during the 20th century would come to crystallize the political crisis that swept the countryside.

Three

Building the Modern State in North China

By a happy coincidence, my study begins precisely at the turn of the century; this moment dramatizes the notion of a state moving to break with the past and begin a new epoch. Much of what happens to rural society in the next half-century originates in the historical events of the time: the failure of the Boxers, the heavy indemnity payments imposed by the imperialist powers, and the subsequent resolve of important sections of the state to launch a program of state strengthening—roots, branches, and all.

These developments culminated in the modernizing drive known as the late Qing reforms (xinzheng), which attempted to transform the relatively weak institutional involvement of the 19th-century Qing state in rural society. Roger Thompson's study of the reform efforts of Qing statesmen in the first decade of this century reveals the widespread presence of modernizing ideas in the late Qing administration, especially among the provincial leadership. An influential memorial by provincial Governors-general Liu Kunyi and Zhang Zhidong, written in response to the post-Boxer imperial edicts of 1901 calling on officials to offer reform proposals, declared: "Three things are essential to a nation: the first is the government, the second wealth, the third power. If a nation has good government, it can strive to achieve prosperity and strength; a hitherto prosperous and strong nation can become poor and weak. The way to attain good government is to reform native institutions; the way to attain wealth and power is to adopt Western methods."[1]

Thompson's work also examines the different approaches to

reform, contrasting especially the efforts of Governor Zhao Erxun in Shanxi, who sought to build on traditional Chinese models of reform, with those of Yuan Shikai, Governor-general of Zhili. Yuan's reforms were based on Japanese and Western models, and he relied on returned students from Japan to formulate moderniz- ing policies. Many of his protégés would hold important posi- tions in the Republican administration after 1911.[2] More relevant here were Yuan Shikai's rural reforms in Zhili and Shandong. During his governorship of Shandong (1899–1901) and in his early years in Zhili (1901–7), police and educational institutions were vigorously established in rural areas.[3] These measures ushered in an era of state making in this region, but the consequences of reforms intended by policymakers came to be interwoven with unintended, and even unforeseen, results, creating immense ten- sion in rural society.

The purpose of this chapter is to analyze the problems of build- ing the modern state at the regional level. The pre-communist 20th-century state in China was a complicated structure of levels and interests. Some represented formalizing and rationalizing agencies, such as the provincial policymakers discussed above, who tended to advance the stuctures of the state toward the ideals encompassed by the state-making concept; others saw the expand- ing state as a source of entrepreneurial gain. There was also competition within and between different levels of administration in the province and the county. Ideas of "state making" drawn from the European experience, valuable as they are, cannot ac- count for the full complexity of the Chinese experience. Taking the state-making ideas as my point of departure, I introduce the notion of "state involution" later in this chapter to try to capture some of this complexity.

Reorganization and Extension of Local Administration

With the increasing intervention of the state in rural society, its traditional fiscal preoccupations became both sharpened and com- plicated. The need to develop modernizing projects and, more important, to finance them and pay off the Boxer indemnity made even more pressing the solution of the two problems outlined earlier: tax evasion and tax engrossment. Moreover, these problems now became embedded in a discourse on nation building and state strengthening that, among other things, lent force to the ideal of the bureaucratic penetration of society.

The 20th-century regimes saw the solution to their problems in the formalization and extension of local administration in keeping with the ideal of a bureaucratizing state. The problem was enforcing compliance among the lower orders of the bureaucracy. Max Weber set out three conditions for such compliance in a modern bureaucracy: an assured salary; an opportunity for a career that was not accidental or arbitrary; and a strong status sentiment among officers that would make them willing to be subordinate to their superiors.[4]

In the 19th century, some reform-minded administrators sought to deal with the problem of curbing the autonomy and power of subadministrative personnel by bureaucratizing them. The statesmen of the Tongzhi Restoration (1862–74) were particularly concerned with this problem, and the efforts of one of them, Ding Richang, would certainly have drawn Weber's attention had he known of Ding. Ding believed that clerks and other subordinates were able to abuse their power because they were barred from official careers. This not only made it difficult to supervise them but also rendered moral sanctions useless. He proposed that they be given proper salaries, that regular examinations be held for their appointments, and that promotion be based on periodic assessments. In other words, he wished to create a career service for them within the bureaucracy. For a variety of reasons, these proposals were never implemented.[5]

The task of the reformist state included more than bureaucratizing subordinate personnel at the county level. It would also have to formalize the apparatus of subcounty government in order to make it more amenable to state interests. This may well have been the more pressing of its tasks since this level was destined to deal most intensively with the rural populace. In recapitulating the administrative reorganization of rural society undertaken by the state, I will pay special attention to how it sought to ensure public accountability in relations between the village and the state.

The earliest reports suggest that subcounty police and educational facilities were first established around 1901 in Shandong and 1903 in Hebei.[6] The taxes levied on the village for these expenses

began to accelerate with the formation of local assemblies dominated by the gentry. As Philip Kuhn has shown, gentry management of local community projects had been common since at least
the late 19th century, but the practice was legitimated by the official
constitutional movement in 1908–9.[7] The 1909 regulations spelled
out all the new revenues that local self-government councils were
entitled to and in addition, empowered council leaders to make
further appropriations in case of shortfalls.[8] This may have been
the original sanction for the notorious irregular levies (*baidi tankuan*)
that peasants found so irksome in the years to come.

Following the establishment of the Republic, the first real efforts
at formalizing local administration were undertaken. At the county
level, magistrates' examinations were introduced in 1913. Odoric
Wou's study of Henan shows that these exams produced a younger breed of professionally trained administrators as opposed to the
classically trained scholars of the Qing. Moreover, subordinate
personnel were to be selected by the county with the approval of the
self-governing councils.[9] By the middle of the warlord period,
however, over 50 percent of the magistrates had not been selected
through the examinations, and a substantial proportion of them (20
percent in Shandong and 31 percent in Hebei from 1911 to 1928)
were natives of the province they served in.[10] Thus, the bureaucratic rule of avoidance of the imperial administration no longer
operated, and the results of the rationalization efforts were mixed at
best.

Attention was also directed to the ward. Although subcounty
wards (*qu*) had been established in many places even before the fall
of the Qing, in these early years the local self-governing councils
collected their levies through the existing, informal structure of
subcounty administration. These included functionaries at level
one and level two of the old apparatus of subcounty rule (see Chapter 2), as well as agencies like the militia, which the gentry had
controlled since the late 19th century.[11] During the first years of the
Republic, the ward was a unit of local self-government, but with
the rescinding of constitutional bodies by Yuan Shikai in 1915, it
became the lowest formal unit of the government, and in theory at
least, it was under the strict supervision of the county.[12]

The wards were established between 1908 and 1914, often at level
one of the old structure, the xiang and the bao located in the larger

market towns in the county. The administration was led by a headman who maintained a small clerical staff and a police force. It was empowered to impose taxes and collect them with the help of the police. It proved to be the most notable achievement of the state in the early Republic. The ward was temporarily eclipsed by the establishment of the township (*xiang*) under the Township Self-government Law in 1921. But the township law was implemented only fitfully, and the ward basically remained an institution respected by all regimes and armies that captured power in North China because it was the most efficient means available to ensure the extraction of revenues.[13]

When the Nationalists captured power in the north in 1928, they were determined to institutionalize local government at the level of the ward. Initially the wards were expected to be self-governing bodies with elected officials, but by 1933 they had become "purely administrative arms of the county government."[14] First, the number of wards in some counties was reduced in an effort to acquire greater bureaucratic control over them. Next, the number of personnel was increased. By 1933, the police force was expanded to a troop of over 16 men, and the office of police chief, with powers separate from the ward headman, was established.[15] The separation of the two offices may have been an attempt by the state to prevent concentration of power at this level.

Nationalist policymakers did not conceive of the role of the ward narrowly in terms of state strengthening; rather, they emphasized its role in the grand design of nation building. Its tasks included not only population registration, land investigation, taxing, and policing but also supervising the construction of the infrastructure of a modern nation: education, participatory institutions, and an integrated economy.[16] However, it was the extractive rather than the nation-building role of the ward that was to predominate . Thus, although the ward coordinated rural self-defense, confirmed appointments of village headmen, and arbitrated quarrels that village authorities could not resolve, its most important function was to levy taxes and enforce their payment by the village. This it did both for higher authorities, including the military, and for itself.[17]

But even as extractive organs, were the wards the bureaucratic institutions they were supposed to be? The ward headman was a submagistrate appointed by the province, and he was subject to the rule of avoidance and not allowed to serve for more than three years in the office. Moreover, he received a salary of about 50 yuan a month.[18] In reality, however, the bureaucratic organization at this level was exposed to many of the weaknesses that had afflicted the lower levels of the bureaucracy in the past. First, the ward headman's salary was considered inadequate, and headmen were said to make several times that amount from other sources. The salaries for the police and other personnel, who received 20–30 yuan a month, were even more inadequate. Perhaps in recognition of the inadequacies of these salaries, the police were expected to collect fees whenever they went into the villages. Small wonder, then, that the largest item on the expenditure side of village budgets was the expense of maintaining the ward, which included police and "entertainment" expenses.[19] Moreover, the wards levied taxes on an ad hoc basis and without supervision or audits.[20] Extension of state control thus meant only partial bureaucratization.

A second level formally recognized by the state was the village. In the early 1900s, the county administration recognized the village headman and his assistant and, in some places, a leadership council.[21] Village leaders were now responsible for managing the new schools, constructing roads, and undertaking various projects designed to bring the village within the ambit of the state-led nation-building process. The village governing council was perceived as an important community managerial resource that would handle the financing of these projects, as well as the tax levies imposed on the village as a whole (tankuan) by higher levels of the administration, particularly the ward.

After 1928, the Nationalists sought to impose a more ambitious plan for bringing all of rural society within a distinctly formal relationship with the state. Moreover, as heirs to the quasi-democratic ideological tradition of Sun Yat-sen, they were committed to the idea of self-government, although, practically speaking, little power was conceded to local groups. In the end, the Nationalist government adopted a model of self-government greatly influenced by that of the warlord Yan Xishan in Shanxi, where the powers of self-government bodies were severely curtailed.[22]

The model implemented by the Nationalists was the *xiangzhen* system: the *xiang* (township) and the *zhen* (municipality) represented the highest levels of village or town self-government and were to deal directly with the state. Below the township and the municipality were the *lü* and the *lin*, a 25- and a 5-household unit, respectively. The lin elected a representative to the lü, which in turn elected a representative to the township. The township was to be composed of 100 to 1,000 households. In practice, however, it rarely exceeded more than 250 households until the Japanese occupation. This was the lowest unit empowered to perform the tasks of nation building and to levy taxes, as well as to supply taxes to higher-level units.[23] Since the population of most villages was not incommensurate with the 100–250–household size of the township, a size prescribed for most of the 1930s, in practice the natural village continued to exist and to function as it had done before. It was only under the Japanese that the institution of the large township of 1,000 households (*daxiang*) was strictly enforced, and this, as we shall see, would have important consequences for local leadership.

The recognition by the state that the focus of state-society relations would be the interactions of ward personnel and village leaders led to the eclipse of the rural agent (difang) as the figure linking the state with the countryside. As mentioned above, this agent, though by no means an eminent powerholder, was capable of monopolizing the channels of communication between the village and the state. Once the village government became the recognized agent in all dealings with the state, he was often reduced to playing the role of an inconsequential messenger. In some places, he lost his communication and investigative functions to the ward police; elsewhere, the post was simply abolished.[24]

More significantly, as the formal status of the village grew, the role of protective-brokerage arrangements formed across villages to control the rural agent diminished to some extent. My language is advisedly cautious here because the rural landscape represents a tissue of contradictory forces—many deriving from the interplay between the intended and unintended sides of state penetration— that worked to make and break the power of protective brokerages.

Indeed, in one sense, the state was doing both. The state intended to link bureaucrats directly with the lowest level of rural settlement, the village. At the same time, ever-increasing revenue pressures led it to extend a form of protective brokerage to the village. The management of what came to be the most important source of revenue from land, the tankuan, can be seen as a form of protective brokerage. This system of levying taxes differed fundamentally from the land tax and its surcharges; it was applied by the state not to an individual landowner but to a village as a whole. The village had to devise its own means of allocating this burden. But, as we have seen, protective brokerage was by no means an unambiguous solution to the state's problems of tax evasion and engrossment.

What was unique about the tankuan levy, from the point of view of the state, was that it could be applied without knowledge of the actual landholdings of a settlement—thus making irrelevant the problem of evasion. As explained more fully below, a state agency levied tankuan whenever it needed funds, leaving to the village government, and the fairness of its institutions, the means of payment. In this way, the state did not have to concern itself with rapid changes in a fluid land market, and at the same time, it was able to link tax responsibility to an accountable community leadership structure. But although the state was thus able to finesse the problem of evasion, it created a new problem: the levying of taxes with little regard to the actual taxpaying capacity of a village.

From the point of view of the village, then, the new arrangement, with the tankuan at its core, represented a different and more atomized kind of protective brokerage. The state would deal with a single village, which now had a formal, unmediated administrative link with the state. In its new transactions with the state, the village could borrow little of the strength of the cultural nexus that it had once used to resist the incursions of entrepreneurial brokers. Over the course of the Republic, the efforts of villages to construct old-style protective-brokerage arrangements would be severely tested as the inner logic of state strengthening, among other factors, released large numbers of entrepreneurial and even predatory brokers to press on all lines of communication between the village and the government. To understand how this happened, it is necessary to analyze how the regional state expanded its fiscal resources.

Provincial Finances in Hebei and Shandong

The fiscal problems of the Qing state had caused the central government to suffer an enormous decline—by almost two-thirds—in the real value of the revenues collected from the land tax and its surcharges, or direct taxes, in the 150 or so years from 1750 until the early 1900s.[25] Prices almost consistently outran the land revenues of the imperial state until around 1905. Since the greater part of local government (province and county) income came out of the land tax and its surcharges during much of the period, the declining real values of tax revenues affected local government as well.[26] However, the story with commercial, or indirect, taxes was very different. The rate of growth of these taxes began to accelerate in the latter half of the 19th century at both the central and local levels in response to the great crises of the mid-century.[27]

Then, as we have seen, the modernization efforts of the early 1900s suddenly began to create a much greater role for state organizations in local society, both from an organizational and from an extractive point of view. For example, from 1903 to 1911 in Ding county, Hebei, prices rose by 7.5 percent and the burden of the land tax and its surcharges grew by 35 percent.[28] Although there were some reversals in individual years, the secular trend from this time on was toward an increase in the budgets of local governments. In this section, I investigate the growth of state financial strength at the provincial level.

Before I plunge into local finances, however, it will be useful to clarify the role played by the central government during this period, especially as it affected provincial finances. Notwithstanding the reform efforts of the Yongzheng emperor, the most striking feature of central-local fiscal relations during the Qing was the absence of a clear separation of sources of revenue between different levels of the administration. Beginning with the fiscal reforms of 1909 and through successive legislation until 1916, the government did specify distinct sources of central government and provincial government revenues. However, the sources of revenue for levels below the province remained undifferentiated, thereby giving the province enormous powers over the lower levels.[29]

Fiscal relations between the center and the province were relatively stable during the years of Yuan Shikai's rule (1912–16), but during the succeeding period under the warlords (circa 1916–27), the military governors of the provinces often kept a good proportion of the land revenues that theoretically belonged to the center.[30] Under the Nationalists, revenue from the land tax and its surcharges became a provincial item, but we should not draw hasty generalizations about the financial weakness of the central government in North China as a result of this. For instance, consider the distribution of tax income among different levels of the government in 1929 and then in the mid-1930s in Ding county, Hebei:[31] the revenues of the central government increased by over 150 percent during these five or six years, a rate of growth that was greater than that of the central government's income for the nation as a whole.[32]

Hebei and Shandong were important provinces from a fiscal point of view. In 1931–32, Hebei had the second highest provincial expenditures in the nation, and Shandong, the seventh.[33] Table 1 traces the growth of real income and expenditures in the two provinces and also indicates the percentage change over the preceding year recorded in the table.[34] The most striking feature about the table is the timing of the increases in provincial revenues. There is a clear cascading pattern that occurs over three distinct periods in both provinces corresponding to three different political regimes in Republican China: the early Republic under Yuan Shikai (represented by the years 1913, 1914, and 1916); the warlord period (1919 and 1925); and the period of Nationalist rule (the remaining years). Within this configuration, it becomes particularly clear that although there was a rather slow rate of growth of provincial income with periodic declines within each period, there were rather startling increases in provincial income from one period to the next.

The average annual rate of growth of provincial revenues in Hebei from 1913–16 to 1931–34 was 42 percent. In Shandong, it was 56 percent over the same period. These rates are dramatically higher than the annual rate of growth of gross domestic product in the nation, which was only 1.08 per cent for the period 1914–18 to 1931–36.[35] The enormous expansion of provincial income suggests the increasing control of the province over the resources of society, and through increases in expenditures, the weightier role it was playing in society as well. This is a point of considerable importance. The bureaucratic power of the central state had become parcelized, but in the process the fiscal foundations of the provincial units had been strengthened, a fact that would enable them to play a more important role than they had heretofore.

Although the growth of provincial financial power is significant in itself, it is, nonetheless, important to see to what extent this growth represented merely the transfer of revenues from the central government to the provinces. Put another way, how much new revenue was the province able to generate? It is well known that the land tax became the de facto revenue of the province during the warlord period and its de jure revenue during the Nationalist period. Indeed, further investigation revealed that for the first three years shown in Table 1 (1913, 1914, and 1916), the income values for Hebei do not include the revenues from the land tax. This is because until the death of President Yuan Shikai in 1916, the center continued to receive the bulk of this revenue (although the province was collecting a surcharge on the land tax usually in excess of the 30 percent permitted by the Yuan Shikai government).[36] Of these three years, we have estimates for the land tax collected in Hebei only for 1916. But this datum adequately serves as a baseline.

When the value of the real land tax revenue collected in Hebei in 1916 is added to the other values in Table 1, the results are as shown in Table 2. The picture here is far less dramatic than that shown in Table 1. Land tax revenues declined in 1925 not only over 1919 but also over 1916. Some caveats, however, are in order. These figures for provincial income in the warlord period may conceal more than they reveal; although the province was retaining much of the land tax, it did remit some amounts to the center. This was especially the case with Hebei, which was usually controlled by Beijing. In other words, Hebei province was probably generating more revenues than the figures show, but exactly how much more is a mystery because we do not know what proportion of the land tax revenues the province passed on to the center. Moreover, the military governors of the northern provinces, including Hebei and Shandong, often levied taxes and provisions that did not appear in formal budgets; it would be impossible even to hazard an estimate of these. Revenues from sources other than the land tax, however, increased by as much as 40 percent during this period. Thus the growth of the state—the provincial state, to be sure—from 1916 to 1925 proceeded on a partial basis; revenues increased in certain sectors while stagnating or even declining in others. The annual rate of growth of new revenues in Hebei during the warlord period (1916–25) was 2.7 percent, still ahead of the GDP.

However, there continues to be a leap in provincial government income from the early and middle periods to the Nationalist period, by over 10 percent per annum from 1916 to 1931–34, even though land tax revenues either declined or increased only marginally. The

TABLE I

Real Incomes and Expenditures of Hebei and Shandong Provinces and Yearly
Percentage Change, 1913–1934

(yuan)

Year	Real[a] income	Percent change	Real expenditure	Percent change
		HEBEI PROVINCE		
1913	1,625,484		8,255,433	
1914	5,776,648	255%	3,220,212	−60%
1916	2,644,561	−54	2,131,015	−34
1919	10,899,222	312	19,438,756	343
1925	9,603,207	−12	11,267,475	19
1931	31,131,782	224	31,132,598	176
1932	20,576,769	−34	20,576,769	−34
1933	25,517,821	24	25,517,821	24
1934	16,056,000	−37	15,735,023	−38
		SHANDONG PROVINCE		
1913	1,877,047		2,088,419	
1914	2,658,095	42%	2,658,095	27%
1916	2,321,067	−12	1,316,889	−50
1919	11,953,867	415	9,478,228	620
1925	10,696,957	−10	17,789,884	87
1931	20,053,039	87	20,053,039	13
1932	21,733,853	8	21,733,853	8
1933	23,341,584	7	23,341,584	7
1934	25,610,000	10	25,610,000	10
1935	23,689,666	−7	24,887,446	−3

SOURCES: Zhang Yifan 1935a: 6, 1935b: 5.

[a] All real values in this work have been converted from nominal figures by utilizing an index of purchasing power for North China, compiled by a Nankai University team, based on wholesale prices in Tianjin ("Index Numbers" 1937).

TABLE 2

Real Income of Hebei Province and Yearly Percentage Change, 1916–1934

(yuan)

Year	Land revenue	Percent change	Other revenues	Percent change	Total revenues	Percent change
1916	8,181,696		2,644,561		10,826,257	
1919	7,165,412	−12%	3,733,810	41%	10,899,222	0.6%
1925	5,971,422	−16	3,631,785	−3	9,603,207	−12
1931	3,971,440	−33	27,160,342	648	31,131,782	224
1932	5,632,143	42	14,944,626	−45	20,576,769	−34
1933	6,306,931	12	19,210,890	28	25,517,821	24
1934	5,446,864	−13	10,609,136	−45	16,056,000	−37

SOURCE: Shenbao nianjian 1935: G–41. See also Nongcun Fuxing Weiyuanhui 1934: 20. All the figures have been deflated by the Nankai index.

critical element here is revenue from sources other than the land tax. The initial increase in yields, by a factor of 7.5 from these sources between 1925 and 1931, moderated considerably over the next few years as the Great Depression set in. But even after the highly successful tax cuts implemented by the provincial government in 1934 following the Second National Financial Conference, the increase in this category over 1916 is 300 percent and over 1919 is 184 percent. This is in keeping with the view that the Hebei government's experiments with the system of commercial taxation beginning in the mid-1920s were highly successful.[37]

For Shandong, we unfortunately do not have specific land revenue values for either 1919 or 1925, but the trend from 1916 until the Nationalist period is much the same as in Hebei, although the increases are far less dramatic. From 1916 to 1934, land tax revenues in Shandong increased only by 28 percent, whereas other revenues increased by 246 percent. Total new revenues in the period from 1916 to 1931–34 increased by about 50 percent or just under 4 percent per annum. Incidentally, the land tax accounted for a much higher proportion of revenues in Shandong than in Hebei.[38]

Thus, the bulk of the increase in provincial income, especially after 1919, came from outside the land tax, a situation unlike that in Jiangsu, where the weight of the land tax, including the provincial surcharge, almost doubled between 1915 and 1933.[39] The principal component of the taxes outside the land tax was the *juanshui*, the indirect taxes, which included the deed tax, professional taxes, and excise taxes. The *juanshui* accounted for an annual average of 31 percent of provincial income in Hebei between 1919 and 1925 and 23 percent in Shandong between 1931 and 1934.[40] These taxes affected the peasantry as much as any other group. This was true even for the professional taxes on merchants because merchants passed on any additional taxes to consumers.[41] Moreover, as Susan Mann has noted, commercial taxes affected peasants by threatening to destroy the structure of local trade on which peasant households depended.[42]

Data on provincial expenditures are not available in any great detail, but it is nonetheless possible to form some general impressions of the character of the intervention of provincial government in local society.

Military spending, reflecting conflicts between competing state organizations, was an important item in the expenditures of both Hebei and Shandong, especially from 1919 to 1930. From 1920 until 1925, military expenditures constituted approximately 50 percent of total provincial expenditures in Hebei and closer to 60 percent in Shandong. Spending on warfare during these years created major deficits in the Hebei budget in 1920, 1924, and 1925 and in 1922 and 1925 in Shandong.[43] The northern warlords fought the An-Zhi war in 1920, the Feng-Zhi war in 1922 and the second Feng-Zhi war in 1924. Deficits from these adventures led to growing public debts (forced loans from banks and merchants), the interest payments on which ensured ballooning provincial expenditures.

Military spending is not necessarily contradictory to the expansion of state power during the early stages of state making. As Rudolf Braun and others have pointed out, in 18th-century Europe military costs were not only by far the largest item in the state budget, they generally exceeded the sum of all other public expenses. Braun calls warfare "the moving motor of the whole development of public finance."[44] The huge deficits created by such military expenditures led not only to the evolution of a tax system but also to the raising of public loans and the funding of public debts. The successful states were able to control the resulting strains by creating an institutional framework in which fiscal obligations came to be regarded as part of public duties. Having attained a certain stable level of extraction, the managers of these states were then able to put their finances on a sound institutional basis.[45]

What was the extent of financial rationalization in North China before the Nationalist takeover in 1928? From 1911 until 1928, several efforts were made to streamline the administration of provincial finances and increase available revenues. First, under the Yuan Shikai government, the measure of the levy changed from the silver tael, which had a fluctuating silver content, to the more standardized dollar (yuan). In 1914, the arbitrary rates of conversion for grain levies were eliminated in favor of a single currency system in which all taxes were levied. Finally, the first measures were undertaken to convert banner and other tax-free lands into taxable lands, to ascertain and consolidate the many surcharges, and to carry out a land investigation.[46]

Many of these proposals and plans began to be implemented only between 1917 and 1925. In 1917, Hebei counties established a collection office under the county finance department, supervised by the magistrate and finance officer. The office had a staff of approximately 35 and was intended to replace the traditional broker. In 1922, specialized departments were created to collect tax arrears, to make new revenue registers, and to increase taxable lands. These measures, however, did not amount to much in the sphere of land tax revenues. This is evident not only from the marginal increases in these revenues but also from the continued presence of brokers and their entourages throughout the period.[47] The organizational changes designed to increase commercial revenues, in particular the creation of the short-lived Committee to Order Zhili Provincial Finances under Governor Yang Jiangde in 1924–25, had more positive results.[48]

Under the Nationalists, all military expenses theoretically belonged to the center. However, provincial military expenses did not disappear. Provinces were expected to make contributions to regionally based national armies, the precise amounts of which fluctuated according to the needs of these armies. For instance, Hebei and the other northern provinces made substantial contributions to the regional army under Zhang Xueliang's vice-command in 1931 and 1932. Additionally, the province maintained a local security force for which a tax (the *gong'anfei*) was levied. In Hebei, military expenditures based on these two items averaged about 25 percent of provincial expenditures between 1931 and 1934.[49]

Data for nonmilitary expenditures in Shandong are available for the years 1921 and 1931, and these enable us to observe the changing pattern of civilian expenditure (see Table 3). The increase between the two years amounts to an annual growth rate of over 50 percent. This kind of growth is impressive by any standards and clearly reflects the expanding role of the provincial state. The provincial government had increased its capacity to intervene in society by strengthening its administrative and police apparatus. Even more significantly, it was developing the infrastructure of the economy and society, as evidenced by the almost tenfold increase in the category entitled "Reconstruction, communication, and industrial regulation" and by new expenditures on government business enterprises. The increase in educational expenditures also points to this development of the social infrastructure.

TABLE 3

Distribution of Provincial Expenditures in Shandong and Percentage Increase in
Real Expenditures, 1921–1931

Function	Percent of total 1921	Percent of total 1931	Percent increase[a]
Party affairs	—	4%	—
General administration	34%	16	177%
Judicial administration	6	9	757
Financial administration	8	8	448
Police	12	16	686
Education and culture	21	13	254
Reconstruction, communication, and industry regulation	8	14	880
Debt charges	7	3	115
Government business enterprises	—	0	
Miscellaneous	4	9	
TOTAL	100%	100%	486%

SOURCE: Chang 1934: 238.

[a] Real values deflated by the Nankai index (1926–100).

The expansion and penetration of the state and the enlargement
of its domain in China took place in an ideological climate that was
self-consciously modernizing. Various practices and techniques
that can be subsumed under the rubric of rationalization were
implemented and utilized, not only during the Nationalist period
but also during the militant warlord period. Yet, as will be clear
when we look at lower levels like the county, rationalization was
only partly responsible for the expansion of state resources. By the
mid-1930s, it was clear that the contradictions and pressures of
state organizations, operating in an environment of what was
perhaps stagnant per capita income,[50] were to lead to the overwhelming preponderance of modes of expansion that were essentially traditional and, as we shall see, involutionary.

State Making and State Involution

Despite the similarities between the processes of state expansion
in Europe and China, there was, nonetheless, a curious paradox in
the Chinese experience of state making: the expansion of the fiscal
power of the Chinese state occurred concomitantly with growing
anarchy in local society. In other words, the ability of the state to
control local society was less than its ability to extract from it. The

concept of state making can only partially explain these developments. We need to develop a concept capable of explaining the paradox of simultaneous success and failure, growth and disintegration, within the same structure.

What I call "state involution" is an alternative to state making as a means of conceptualizing the expanding and modernizing role of the state in 20th-century China. In state involution, the formal structures of the state grow simultaneously with informal structures, such as the entrepreneurial state brokers discussed previously. Although the formal state depends on the informal structures to carry out many of its functions, it is unable to extend its control over them. As the state grows in the involutionary mode, the informal groups become an uncontrollable power in local society, replacing a host of traditional arrangements of local governance.

I adapt the concept of involution from Clifford Geertz, who originally applied it to his study of Javanese wet-field agriculture.[51] According to Geertz, involution is a process whereby a social or cultural pattern persists and fails to transform itself into a new pattern even after it has reached definitive form. In Java, the expansion of agriculture throughout the colonial and postcolonial period, which took place under more or less constant returns to scale, manifested itself in a baroque elaboration of the existing institutional pattern. Although this did not lead to a serious drop in per capita income, it nonetheless inhibited the possibility of economic growth (in terms of per capita yield).

State making occurs where expansion takes place on an efficient basis, whereas in state involution expansion occurs according to a logical procedure similar to the one described by Geertz. I define efficiency in the system of tax administration as follows: the system is efficient when the formal structure of the state acquires an increasing proportion of the resources collected, by whatever agencies, at the source from the taxpayer. Conversely, a system is inefficient when the formal state structure is unable to increase its share (not the absolute value) of the total resources extracted from the taxpayer. In the perfect version of state involution in state finances, we should see a situation in which every unit increase in the revenues of the formal state structure is accompanied by a commensurate increase in the income of the informal structures over which the formal state has little control. In other words, the involutive state cannot develop systems of bureaucratic responsibility at a rate faster than the entrenchment of the informal apparatus of extraction—a process that is itself induced by the increased extraction and intervention of the state in local society.[52]

More broadly, state involution occurs when state organizations expand not through the increasingly efficient use of existing or new inputs (which in this case refers to personnel and other administrative resources) but through the replication, extension, and elaboration of an inherited pattern of state-society relations—in the case of China, through entrepreneurial brokerage. When the Chinese state resorted to brokerage to fulfill its goals of expansion in the 20th century, not only did the strata of brokers encrusted on its edges swell numerically, but there was a deepening effect as entrepreneurial brokerage penetrated levels of social organization untouched previously, such as the village.

State involution does not occur where the state seeks a restricted role, as in traditional China, and where efficiency is not in itself an absolute value. It is thus inappropriate to apply the notion to feudal and colonial situations dominated by a paternalistic state, or at least by a state not committed to the rapid and continuing increase of its control over material and symbolic resources (such as education). Many of these feudal and colonial societies lack another important condition of state involution: the domination of local state forms by entrepreneurial brokers who derive their power and profit from the functions they perform for the state, but who are not easily accountable to the formal agencies (or democratic processes) of the polity. Rather, the domination of local state structures by social elites with independent bases of power typically developed in feudal societies where the state and social power at the local level were perfectly fused.

A modernizing and bureaucratizing state, though inevitably partial to certain elites, seeks to develop a structure of power that is autonomous from these elites. That is, after all, the ideal of "differentiation" of fully bureaucratic states—differentiated, at least formally and structurally, from society. Although the involutive state seeks to differentiate itself from social powers, it is unable to bureaucratize itself fully. Either it finds it easier to expand its resources by intensifying the use of existing brokerage formations, as in Republican China, or it is unable to contain the proliferation of entrepreneurial brokers choking the path of expansion on which it is launched.

These brokerage formations exist in the state structures of much of the developing world. In India, for instance, the ordinary person often needs the services of an intermediary in order to approach a bureaucrat or to get some official business done. Frequently, the intermediary is a government functionary or a professional broker whose investment and source of livelihood are his connections in the "office," which he nurtures with great care. In societies where such brokers are dominant, the state not only loses potential revenue to the broker, but precisely because the broker needs to buy his access to the bureaucracy (through bribes, commission sharing, and the like), the state also forgoes control over a significant proportion of the income of its bureaucrats. The more serious political consequence of this phenomenon is that as bureaucrats turn their attention increasingly to these alternative sources of livelihood, they become quasi-brokers themselves and cease to identify with the goals of the state. State involution climaxes at a level where the proliferation of entrepreneurial brokerage across society becomes a barrier to the rationalization of state organizations, which are now doomed to modes of expansion that are often oppressive and disruptive of local society.*

Thus the significance of the growing role of the state in provincial finances in North China must be reconsidered in light of what

---

*Despite its lack of complete fit with the Geertzian notion, I retain the term "state involution" because I have been unable to find a single expression to better describe the phenomenon. Needless to say, I use the word "involution" metaphorically—it applies not to an economic process but to a political one—much as Geertz himself transformed the idea from a cultural to a "cultural-economic" one. And like all metaphors, it draws attention to a phenomenon that ultimately differs from the original referent. Therefore, I urge readers to pay more attention to the phenomenon than to the term. The most important features the phenomenon I describe shares with agricultural involution are (1) the idea of expansion without real growth (constant returns to scale) and (2) the replication and elaboration of a given form—entrepreneurial state brokerage. What sets it apart is (1) the idea that there are formalizing and rationalizing agencies that are often in conflict with the involutive forces in the state and (2) the idea that dysfunctionalities appear simultaneously with the process of state involution; in the Geertzian notion the negative consequences appear potentially in the shape of an impending crisis of over-population and shrinking resources.

made this growth possible. The study of local finances at the county level and below reveals a complex involutionary process at the base of this growth that would release powerful forces reaching beyond the county seat into the villages themselves.

County Finances in Hebei

Although there was some demarcation of central and local sources of revenue in the early Republic, provincial and county revenues continued to remain undifferentiated. This led not only to domination of local finances by the province but also to general confusion in county finances.

Thus, for the Republican period as for the Qing, it is important to keep in mind the difference between formal and informal sources of county income. The most important of the formal revenues of the county were the surcharges levied on taxes. The late Qing practice of granting localities the right to levy surcharges for projects at their own level (like the *haoxian*, literally "meltage fee," and later the police and educational surcharge) became broadened after 1914, when localities were officially permitted to levy a surcharge on many taxes, including the land tax, the deed tax, and other miscellaneous taxes, as long as these surcharges did not exceed 30 percent of the main tax. However, the province arrogated the income from these surcharges for itself. During the warlord period, the county negotiated its share of the surcharge with the province.[53]

After 1928, when the land tax and its surcharges became the de jure revenues of the provinces, the provinces permitted counties to levy surcharges at a variable percentage of the main tax for their own projects. In Hebei, this was approximately 56 percent of the main tax.[54] On commercial taxes, which were mostly farmed out, the county surcharge was not supposed to exceed 50 percent of the provincial tax in each county. However, the surcharge rates frequently increased beyond these limits and may have been about three or four times the land tax in the 1920s and 1930s. This is a significant increase over the approximately 5.15 percent in Qing times and 30 percent in the early Republic.[55] This increase in the surcharge rate beyond the legally permitted limit, then, constituted a category of informal income.

Another source of formal income for the county was one discussed at some length above. This was the *moujuan*, better known among the peasants as tankuan (literally, "sharing the amount," or tax burden). Originally this was a levy (*chaiyao*) imposed in the northern provinces to provision supplies for the emperor, officials, or armies in transit. Although it was used widely to finance the new measures of the 1900s, it was not until 1911 that the share levied on each county was formalized, converted into a cash payment, and made its supplementary income to fund these projects. As we have seen, the uniqueness of the tankuan lay in the manner in which it was levied—on the village community as a whole rather than on an individual taxpayer. The tankuan differed from the permitted surcharge in that it had no statutory basis and the county authorities were expected to confer with the local elite to determine a reasonable levy. Thus, rather than a formal revenue source, it might be more appropriate to think of it as a conventional source of revenue.[56]

However, as the tankuan became regularized, another form of it appeared: the infamous *baidi* or provisional tankuan. A provisional tankuan, which rarely appeared on county budgets, was imposed whenever local authorities—the county, the ward, the military, or even the province—needed funds on a temporary basis. They began to increase during the warlord period as a consequence of the wars that ravaged the region, becoming part of informal local finances throughout the Nationalist period because of the increased activities of the county and resultant shortages in the local budget.[57] Provisional tankuan came to be distinguished from the regular tankuan, which were levied on a seasonal basis and appeared on county budgets. However, like the regular tankuan, they were levied not on the individual taxpayer but on the village or some other collective unit, which then devised its own means of allocating the tax burden.

The provisional tankuan quickly became one of the most arbitrary and vexatious of levies and was, of course, almost impossible to supervise or measure. Yet it probably contributed more to government revenues than many other categories,[58] and more significantly, it constituted an important source of income for government and quasi-government personnel who inserted themselves into the collection process. Precisely because tankuan levies were outside the regular budgetary process and not easily susceptible to public regulation, they tended to become swollen as they made their way down the administrative hierachy. State brokers at all levels of this hierarchy superimposed their own demands on the original levy, and it was extremely hard to distinguish whether this share was to be used for public or private purposes.

What position did the county occupy in the financial picture of the nation as a whole? In 1934, the total income of all counties in Hebei from surcharges on the land tax was 5 million yuan compared with the provincial income of 6 million yuan from the land tax. In Shandong in the same year, county income was 11 million yuan compared with 15 million yuan for the province.[59] Thus the publicized income of the counties was only slightly less than the land tax revenue. After the Nationalist takeover, county income grew rapidly—at the rate of approximately 17 percent per year from 1928 to 1933 in Qinghai county, Hebei—even through the depression years.[60]

Despite this growth, the share of revenue permitted the county was considered grossly inadequate by many contemporary observers of the fiscal system. They believed that the county was deprived of far too much of the tax income and that much more should come back to localities than actually did. According to the figures presented to the Second National Financial Conference in 1934 by Li Jinghan, the county formally collected only 75 percent of the amount the province collected and only 40 percent of what was collected by the central government from the same county. Of the total government income in the mid-1930s, the center received 52 percent, the province 27.5 percent, and the county only 20 percent. Since Li believed that little of the revenues collected by the higher levels of the government was spent for the development of local communities, he advocated fiscal reforms that would grant the county 50 percent of the total tax income.[61]

The distribution of county income sources is presented in Table 4. The most striking feature is the contrast it presents to Table 2, which documents the sources of provincial income in Hebei. Whereas income from non–land tax sources at the provincial level ranged from 70 percent to 87 percent of total revenues between 1931 and 1934, at the county level, the income from the land tax, county property, and moujuan—all sources connected with land—was 62 percent in 1931, 64 percent in 1932, and 76 percent in 1933. It is

TABLE 4

Distribution of Income Sources in Qinghai County (1928–1933)
and Ding County (1929)

Year	Land tax surcharge	Deed tax surcharge	County property	Moujuan (tankuan)	Yashui surcharge	Total[a]
Qinghai County						
1928	57%	12%	15%	—	5%	89%
1929	30	7	8	47%	3	95
1930	31	14	7	40	4	96
1931	45	19	14	3	9	90
1932	36	17	11	17	9	90
1933	39	11	7	30	5	92
Ding County						
1929	26%	4%		17%	22%	69%

SOURCES: For Qinghai County, Feng 1935: 700; for Ding County, Gamble 1968: 183.
 [a] For Qinghai County, the remaining 4 to 11 percent is made up of a multitude of miscellaneous duties.

hard to tell how generalized this phenomenon was. Ding county did record higher income from commercial taxes (*yashui*) in 1929 than did Qinghai county, and Sidney Gamble shows that a relatively high proportion of Ding county income derived from special excise duties (the animal, cotton, peanut, and wood taxes generated 28 percent of total county income). These taxes perhaps enabled Ding county to apply lower moujuan assessments than Qinghai.[62]

A nationwide study of the sources of county income in thirteen provinces shows a picture closer to Qinghai than to Ding county. Surcharges on the land tax accounted for over 60 percent of the income, and commercial taxes for less than 1 percent.[63] Although this piece of evidence tends to confirm the image that county income derived mainly from direct taxes, it also reaffirms the general impression of the success that the Hebei government had with indirect taxes from as early as the 1920s through the 1930s. Nonetheless, even here the provincial government gained much more from this source of income than did the lower levels.

What was the pattern of county expenditures? Table 5 presents the results of a study of the distribution of county expenditures by C. M. Chang for 130 counties in Hebei in 1931 and the average percentage distribution for samples from thirteen provinces in the early 1930s presented by Sun Shaocun. The chief difference between Hebei and the nationwide average was spending on police and defense. The Hebei counties spent almost twenty percentage points more on this item than the average county in the nation. Expenditures on police and defense were proportionately higher in the northern provinces, reflecting, perhaps, the greater state of disorder and military violence in these provinces. In Shandong, for instance, they accounted for 32.43 percent of county expenses; in Jiangsu for only 18.65 percent. The general pattern of distribution in Hebei is borne out in the case of Qinghai county, for which we can also a construct a time series (see Table 6).

Several points should be noted in connection with Table 6. Education was clearly an extremely important function of local government. The bulk of these funds for education was concentrated on the development of primary schools.[64] Interestingly enough, a greater share of the budget was spent on education during the warlord period than under the Nationalists, although, of course, the absolute amount spent on education was probably greater during the Nationalist era. Local security was the other top item, and in 1929 this item (police and security) constituted almost 75 percent of the entire expenses of the county. Both of these items conform to the general picture we have for Hebei as a whole. Both also tended to diminish in relative importance as other modernization projects began to mushroom through the 1930s. The gradual growth of ward expenses suggests the effort to strengthen local government at this level.[65]

One feature of county finances that came under heavy criticism from contemporary observers was the shortage of resources available for each governmental activity undertaken, a phenomenon that was seen to be largely created by the government itself. Instead of utilizing the increased revenues to consolidate or improve previously existing functions and departments, in the 1920s and 1930s the county was under tremendous pressure from the province to create departments and bureaus with additional, "modernizing" functions, such as the departments of land registration, sanitation, roads and bridges, party training, and many others. Each of these departments was allocated such paltry amounts that for a serious administrator the situation was a veritable nightmare. For instance, a county department of water control and forest con-

TABLE 5
Distribution of County Expenditures, Hebei and Nationwide, 1930s

	Hebei, 1931		Nationwide early 1930s: Percent
Function	Amount (*yuan*)	Percent	
Party affairs	58,787	0.71%	1.27%
Financial administration	237,088	2.85	3.31
Police and defense	3,235,450	38.92	19.58
Education	3,167,711	38.10	31.77
Self-government	902,556	10.85	4.81
Modernization	542,667	6.53	5.80
Charities and relief	54,270	0.65	4.02
General administration	21,116	0.25	15.44
Other	94,595	1.14	14.00
TOTAL	8,314,240	100.00%	100.00%

SOURCES: For Hebei, Chang 1934: 236–37; nationwide, Sun Shaocun 1936: 39.

TABLE 6
Distribution of Expenditures in Qinghai County, Hebei, 1919–1933
(percent)

Function	1919–23[a]	1924–28[a]	1928	1929	1930	1931	1932	1933
Education	41.19	43.36	47.80	23.69	22.38	37.98	31.44	21.68
Police	48.75	36.72	49.67	27.32	19.36	33.25	20.78	23.59
Security	—	—	—	47.13	39.64	2.59	17.01	29.54
Modernization projects	7.29	3.14	2.20	1.73	9.75	18.14	13.20	7.66
Ward government	—	12.34	—	—	8.87	7.54	14.84	15.88
Other	2.77	4.44	0.33	0.13	—	0.50	2.73	1.65
TOTAL	100	100	100	100	100	100	100	100

SOURCES: Feng 1935: 708; see also Feng 1938e: 1041–42.
[a]Annual average.

servation was granted the niggardly sum of 480 yuan, an amount that would barely pay the wages of two clerks.[66]

Indeed, so great was the pressure to develop the facade of modern government that it entailed administrative redundancy, exacerbating the shortage of available resources. Modern-style fire brigades coexisted with traditional fire prevention organizations. Police organizations existed at the county, township, and ward levels—the last of which also supervised the militia—with over-lapping jurisdictions and little coordination. Critics felt that all of these security arrangements could have been more economically and efficiently organized under a single administrative center.[67]

All this expansion meant a vast increase in the number of personnel, which in turn restricted the funds available for equipment and projects. In a study of four counties including Qinghai, Feng Huade discovered that wages alone claimed 70 percent to 80 percent of total expenditure for all items, but particularly for the top three items—police, education, and ward expenses. At the level of the ward, 90 percent of the expenses were absorbed by wages. Moreover, from 1929 to 1931, the real wage bill actually increased, as more and more bureaus and departments were added on.[68]

Among other things, the high wage-to-equipment ratio suggests that government personnel were unable to achieve a high level of efficiency. As an example, Feng cites the case of Qinghai, where there were 150 policemen but only a few modern weapons. He believed that under these circumstances the level of police efficiency was so low that many officers could well have been dismissed without much effect on the performance of the force as a whole. Since most of the county revenues went to pay wages and there was little left over to implement projects, the system of local finances ended up, to a significant degree, as a system supporting the livelihood of an increasing number of state brokers. Local government became what Bradley Geisert called an "employment contraption." Feng summed up the situation succinctly: "This disproportionate distribution of expenditures [on salaries], especially for such items as industrial development [or water control], which by its very nature requires greater outlays on equipment than on salaries, results in the creation of a nominal staff whose function is actually not to function. Under such circumstances, money spent is equivalent to money wasted, although the burden on the peasant is not in the least alleviated."[69]

The responsibility for this situation was more the provincial government's than the county's since the province had ordered the modernization measures. At the same time, the province sought to limit the funds available to the county severely, or rather, to make certain that provincial domination of local revenues was not compromised. It sought to do this in 1928 by establishing financial bureaus at the county level, oriented toward the province and with considerable powers of supervision and control over the county administration. Despite their limited success, these bureaus exercised such great financial pressures on the county that many were reduced to insolvency.[70]

The combined result of these severe pressures was to encourage trends contrary to provincial goals. First, in order for local governments to fulfill just their minimal obligations, the unreported tax income of county governments began to rise rapidly, in the form of higher surcharge rates and more frequent or higher provisional tankuan levies.[71]

Second, the additional government personnel hired as government departments expanded, were, as a result of these pressures, employed under circumstances similar to those in Qing times. The fact that the wage bill was spread so thinly over an increasing number of personnel in the proliferating organizations of local government meant that these personnel were forced to depend on sources other than their formal salaries for their sustenance. The greatest opportunity for state brokers to pursue their pecuniary interests was to be found in the provisional tankuan. There was income to be had here all the way down the hierarchy of collection. Personnel at each level added on their share to the levy, which may have emanated at any point in the hierarchy and which was extremely difficult to supervise.

Tankuan also provided the channel through which the most significant and novel aspect of the involutionary process took place in Republican times—the extension of the brokerage pattern downward to the ward and the village. Brokers at the level of the ward and in the village added on their share to the downward movement of both civilian and military levies and subtracted them in the upward movement of taxes. Official reports of the Administrative Yuan in Nanjing, elaborating on the severity of tankuan demands (which they describe as "the greatest cause of the suffering of the people"), repeatedly demonstrate this swelling or "piggyback" effect. For instance, it was reported that the forty villages and towns of Shanchuan ward in Xingtai county, Hebei, had already spent several times the budgeted amount for security expenses by the middle of the fiscal year in 1933. The increases apparently originated at the ward level and were absorbed by the militia.[72] In another example, villages paid dues that were five times the formal tankuan levy. The difference was allegedly engrossed by police and self-defense personnel. There are many such cases to be found in the literature, especially at the village and the ward level, indicating the burden of this levy. They also illustrate the manner in which this levy became an important foundation sustaining the entire structure of formal and informal government by means that were essentially unsupervised and arbitrary.[73]

The Republican state, even at the regional level, was a complex structure encompassing contradictory interests and tendencies: contradictions among formalizing and entrepreneurial agencies, competition between province and county. The purpose of this chapter has been to identify the inner contours and dynamics of this structure. If there was overwhelming dominance of state-involutionary forces here, especially at the lowest levels of society, it took place, not despite, but perhaps because of the pressures and conflicts among these different interests in a state struggling to enhance its command over society.

The modern Chinese state no more began in 1900 than the old state died in the Republican revolution of 1911. New state policies produced new results, but they also produced unforeseen effects. These effects would return the new state to the weary world of the old empire, but dizzied by the brilliance of prospective modernity, state makers would find themselves closing off the old paths of solving these problems. It is to these paths in the cultural nexus of power that I now turn.

Four

Lineages and the Political Structure of the Village

Until lately it might have been considered preposterous to regard lineages in North China as a significant factor in the cultural nexus. Supposedly, their most remarkable feature was their weakness compared with that of lineages in the Yangtze valley and further south. Unlike those in the north, lineages in the south were said to control great amounts of property, to be spread over several villages, and to maintain ties with higher-level units. Together, collective property and a supra-village network in the south provided the basic arena of rural politics and conflict, channels for upward mobility, security for the poor, and a powerful corporate identity lacking in the north.[1]

It has recently been argued that large, complex, and corporate lineages were perhaps more the exception than the rule in China, and were confined to certain locations in the south and southeast.[2] Others have shown that in the New Territories—supposedly the heartland of the dominant lineage—multi-lineage villages, functioning much like those in the north and elsewhere were just as common as the dominant-lineage village.[3] The critique of the older paradigm of lineage studies, however, goes even deeper than these arguments. Steven Sangren has mounted a radical critique of the ideology of patrilineal descent that informs the concept of the dominant lineage found in the earlier studies of Maurice Freedman and Hugh Baker. Sangren argues that the study of Chinese agnatic groups has been dominated by formal principles and jural ideas about lineages at the expense of the practical norms, functions, and operational procedures of these groups. Attention to the actual practices of these groups not only exposes the reification and theoreticism that social analysts have adopted from the Chinese ideology of patrilineal descent, but also shows how lineages embody the broader organizational principles of Chinese society.[4]

These arguments provide a rationale and context for studying kinship organization in North China that the older paradigm did not. Freed from the hold of the dominant-lineage ideal, which reduced lineages in North China to pale and rudimentary versions of their southern counterparts, northern lineages can now be shown to play meaningful and important roles in rural communities without necessarily being large, complex, or endowed with great amounts of property and a strong collective identity. Accordingly, I use the term "lineage" in a loose way: as a corporate group demonstrating descent from a common ancestor, usually through some corporate property and ceremonial ties, and often residing together.

At the same time, however, I intend to show that the older paradigm contained powerful insights, important particularly for a historical approach to Chinese lineages, that an overemphasis on the functional aspects of Chinese lineages might lead us to neglect. I refer to the native Chinese ideology of patrilineal descent itself, which more or less fits what Patricia Ebrey has called the *zong* orientation.[5] As the "official" ideology of kinship in the sense of Pierre Bourdieu, patrilineal descent does not exhaust the ways in which kinship was practically used and understood in northern villages. But just as the actual functioning of kinship and lineage organizations is incomprehensible apart from the practical deviations from the norm, so, too, they can hardly be understood without reference to this official model.[6]

It is the normative and ceremonial, as well as the organizational, features of lineages that made them such exemplary institutions in the cultural nexus of power. In many northern villages, lineages had come to define the traditional polity. Lineages and sublineages formed the basic divisions that managed administrative and other public activities, and the principle of common descent governed representation in many village governing councils. At the same time, despite the ambivalence of the imperial state toward them, lineages were significant structures linking villages to the normative universe of the higher orders of Chinese civilization.

State penetration in the 20th century was to have complex ramifications that would significantly alter both the local and the wider
role of lineages in the nexus.

To be sure, lineages were not equally important in all villages. In
some villages, lineages were rather marginal. At the end of this
chapter, I discuss two ideal types of villages—the "lineage-community type" and the "religious-community type"—as ways of
understanding the political systems of Chinese villages and
their role in the cultural nexus of local society in late traditional
times.

The Family in the Public Realm

Recent scholarship has revealed that there is no single concept of
the family in Chinese culture. Although several scholars have
outlined more than two such conceptions, I will sacrifice complexity for clarity and restrict this discussion to two broad categories
that cover most of these conceptualizations. Ebrey's historical
study of Song ideas of the family distinguishes between the *zong*
("patrilineal descent line") orientation and the *jia* ("corporate,
property-owning group") orientation. The zong located the family
in an orientation emphasizing the ancestral cult, the agnatic group,
accurate genealogies, and principles of descent or rank in determining seniority, an orientation that "in spirit" is incorporated in
the modern lineage. The jia was a basic unit of political economy,
unitary in structure and including non-agnates.[7] In many ways, it
resembled the practical family in contemporary Taiwan so ably
analyzed by Myron Cohen.

The Japanese legal scholar Shiga Shūzō has lucidly defined the
difference between the two conceptions. He sees the family as an
economic unit, which he calls the "common living, common budget
group," in which all members have an equal share. Yet from the
point of view of legal rights, this relationship of equal shares in
the family does not exist, as is evident from a simple example.
Two brothers, A and M, live in an undivided house. A has three
sons, and M has one. As a common budget group, the six have more
or less equal shares, but when it is time to divide the property, say
upon the death of A and M, the property will not be divided in four
ways but in two. M's one son will get one half; A's three sons, the

other half. Thus, from the viewpoint of inheritance, the family must be seen from the perspective of the descent line rather than of the economic group.[8]

Arthur Wolf and Huang Chieh-shan have made a similar distinction. In one form, the family is a line—a descent group that holds as corporate all land transmitted by inheritance. "The native view of the line was given its clearest expression in relation to the ancestral altar, graves, and care of the dead."[9] An uxorilocal son-in-law who may be part of a jia is not considered a part of the line. In a second form, the family is the jia (*ke* in Hokkienese). As the unit of production and consumption, it is symbolized by the stove since the jia consists of people who eat from the same stove. They further argue that the association of the jia and the stove means that the family in this sense is seen as the primary component of communities, which are themselves viewed as part of a larger political order. This argument rests on earlier work by Wolf that dealt, in part, with the role of the stove god, considered the lowest-ranking member of the bureaucracy and assigned to watch over individual families. Thus, "to define the family with reference to the seat of the stove god is to place it in the political realm and make it part of the empire."[10]

In many cases, the basic familial unit that participated in public organizations in the village and in formal political organizations on a higher scale like the ward (qu) and the township (xiang) resembled the entity that Wolf and Huang call the jia. Wolf and Huang have warned against taking the concept of jia too literally. I interpret this caution to mean that it is acceptable to envision variations on the basic idea of family members sharing the same stove—as, for instance, that suggested by Myron Cohen in which the family group can be residentially dispersed and yet belong to the same family.[11] This is indeed brought out by the *CN* interview data, which mention cases in which a son has left the family to work in Manchuria or elsewhere for an extended period. However, as long as the property and the stove had not been divided, he continued to belong to the family, which in turn was still seen as the group centered around the stove.[12]

Nonetheless, there were other cases—and telling cases in my opinion—in which the basic unit of community activities was not the family conceived of as a group around the stove or even as the common budget group. In Wu's Shop and North Brushwood, both in Hebei, the basic unit in village political and religious activities was not the jia but the *yuanzi* ("courtyard").[13] In village elections, for instance, this basic unit collectively possessed a single voting right until the institution of the baojia or decimal system of surveillance by the Japanese in 1940–41.[14] In yet another village, brothers who had already divided the family property were entered in the baojia records as a single household.[15]

The courtyard referred to a group of separate families, usually two or three, who lived in adjacent houses or in walled-off sections of the same house. The families in a courtyard were commonly headed by brothers who had divided the family property and cooked their meals separately.[16] Evidently, the courtyard constituted an intermediate level of the common descent group between the family and the lineage segment or the lineage. In some villages, the members of this unit performed various ritual and social functions together. Thus, for instance, although each component of the unit had a stove god, all the other gods and the ancestral altar were shared by the courtyard.[17] Moreover, when individual gravelands were owned apart from the common gravelands of the lineage, these were typically owned by the courtyard.[18]

The following description by Francis Hsu of a large village in Yunnan bears a striking resemblance to the northern courtyard. After having described the division of a family, he writes:

Here division ends. The family altar remains in the west wing of the house. Before that altar all family members worship their common ancestors and family gods as they have always done. . . . Each new unit will reside in that wing or wings of the house which it owns without expecting to move away or set up another altar. *With regard to community affairs, whether religious or social, the larger household remains one unit* [emphasis added]. In any community prayer meeting there will be one contribution from the family, invariably given in the name of the old father, or if he is dead, of the oldest brother.[19]

Hsu sees this pattern as a strategy that enables a household to reconcile individual freedom and competition with the social and ceremonial unity of the big-family ideal. I believe that the meaning of this phenomenon lies elsewhere, but to Hsu's functional analysis we can add several other political and economic advantages that accrued from maintaining an enlarged basic unit.

An example in the *CN* volumes comes from Xingtai county in southern Hebei where gate associations called zha operated and managed the distribution of irrigation water among their members. Leadership in this organization was often in the hands of those who owned the largest number of water shares. The records of these organizations make it clear that some of the shares were held not by individual families but by corporate agnatic units called *men* and *tang*. Sometimes, they were held simply in the name of the ancestor.[20] These agnatic units often consisted of brothers and cousins who had already divided the family property but continued to hold their separate shares as one unit. Collectively, therefore, they continued to be large shareholders and so part of the leadership structure. Sometimes, the brothers within such a unit rotated the leadership position among themselves.[21] The practice of maintaining a large unit probably helped to prevent the number of shares of the unit from diminishing, thereby stemming the loss of political influence within the organization.

Land, too, often continued to be held in the name of the ancestor for legal purposes even after the partition of family property.[22] In this way, the inheritors could avoid paying both the deed tax and the fees of the registration clerk for entering the changes. In parts of North China, the enlarged version of the household became the basis for the taxpaying household, the *hu*. The baojia records of these villages show as many as four different households belonging to a common descent group registered as a single hu.[23] (Incidentally, these findings should alert analysts using historical records from presuming an average standard size for the jia or hu in North China.)

Practical considerations aside, it is clear that in the public affairs of the village, the basic, recognized familial unit was a segment of the common descent group. Since this unit included members only of the descent group, the notion of the basic unit contained within itself the principle of the line. This leads me to believe that, considered in its unmediated form, community in the village was formed as much by groups that were related by the ancestral tie as by domestic groups that were the relevant units of economic activity. The significance of this observation will become clearer when we study the role of lineage groupings as higher-order building blocks of the polity. In turn, the character of the basic familial unit becomes more comprehensible when understood as a segment of a single kin hierarchy unified by the ritual tie expressing common descent.

Lineages in North China

The presence of lineage groups and patrilineal ideology in northern villages was in no small measure a result of their vigorous propagation by scholars, officials, and the imperial center from the Song through the Qing. Regarded as embodying the principles of classical antiquity, the ideology of descent was seen as an ideal moral and ritual medium for regulating behavior and social order.[24] Needless to say, the actual power and authority of lineage leaders derived from combining the symbolic resources of lineages with other economic, administrative, and interpersonal relations in the cultural nexus. Let us look at the ways in which the authority of the lineage was sustained.

The strength of lineages varied. In some areas like south-central Hebei, they appeared to be relatively strong, whereas in some villages near major cities, in what Skinner has called core areas, they were weak. Luancheng county and neighboring Yuanshi county in southern Hebei had many villages dominated by a single lineage or where lineages were an important factor. In Luancheng county, 60 of the 143 villages had single lineages to which over half the village population belonged. The percentage of households with the same surname in these 60 villages was as follows:[25]

Percent	Villages	Percent	Villages
50–59%	26	80–89%	4
60–69%	10	90–94%	4
70–79%	9	95–100%	7

I consider North Brushwood in Luancheng county first because of the villages for which there is detailed information, lineage organization played the most important role in this one. However, unlike in South China where the importance of the lineage was closely tied to its corporate wealth, in this village the most cohesive lineage and the one with the most elaborate organization also happened to be the poorest lineage. Not only did it have little corporate property, but its individual members were poor. This was the Hao lineage of North Brushwood, which contained about

35% of the households in the village. More than 70 percent of the members of this lineage held less than the village average of 14 mou of land. Moreover, the two largest landowners of the lineage owned only 60 mou and 35 mou each.[26] It would appear from this instance that there was no necessary correlation between lineage strength and wealth in North China.

There were four large lineages in North Brushwood, the Hao, Xu, Liu, and Zhao, which had 53, 24, 22, and 20 households, respectively.[27] Together they comprised 119 of the 140 households in the village. The Hao lineage was further divided into five segments. The ceremonial identity of both the lineage and its segments was well marked, despite their poverty. The entire lineage behaved as one unit at New Year's. But during the other lineage ceremonies, the western segment—the largest and oldest—held its ceremony and banquet separately, while the rest performed their ceremony jointly.[28] In general, relations among the segments, at least in ceremonial activities, appeared to vary according to the distance in time of the division—the earlier the split, the less close were relations. The Liu lineage also had five segments, and the Zhao had three, but little is known about relations among these segments.[29]

All the lineages in the village performed the rites of ancestor worship on New Year's day and on Qingming at the beginning of the third lunar month. Three of the four large lineages also met on the Day of the Cold Feast (*hanshihui*), known alternatively as the Gathering of Fathers and Sons (*fuzihui*), when the adult, male members of the lineage gathered together to eat cold provisions.[30] At the banquet, a distinct hierarchy in the seating arrangement, mentioned earlier, exemplified the principles of patrilineal descent. The eldest member of the most senior generation, or the lineage head, occupied the seat at the northern head of the table. Thereafter, each succeeding generation followed the other, with the members of a generation arranged in decreasing order of age. The southern end of the table was occupied by the youngest member of the most junior generation.[31]

Commonly, the ceremonies and banquets among most of the major lineages in all the villages surveyed were financed by rents from small pieces of corporate land owned by the lineages. These lands usually ranged from five to twenty mou. However, occasionally, as with the Hao lineage of North Brushwood, the corporate land of the lineage was woefully inadequate, and the lineage formed a funding association, with members contributing varying amounts to finance the celebrations.[32]

The authority of the lineage in North Brushwood was displayed in various ways. The lineage head played an important role in both the ceremonial and the secular affairs of the lineage. This was unusual in South China, where there were often men who were far more powerful than the lineage head. In North Brushwood, where stratification within the lineage was not steep, there were few people more powerful than the lineage head. For instance, his approval was necessary for adoption, and his presence was usually required during family partition. In partition and adoption deeds, his name always appeared along with that of another witness from the lineage. As if to acknowledge the importance of his position, the state often summoned him to the county court for his opinion on difficult cases involving family matters.[33]

Although the entire lineage was not a distinct unit of cooperation, people in need often turned to lineage mates. In land transactions and loans, a lineage member was often the middleman and guarantor of the contract.[34] Before the prices of agricultural commodities began to rise dramatically in the late 1930s, tenants were often arrested in North Brushwood for rent arrears and defaulting on loans. When this happened, the village head, the guarantor, and the lineage or segment head of the tenant shared the responsibility to bail him out.[35] If he pleaded bankruptcy, Chinese law authorized his creditor to strip him of his personal belongings, such as his clothes, and even the walls of his home. The hapless tenant then approached his lineage, which was obliged to contribute what it could in order to restore to him some means of livelihood.[36]

The authority of the lineage was most clear in the case of land transactions. In virtually all the villages studied, the lineage had first rights to purchase any land that one of its members wished to sell, although this was sometimes ignored in practice.[37] In North Brushwood, however, this practice was taken seriously, and the lineage had the right to annul a sale if a lineage mate sold land to an outsider before offering it to the lineage or if it offered the same price.[38] The *CN* investigators sought to verify this fact and gauge its currency in the county by questioning the chairman of the county Chamber of Commerce:

Q: If a man sells land without seeking the permission of his lineage, can the contract be annulled?

A: Yes. Developing out of their close ties [*renqing*], this custom among the lineage has become a right. Why the villagers persist in such a custom is a question I cannot answer. If a man does not offer the land to a lineage mate, but instead sells it to an outsider, the lineage will demand its right to buy the land. A custom has developed from the importance of human feelings, and from a custom it has developed into a kind of power of the lineage. Although for the county authorities, it does not matter to whom the land is sold as long as official papers are used, in practice, however, the custom [of first offering land to the lineage] has persisted as before.[39]

Finally, in North Brushwood, the lineage functioned as the organizer of class actions. If a landlord, regardless of the lineage he belonged to, demanded a rent higher than the customary rate, the tenants of a particular lineage often collectively decided against leasing land from him. In 1931, for instance, when prices began to fall, lineages successfully engaged in collective action to bargain for lower money rents. Sometimes, in order to swell their ranks, the tenants included others of the same surname as well.[40] Thus, in the absence of any class-based organizations to articulate their demands and in a situation where the lineage was relatively unstratified, the villagers turned to the authoritative principle of patrilineal descent to define the parameters of mutual cooperation and to express their collective demands.

In none of the other villages for which we have detailed information was lineage organization quite so strong as in North Brushwood. However, most of them exhibited many of the same features to a lesser degree. Hou Lineage Camp in northeastern Hebei perhaps resembled North Brushwood most closely in this respect.

Hou Lineage Camp was located less than 50 miles from the Manchurian border. Unlike North Brushwood, it was a relatively prosperous village, mainly because of the remittances of, and the money brought back by, migrant workers in Manchuria, which had been opened to Chinese since the late 19th century.[41] The baojia rolls record 114 households. The Hou lineage was the largest, with 84 households, or 73.7 percent of the population. It was divided into three segments: a large segment consisting of 68 households, another of 6 households, and a third of 18 households. The Hous were followed by the Lius with 10 households, the Wangs with 6, and the Chens with 5. There were a few other surnames, with one or two households each.[42] Another source provides us with information on landholding by lineage members; that is, not the corporate estates of the lineages, but the total land owned by the members of each lineage. The figures for the numbers of households differ slightly from those of the baojia records. Nonetheless, the figures for the households are close enough to give a rough idea of the proportions:[43]

Name of lineage	Total land owned (mou)	Number of households	Mou per lineage member
Hou	2,000	89	22.5
Liu	500	9	55.5
Wang	100	5	20.0
Chen	50–60	5	ca. 11

Although the Hous, who were numerically dominant, owned a large proportion of the total land of the village, the average landholding among them was less than half the average landholding among the Lius. The disproportionate role in relation to their numbers that the Lius played in village politics can probably be explained by their greater average wealth.

All the lineages, except for the very small ones, celebrated a festival called the Gathering at the Graves (*maihui*) on Qingming to pay their respects at the grave sites.[44] The Lius paid their respects and dined together on the Cold Feast Day as well. The Liu ceremony was financed by the interest earned on a lineage fund called the Fund for Respecting the Ancestors.[45] Since the 1860s, the Hous had also had a fund to finance their celebrations. On Qingming, there was a large gathering of the entire lineage, and three pigs were slaughtered for the feast that followed the rituals. However, after 1921, the scale of the ceremony was gradually reduced, mainly, the villagers claimed, because of the general impoverishment in the village.[46]

On further investigation, it appears that the celebrations, financed by contributions from each household in the lineage, were drastically cut around 1920 because of the high tankuan rates and heavy demands by the military.[47] These were the years when Wu Peifu fought some of the most bitter wars against, first, Duan Qirui and, later, against Zhang Zuolin in northeastern Hebei.[48] But clearly, these demands did not affect all the members of the Hou lineage equally. In fact, groups within the lineage that could afford them continued the festivities among themselves. The segments of the Hou lineage, in particular the largest segment of 68 households, were further divided into subsegments known as *xiaogu*, referring to all members within the five mourning grades. After the pan-lineage ceremony was canceled in 1921, many of the xiaogu formed associations to buy a pig and offer it to their own ancestor. Subsequently, each group dined together at its own particular gravesite. However, not all the small associations could afford the banquet,[49] and they were excluded from the celebration of this important lineage ceremony.

Thus, when the cost of organizing the large celebration became too high for some in the lineage, those who could afford to have a ceremony split off from the others. This process was basically similar to that described by Freedman for South China, where lineage segmentation was expressed in terms of economic differentation.[50] What is noteworthy about the Hou Lineage Camp example is the manner in which the interplay between lineage segmentation and stratification represented a response to external pressures faced by the lineage. It also reveals the manner in which the segmentary nature of lineage hierarchies used common descent as an authoritative principle of organization even when lineages were threatened.

In Hou Lineage Camp, the lineage head was not as powerful or as influential as his counterpart in North Brushwood. Rather, wealthy and educated individuals exercised an important influence in the lineage. Nonetheless, the lineage head's signature was required on family partition, adoption, and, sometimes, land sale deeds; and as in North Brushwood, he was summoned to the county courts to be consulted in difficult cases involving the lineage.[51] As for lineage charity, the small plots of corporate land that a lineage may have owned were leased out to poorer lineage mates, either at a nominal rent or with the provision that the tenant finance the lineage ceremony during Qingming. Although informants claimed greater lineage generosity in earlier times, in the 1930s the main form of

charity among lineages in Hou Lineage Camp was isolated instances of assistance to disabled relatives.[52]

In economic matters, an effort was made to sell land to members
of the same lineage. When land was sold to an outsider, the buyer
dined the seller, the middlemen, and some lineage members. In
the more distant past, the buyer had invited as many members of
the seller's lineage as he could afford.[53] Presumably this was a way of
publicizing the transaction and legitimizing it so that the lineage
would not have the opportunity to exercise its customary right to
dispute the transaction.

Many short-term loans were contracted between lineage members, and even when interest was charged, as in the case of loans for a
year or more, the interest charged was approximately 10 percentage points less than that charged by an outsider.[54] Whereas loans
were frequently contracted between members of the larger lineage,
most other forms of economic cooperation, such as the sharing of
implements, occurred within the segments mentioned earlier.[55]
Before we exaggerate the importance of the segment, however, we
would do well to note another condition of economic cooperation
that villagers often mentioned: people who cooperated with each
other in economic matters had to control relatively equivalent
amounts of resources; otherwise there would have been an imba-
lance in the exchange over the long run. Doubtless this condition
disqualified many members of the same segment from cooperating
with each other.

Another village in which the lineage played an important role
was Xia Walled Village in Shandong. The dominant lineages in
this village of 130 households were the Wang with 51 households,
the Ma with 30, and the Wu with 18.[56] All the lineages in this village
held their important ancestral ceremony, not at Qingming, as in the
other villages, but at New Year's, when they held a ceremony called
the Gathering to Worship the Ancestors (*zongzuhui*)[57] The Wu
lineage possessed a genealogy—one of the few found in the *CN*
villages—that circulated among its members. After the ceremony
at the graves, the household that held the genealogy entertained the
other households of the lineage. Since the poorer households could
not afford to entertain the others, the genealogy did not circulate
among them. However, they were included in the entertainments.[58]

The authority of the lineage head was not so marked as in North

Brushwood, but he often mediated disputes over family partition.[59] The corporate lands of the lineages in this village, which were not more than a few mou each, were leased out to a poor member of the lineage. Even lands that belonged to individual members of a lineage were most often leased out to lineage mates. This was especially the case with sharecropping arrangements because sharecropping required a great deal of trust between landlord and tenant. Otherwise, it was feared, the tenant might claim to have harvested a smaller amount than he actually had.[60] It was common to ask a fellow lineage member for a loan, and contracts were not required when one sold land to a lineage member within the five mourning grades.[61]

In the remaining three villages, lineages played a much more limited role than in the ones described above. Lineages appeared to be weak around major cities,[62] and these villages were located close to large metropolitan areas: Sand Well is in Shunyi county, which borders Beijing on the north; Wu's Shop Village is in Liangxiang county, which borders Beijing on the south; and Cold Water Ditch is in Licheng county, which borders Jinan in Shandong. Their closeness to these regional cities made for an active land and labor market in these villages. This introduced a certain fluidity in population and complicated the original patterns of residence and landholding according to lineage blocks (see the next section). However, it is hardly likely that proximity to urban areas was the only factor at work here. Historical factors, such as the formation of Manchu banner villages with tenants of diverse origins, also contributed to limiting the role of the lineage.

This is not to say that lineages did not exist in this second group of villages. In fact, the Li lineage in Cold Water Ditch had a genealogy and an ancestral hall. However, neither was being put to any use at the time of the *CN* survey.[63] Moreover, neither the lineage nor its segments seemed to have any form of collective worship. Ancestral worship was performed mainly on a family basis. Although the lineage did have collective lands, many of the grave sites were located outside the collective area. In principle, this was supposed to happen only when there was no space left in the collective area. In practice, however, individualization had occurred because of the popularity of geomancy (fengshui) in this area, which involved the frequent shifting around of graves.[64] Individualization represented an attempt to separate the fortunes of a particularly prosperous or ambitious family from the main line. This shift in focus away from the lineage or segment to the individual household was also the case in Sand Well and Wu's Shop,[65] the two other villages where lineages were weak. These were also villages in which lineages appeared to play no role in the political process.

To sum up, despite the absence of large amounts of corporate property in the first set of villages—North Brushwood, Hou Lineage Camp, and Xia Walled Village—lineages played an important role in the lives of the villagers. In social and economic matters, there was a good deal of cooperation among lineage mates. This was particularly evident in life-cycle ceremonies, in the market for small loans, and in the sale of land. The authority of the lineage head varied from village to village, being most developed in the extremely poor village of North Brushwood and less so in the richest of the three, Hou Lineage Camp.[66] But what is particularly noticeable is the ceremonial core defining the unity of the lineage at least through the first decade of the Republic. And these efforts to solemnize the descent group ritually at whatever segmentary level was possible continued even through the trying circumstances of the late Republic.

Although the jia orientation was deeply embedded in Chinese culture at all levels and in some ways was a part of the Confucian ideal, the classical zong orientation, as embodied in the lineage, appeared as the more official version of kinship in rural society. This was partly because lineages shared more explicitly in the Confucian values sanctioned by the imperial order, such as filial piety and the ancestral cult. But this orientation was also ideologically orthodox because, by virtue of its ability to nourish proper attitudes and social stability, it was propagated and projected in moral and ritual terms. And it is precisely these perceived ideological qualities—normative representations in the cultural nexus reproduced by the segmentary lineages—that came to legitimate the lineage in its role as an organizer of public life in the village.[67]

Kinship Space, Administrative Forms, and the Village Polity

The variable importance of the lineage is brought out most sharply by the role it played in the political system of the village. As we might expect, there was a correspondence between villages in which lineages were important in general and those in which they were an active factor in the organization of the political system. Thus, of the six *CN* villages, lineages played a significant role in the political life of North Brushwood, Hou Lineage Camp, and Xia Walled Village and a markedly less significant role in Cold Water Ditch, Sand Well, and Wu's Shop.

In order to manage administrative and other public activities, villages were divided into groupings of territorially contiguous households. In North Brushwood, Hou Lineage Camp, and Xia Walled Village, as well as in many others for which there is some information, territorially contiguous households were also agnatically related units. I call this phenomenon "kinship space." In these villages, lineages or their segments formed the basic political divisions (small lineages with fewer than three households or so were grouped together to make one or more division). Accordingly, each of these basic divisions of the polity provided one or more representatives to the village governing councils. Thus, at this level, agnatic kinship defined the principle of representation in the village councils. In other words, kinship space overlapped with "political space."

The historical relationship between state-sponsored administrative forms, such as the territorial and numerical baojia and lijia systems, and "indigenous" groupings of rural lineages and temple organizations is, as yet, mostly uncharted territory. It seems that while a vigorous imperial bureaucracy sought to promote lineages as keepers of the moral and social order, it also sought, as part of its general policy against the concentration of power, to keep them out of public administration.[68] Thus, during eras of administrative strength, the numerical systems of surveillance probably worked to counterbalance the power of lineages, but by the late 19th and early 20th centuries, the evidence from North China suggests that the relationship between kinship space and imposed territorial forms had definitely become a complementary one—and among the most intriguing relationships in the nexus.

Philip Kuhn has suggested that territorial organizations and indigenous networks may interact in various ways.[69] In local administration, for instance, networks may come to define the territories with which they are associated and vice versa. Thus, in northern India during Moghul times, although the unit of taxation, the *pargana*, was territorially bounded, what defined the ground was the reach of the dominant lineage because basically the revenue was farmed out to the lineage elite. Territorial divisions can also be imposed with no initial regard for the contours of local society, as in the case of the Chinese tax division, the *tu*. In this situation, new networks may emerge or old ones may be strengthened in order to fulfill certain functions associated with the territorial organization.

The interplay between kinship space and numerical or territorial forms invites consideration along these lines. In the villages under study, one frequently comes across terms like *pai* or *shijia* to designate the basic political divisions in the village. These terms were derived from the names of subdivisions of earlier administrative systems, notably the baojia and the lijia systems. In mid-Qing times, the pai was the unit of ten households in the baojia system,[70] and shijia self-evidently refers to ten households.[71] Interestingly, the alternative term for shijia in some villages, the *zu*, is not an administrative term but a reference to a lineage segment.

These units conformed only loosely to the numerical or territorial principle embodied in the original administrative form. Rather, in the late 19th and early 20th centuries, they appeared to be more representative of descent groups. First, these divisions did not necessarily consist of ten households, and second, they sometimes included families separated from the division physically but related agnatically to the members within it.

The overlapping of the two principles of organization was most perfectly expressed in a southern Hebei village in Xingtai county where lineages were relatively strong. In the village of Dalucun, the four important lineages were organized into four administrative units that were territorially discrete and were known as pai. The pai had no formal headmen, but each was effectively directed by the respective lineage head, under whom were several functionaries. These people handled the affairs of the lineage as well as of the unit. Moreover, each of the four lineages had an ancestral hall in its pai that not only functioned as the ceremonial expression of lineage identity but also marked its distinctness as an administrative unit.[72]

Two historical processes were probably at work to produce this overlap. In the first and simpler process, the territorial forms were absorbed into pre-existing kinship networks from the beginning. This might have been the case in South China, which is known for its powerful lineage organizations. Katayama Tsuyoshi has shown that during the late Qing and the Republic, the *tujia* units in the Pearl river delta, which were equivalent to the lijia units, corresponded exactly to lineage and lineage segments. He basically argues that the fiscal relationship between the state and the individual was mediated by the lineage in this area.[73]

In the second process, as government surveillance over administrative systems in the village like the baojia and the lijia weakened throughout the 19th century, lineage groups within these units grew and began to dominate them. This appears to have been the case in Hou Lineage Camp, where units called the shijia or zu sent out political representatives. Although the shijia, a vestige of an earlier administrative division, literally denoted a ten-household unit, in fact it included more than ten families. Usually it represented a segment of a lineage or a lineage itself and might even incorporate an occasional family in the segment that did not reside in the same neighborhood.[74] If there were fewer than ten families in a lineage, then two or more lineages combined to form a single unit, but there was a marked preference for the shijia to consist of lineage mates.[75] The administrative forms were losing their purely territorial character and beginning to provide instead a primarily organizational focus for the lineage.

In either case, the material suggests that leadership of the state-sponsored decimal system could become an attribute of the lineage system. The political certification from higher authorities that these administrative titles and forms carried most likely motivated lineage leaders to build around them or absorb them as additional political resources available at the village level. At another level, the interchangeability of the terminology for kinship space and administrative units suggests that these two forms lay within a lexical and semantic continuum in rural society, which probably reinforced the tendency to view lineages as "orthodox" and "official." Together these features enable us to see how lineages, as exemplary institutions within the cultural nexus, functioned as a legitimate medium for organizing the polity. Even if the imperial state viewed this tendency with occasional suspicion, there is no doubt that the state continued to benefit from the fact that the ideology of patrilineal descent in the villages served to legitimate the orthodox order on which the state rested.

An example from Sidney Gamble's survey of North China villages illustrates how lineage organization of the village polity evolved historically. He writes of Village A, which is northeast of Beijing and was founded by the famous eunuch Wang Yan of the Ming dynasty:

He [Wang] bought a large tract of land around the temple [in Village A] and sent two of his nephews, one fraternal and one sororal, and their families to look after the land and the temple. They were the first families in village A. Since both families had the same grandfather, the temple and land belonged to both and were the common property of the entire village. Even so, the two families and their descendants evidently recognized that they belonged to different patrilineal lines, for as the clans grew each expanded in a separate part of the village and continued to maintain the division through the years. At the time of the study they were completely distinct, the Sungs in the eastern part of the village and the Changs in the western part (the names have been changed). Politically, the Sung patrilineal line, descended from Wang Yen's fraternal nephew, was dominant with a seven-to-three, and later, a three-to-one representation in the village association or leadership group.[76]

In the *CN* villages, the village in which the residential pattern most clearly followed the kinship principle was, as might be expected, North Brushwood—the village in which lineages were most important. We are fortunate in having a map of the residential settlement of the village (see Map 3). The northeastern section of the village has a main street running north–south. The doorways of the Zhang family mainly open out onto this street. The doorways of the Hao lineage mainly open onto another major street running east–west in the northern part of this section. Whenever, in this original and main part of the village, a household of one surname appears on a street dominated by households of another surname, to the extent that it can avoid doing so, the doorway of that house does not open out onto the street occupied by the dominant surname. In Map 3, I have marked the houses in which this is the case. The pattern suggests a conscious attempt by lineages or their segments to maintain their distinctive identity through separate residence.

Another major street, which runs parallel to, and south of, the one dominated by the Hao lineage, is the domain of the Xu lineage. At the western end of this street is a north–south street, occupied on the northern half by the Xus and on the southern half by a segment of the Haos. In the southwestern section of the village, the major north–south street is dominated by the Lius. The east–west street here is shared by the Wangs and the Zhaos, but even here, they occupy more or less distinct blocks.

Interview data confirm that this residential pattern conformed closely to the norms of the villagers. They expressed a preference for lineage coresidence and even tried to own cultivable land adjacent to each other, although this was not always possible.[77] In addition to the ways discussed above in which the lineage played an important role in the life of this village, the kinship space was also the locus of the management of certain tasks, such as crop watching and night watching, which were carried out at the village level in many other settlements.[78]

Perhaps the most important function in the kinship space was the management of the annual Lantern Festival (*shenzhahui*). In general, North Brushwood had few if any community festivals involving the village as a whole, but until the early 1940s each of the kinship groups held a Lantern Festival, which lasted for the fifteen days from the first day of the year until the first full moon. A committee was formed within each neighborhood to raise contributions from the residents and manage the festival. The residents set up an altar for the gods of heaven and earth in the center of their street, and there they hung huge lanterns, burned incense, and made offerings to the gods. Around 1940, the festival was abandoned because of soaring costs.[79]

Leadership in North Brushwood was based on lineage representation. Before the reintroduction of numerical systems of organization into the village in 1929 when the Nationalists captured power in the north, the governing council of the village consisted of 12

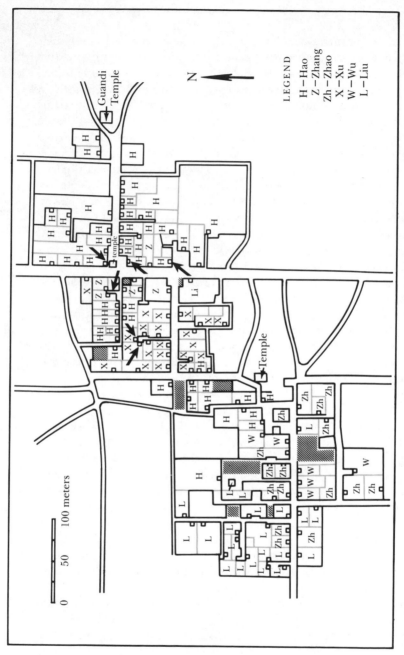

Map 3. Residential Map of North Brushwood Village. See accompanying text for explanation of arrows. From *Chūgoku nōson* 1981, vol. 3.

LEGEND

H – Hao
Z – Zhang
Zh – Zhao
X – Xu
W – Wu
L – Liu

councillors called *dongshi* or *gongzheng*. There were two representatives each from the five largest lineages, and two from the rest. The position of the representative of the lineage was usually hereditary, and in cases where there was no successor, the councillors chose a representative from the lineage that lacked one.[80] This mode of selection, which seems to have been prevalent in most villages of this type, suggests that although kinship units provided the framework on which the political system was constructed, recruitment into the leadership group was not determined collectively by the lineage group but by the elites within the lineages.

In Hou Lineage Camp, as in North Brushwood, there was a distinct tendency for members of the same lineage, and in the case of the Hou lineage for members of the segment, to reside contiguously and form a kinship space. Before 1911, the village was run by a governing council of eight or nine councillors called the *huishou* or *dongshi*.[81] Each councillor represented a unit called the shijia or zu; as discussed above, lineage forms had begun to dominate what were originally administrative forms.

Before 1911, the governing council was a collegial body without a formally designated head. As in North Brushwood, although the councillors basically represented the lineage groups, the lineages themselves did not select them. When one of them died, his successor was selected by the remaining councillors and subsequently presented to the unit for approval.[82] Of course, no cases of disapproval were reported. The functions of the councillors included supervising the periodic digging of a canal to prevent flooding, organizing the crop-watching and the night-guard systems, mediating disputes in the village, and providing the link between the village and the state.[83]

The third *CN* village in which kinship space defined the principle of representation in the polity was Xia Walled Village. Descriptions of the village indicate that there were three main residential divisions in the village, called pai, each of which was dominated by a single lineage. Thus, the eastern pai was dominated by the Ma lineage, the central pai by the Wang lineage, and the Western pai by the Wei lineage. Before 1929, pai representatives from each of these residential segments formed a governing council. The manner in which the representatives were chosen indicates the nature of decisionmaking in the kinship space.[84]

Q: Do the leaders of the lineage become the head of the pai?

A: Before 1929, the lineage conferred and selected a well-qualified member, and then the leaders of the lineage reported their choice to the village headman. Thus, the person who became the head of the pai would have to have been recommended by the powerful lineage living in the pai. Later on, all the members of the pai went to the village association and formally elected the representative who had been chosen previously.

The few ethnologies describing kinship in North China contain several cases that reveal the particular collocation of kinship space and the public realm described above, most notably those of Martin Yang, David and Isabel Crook, and Tian Deyi.[85] Indeed, according to R. F. Johnston, who wrote at the turn of the century about the Weihaiwei area in Shandong, which appeared to have a particularly large number of single-lineage villages, it would be inaccurate to speak of any public property, such as wells and roads, of the village as such. Rather, it was more appropriate to see these properties as belonging, wholly or separately, to the lineage or lineages.[86] Although this was patently not the case in many other parts of North China, his generalization does point to the prevalence of the phenomenon I have tried to elucidate above.

The three remaining *CN* villages did not have the particular residential pattern described above, probably because they had much greater population mobility than the others. Nonetheless, large blocks in Sand Well were dominated by single surnames, which suggests the presence of greater surname homogeneity in these neighborhoods in earlier times.

Lineage Politics and State Penetration

We have seen that leadership councils in many villages were often the product of an unspoken compromise between the dominant lineages organized in their kinship spaces. What was the nature of power relationships among lineages reflected in these councils and how were they affected by state penetration in the 20th century? Emily Ahern has suggested a typology of interlineage relations in China. In villages with a single dominant lineage, she posits that internal segmentation is highly developed and the ritual identity of the segments takes precedence over the unity of the lineage as a whole. Lineage identity is strongly developed in villages of a second type in which several lineages of roughly equivalent strength need to cooperate, but also compete with each other. A third type is one in which a community is made up of several lineages, one more powerful than the rest. Here the powerful lineage may either dominate the others or political competition may center around an alliance of the smaller lineages against the dominant lineage.[87]

The patterns of relationships among lineages in northern villages is comprehensible within this typology as long as the three types are seen as points in a fluid continuum of possibilities. Thus, in Hou Lineage Camp, and to some extent in North Brushwood, one fairly strong and deep lineage with well-developed segmentation coexisted with a number of other lineages. Xia Walled Village, among others, lay somewhere between the second and third types. In order to understand the dynamics of interlineage relations in the villages of North China and the impact of the state on them, I outline a trajectory of their development. The sequence of phases in this trajectory begins with Ahern's first type, is followed by her third type, and ends with her second type.

In light of Yamagata Kanki's findings that most villages in North China began as single-lineage settlements,[88] it is not unreasonable to take the single, dominant-lineage type as our analytical starting point. The lineage need not necessarily have been the original settler; it may just be the survivor.[89] At any rate, we should expect to see a dominant-lineage type of development in these villages until such time as other agnatic groups become an active presence. Thus, from a processual viewpoint, we can now understand why villages have characteristics of both the first and the third types—they are moving from one to the other. Hou Lineage Camp, with its pattern of dominant-lineage segmentation coexisting with other lineages, may be placed somewhere in this phase of development. In the second phase, we see interlineage relationships much as in Ahern's third type: dominant lineage versus an alliance of smaller ones. In Xia Walled Village, the third *CN* village where lineages were strong, the division of the village into three sections, each of which was dominated by a single lineage, originated in lineage conflict. Before this division, there was a great deal of quarreling in the village because the allegedly dominant Ma lineage oppressed all the others. Consequently, the village was divided, and the system of representation described earlier was introduced.[90]

Another example of a village in the second phase moving toward the third phase of roughly equivalent lineages competing and cooperating with each other comes from Shangkouzimen in Qinghai county south of Tianjin. Thirty of the 85 households in this village belonged to two Li surname groups. The leadership council in Shangkouzimen consisted of a village headman and five councillors, one from each lineage.[91] However, until the 1930s, the governing council had been composed predominantly of the Lis. For reasons that are not entirely clear, the system of representation changed to the one described above. The villagers felt that it was convenient to have a representative from each lineage since a person from a particular lineage "understands matters relating to his lineage better than an outsider."[92] It is possible that as the nature of decisions made by the village leadership, for instance, those concerning tankuan rates, began to affect the material lives of the people to a greater degree, other lineage groups who had acquiesced in a situation dominated by the Lis now claimed greater representation.

The transition from phase two to phase three was, of course, not inevitable, particularly if the growth of the other agnatic groups was arrested. But when it did take place, it was either because of an expansion in the numbers of minority agnatic groups or, as in the case of the Lius in Hou Lineage Camp, because of the growth of their economic power. And it was often accompanied by strife. Lineage strife in North China, though rarely as large scale or as violent as among the embattled lineages of South China, was especially prevalent during this transition. Doubtless, given the tit-for-tat pattern of lineage feuding, rivalries might also be expected to continue through the third phase. However, the need for cooperation in running village affairs during this phase mitigated or contained the development of these rivalries.

David and Isabel Crook's description of Ten Mile Inn in Shanxi, just a few miles away from the southern Hebei border, is pertinent here. Most of the households in the village belonged to three lineages. The Wangs lived in the lower village, and the Fus and Lis lived in an upper section called the Fort. Each had an ancestral hall in its own part of the village. On the first full moon of the year, each lineage organized lavish celebrations that included mock battles. The Crooks write that these battles sometimes broke out into real fights, "for they symbolized the rivalry which was especially noticeable between the lower village, where the Wangs were in a great majority, and the Fort, which was the stronghold of the Fus and the Lis. Even the two fort clans were often at loggerheads."[93] The nature of lineage rivalries, as well as the effort to contain them through ritualization, suggests that interlineage relations in Ten Mile Inn were either at an advanced stage of phase two or in phase three of the trajectory.

What was the impact of 20th-century developments, in particular the penetration of the state into village life, on this configuration of lineage power and the trajectory outlined above? Coincidentally, there were three stages of state penetration. In the first stage, from about 1900 until the Nationalists reinstituted the numerical systems of surveillance in 1929, the introduction of new resources and issues that accompanied the state's effort to expand the public sphere in the village tended to exacerbate lineage competition. In the least spectacular cases, such as in Xia Walled Village, the village headman was presented with opportunities to favor his lineage in the allocation of tankuan rates and labor service dues. As long as he stayed within reasonable limits, however, nobody created a fuss.[94]

Martin Yang's description of conflict in Taitou, a village in eastern Shandong, provides a more dramatic example. There were three major lineages in Taitou and a few small ones. Although the largest lineage, the Pans, who were divided into several segments, no longer lived in a consolidated area, the two other important lineages, the Chens and the Yangs, did for the most part live in their kinship spaces.[95] The major rivalry in the village was between the Pans, who were numerically preponderant, and the Chens and the Yangs, who were lineages on the rise. Feuds had broken out sporadically between the Pans and the Chens over matters relating to lineage honor. All in all, Taitou appeared to be between phase two and phase three of the trajectory. With the widening of the public sphere, conflicts over the control of public resources became more important. For example, no election was considered valid in Taitou unless some representatives of each lineage were present.[96]

A major incident centered on control of the village school. The village school had been owned by the Pans, but after a time the Chens and the Yangs set up a school of their own because they felt that their children were not being treated as well as those of the Pans in the Pan school. With the modernization projects of the government in the 20th century and the entrance of missionaries into the village, the picture became more complicated. The Pan school became a public school that received recognition and subsidies from the county government; the other school became an institution of the Protestant church in the village. The introduction of these new elements enhanced the stakes involved in the competition over public resources. Although, for a period, conflict was averted by demarcating from which area students were to attend the schools, animosities were rekindled when attempts were made to combine the resources of the two schools. The Pans became suspicious that the merger was an attempt to upset their position, and hostilities between the lineages grew to the extent that the village headman, who was a Pan, was forced to side with his lineage.[97]

Lineage conflict was also aggravated in Hou Lineage Camp, whose two principal lineages were the Hous, who were numerically dominant, and the Lius, who were more wealthy. An indication of the hostility between the two can be seen on a plaque donated in 1880 to a respected leader of the village surnamed Hou as a token of thanks for performing many commendable services for the village. The services included mediating disputes, aiding the poor, and assisting villagers involved in legal cases. The interesting part of the plaque is the list of 45 contributors. Four of them were councillors: two Hous, one Kong, and one Chen. Five contributors were from outside the village. Of the remaining, 27 were surnamed Hou, and 9 were drawn from all the other surnames of the village—all except for the Lius. The Lius are conspicuous by their absence because they were a powerful group. They were the second largest lineage in the village, and their average per capita landholding was over twice the village average. The explanation that the informant provided for their absence was simply that they were on bad terms with the Hous.[98]

The old rivalry between the Hous and the Lius assumed a new dimension with state intrusion and the changed circumstances of the 20th century. In 1921, because of the dramatic increase in tankuan rates and the consequent inability of those holding poorer-quality land to pay the same rate as the others, the village conducted a survey of the land owned by all the villagers.[99] Although the ostensible purpose of the survey was to grade the land into different categories, in the course of the survey a great deal of land that was unregistered (*heidi*), and thus untaxed, was disclosed. Three of the councillors belonging to the Hou lineage wished to take the offenders to court. Among the offenders was the village headman, who was a Liu. After lengthy discussions in the council, however, the matter was dropped, and completely new village land records were drawn up. Nonetheless, the old rivalry between the two lineages took a turn for the worse. The village headman and assistant headman were made to resign and were replaced by two men from the Hou lineage. Moreover, there was not a single Liu on the new governing council, and the Hous and the Lius ceased to be on speaking terms with each other for several years, despite several efforts at mediation.[100] This case is also interesting because of the manner in which lineage leaders utilized connections in the political hierarchy, demonstrating the interlocking character of the cultural nexus; I will return to it later.

Thus, during the initial stage of state penetration, the expansion of resources in the public sphere tended to heighten traditional lineage rivalries where these existed. With reference to the trajectory outlined earlier, heightened lineage competition probably hastened the transition to stage three in villages like Shangkouzimen whose councils had until recently been dominated by a single surname. Given the chance of pushing through a transformation to the third phase, minority surnames may have found the impetus to do so in external circumstances such as state penetration. In villages already in stage three or rapidly approaching it (that is, villages in which the leadership council reflected a compromise among major lineage groups), this heightened competition could threaten to destabilize the village's political structure, which depended on lineage cooperation. This was the case in Hou Lineage Camp and Taitou. No doubt, countervailing forces, such as the need for collective defense, might have worked to mute lineage rivalries,[101] but the competition for new resources and over new issues tended to divide along old lines.

It was perhaps at least partly for these reasons that the Nationalist state sought to replace traditional political arrangements based on institutions such as lineages. This represented a second stage of state intrusion and affected the system of lineage representation in one of the three *CN* villages with strong lineages. In 1929 the Nationalists instituted the *lülin* units in which 5 households formed a *lin* and 25 households formed a *lü*. These administrative arrangements appear to have largely replaced the traditional political system in North Brushwood. In En county, where Xia Walled Village was located, the county authorities did not implement these measures, but they did implement the baojia system after the Japanese takeover.[102] But whatever gains the state may have achieved in establishing a formal administrative relationship with the household were rapidly eroded by the heavy pressures of taxation and political arbitrariness, topics we will study later. Meanwhile, the disarticulation of the village polity from lineage hierarchies robbed this polity of the legitimacy gained by association with the official and orthodox traditions of the old order. By the same token, it deprived the state of a symbolic channel to communicate its normative goals in local society.

Nonetheless, judging from the resilience of indigenous kinship hierarchies and the history of their relations with imposed administrative forms, we might expect that these administrative forms could not displace kinship polities for long. It was observed earlier that local administrative units tended to become attributes of the lineage system. In fact, in Hou Lineage Camp this is precisely what seems to have happened. In 1940, the jia of the baojia system, with which the Japanese had replaced the lülin system, was found to correspond closely to the traditional kinship space of the zu or shijia.[103]

This time, however, the traditional political roles of kinship hierarchies were not fated to survive. The main reason for this was the introduction of the large township (daxiang) by the Japanese in 1941 in the last stage of state penetration (discussed at length in later chapters). The creation of this artificial unit of 1,000 households destroyed village-level systems of representation by concentrating decisionmaking functions within itself. As long as the township could retain these functions effectively, lineage groupings would be denied a role in the political process. Nonetheless, given sufficient time, kinship hierarchies might have extended beyond the village and developed human and political resources in order to adapt to the higher scale of the township. The trajectory of development of interlineage political relations might have entered another phase.

Two Ideal Types of Villages

In contrast to the villages where kinship space was closely tied to the political life of the village, in the second group of villages—Sand Well, Cold Water Ditch, and Wu's Shop—there was a markedly greater emphasis on ceremonies of a village-wide character, and as a corollary, leadership was not expressed through the framework of lineage representation. Rather, the dominant organizational forms through which the village elite expressed its social responsibilities and leadership aspirations in late Qing times were religious ones.

The study of religion is taken up in the next chapter. Here, I would like to continue the discussion on the polarity of village types in late imperial times. As with all such categorical divisions of social types, it would be foolhardy to claim that they were logically exclusive of each other. Rather, they were no more than two ideal types on the poles of a spectrum. In varying degrees, both religious and lineage ideology served to integrate all villages with the higher orders of society. Even in the case of the two most representative villages of each ideal type, North Brushwood and Sand Well, representing the lineage-community type and the religious-community type, respectively, elements of each could be found in the other.

In North Brushwood, for instance, a festival held each year on the birthday of the goddess Guan Yin had no connection with the lineages. Significantly, however, most of the participants in the ceremonies were women, and the festivities were not confined to the villagers.[104] More significantly, perhaps, those selected to organize the festival did not belong to the leadership council of the village.[105] For these reasons, I shall continue to consider North Brushwood as a lineage community. Conversely, in Sand Well, there were elements of the lineage community. The three most populous lineages here comprised 36 of the 70 village households.[106] At any point in time, members of these lineages occupied between half and two-thirds of all leadership positions, suggesting that there may still have been some vestigial consciousness of a system of lineage representation. However, as we have seen, lineages or segments did not form the basis of the political division of the village.

Although I have classified Hou Lineage Camp as a lineage community because of the importance of lineages in the pattern of residential settlement and the political structure, it was the village in which the coexistence of the two types was most clear. There were two religious ceremonies in the village that were not strictly village-wide because only the village leadership council took part in them.[107] Their existence does indicate, however, that village leaders played an important role in religious activities. A temple stele of 1864 noting that the councillors took the lead in repairing the temple confirms this observation. Interestingly, however, the four councillors who initiated the move were all surnamed Hou, and one of their ancestors had contributed the temple lands.[108] Therefore, although religious ceremonies in the village symbolized the community, the community was clearly dominated by a single lineage.

As mentioned earlier, Hou Lineage Camp benefited greatly from the opening of Manchuria to Chinese settlers and sojourners in the late 19th century. This factor contributed to the emergence of wealthy and powerful individuals in the village who were not from the Hou lineage. These people often belonged to shallow lineages, and one of them had no lineage in the village at all. It is likely that they sought to found their authority in the village in organizations and activities unrelated to the lineage. Thus, historical circumstances such as these in Hou Lineage Camp no doubt contributed to the coexistence of lineage and religious organizing principles in many villages of North China.

Finally, the lineage framework, or for that matter the religious framework, cannot exhaustively explain the nature of leadership or the actual distribution of power in the village. These ideal types help us to understand the most important institutional bases on which legitimate power was organized in the cultural nexus. In religious communities—where leadership was expressed through religious organizations—class background, influence, and ability were important in determining the leaders. Since kinship did not structure the basic political divisions of the village, it also failed to provide village leaders with an adequately cohesive constituency.

Consequently, they turned to community functions in the village to express their social responsibilities; before the 20th century, the most important of these were religious activities.

In lineage communities, kinship provided the framework for recruitment and thus determined the shape of the polity. However, the inner contours of this polity were affected by material factors. The lineage members did not necessarily determine who among them would represent them. In most cases, village leaders recruited their own successors from the appropriate lineage, and they usually chose someone from the elite, like themselves. Thus, wealth and personal prestige were also significant in influencing the distribution of power. These considerations illustrate the importance of the fusion of kin and economic criteria as an organizing principle of Chinese social life.

Five

Religion, Power, and the Public Realm in Rural Society

Even an extremely superficial reading of the *CN* surveys will persuade the reader of the importance, as well as the rapidly changing character, of popular religion in early-20th-century rural China. Yet there are few guides to lead us through a simultaneous understanding of the social and the historical roles of religion in village society. Until recently, ethnographic studies of folk religion, although illuminating the linkages between religion and other social structures, have stressed the functional and system-affirming character of this religion. The appearance in the mid-1970s of major historical works on millenarian movements quickly brought to light the lack of a dynamic vision in the ethnographic studies. However, as specialized studies of religion in rebellion, these historical works, in turn, were unable to give us an adequate image of the social and historical roles of religion in general.

In this chapter, I seek to unite the sociological and historical perspectives into a single study of religion as an evolving social phenomenon. Drawing from the sociological perspective, I examine the interface between religious and other social phenomena, in particular, power. Drawing from the historical perspective, I emphasize that this interface changes constantly. In the early 20th century, such change was brought about most particularly by the epochal intrusion of the state into rural society, which transformed the role of religion long before the Communists set out to do the same.

A Typology of Rural Religion

Religious hierarchies, networks, beliefs, symbols, and rituals are among the most significant and varied phenomena in the cultural nexus of power. Because of their varied roles in the nexus, religious associations experienced different consequences when the state moved in to destroy rural religion. In order to explain these consequences, I classify religious organizations into four categories according to the scale and principle of affiliation. This scheme is superior to a functional classification, which it subsumes, because every organizational type indexes a different mix of power resources, material and symbolic. Hence, each type can be seen to react in a distinctive way to the forces that impinged on it.

The first category refers to religious organizations whose scale of activities is subvillage. Affiliation in these organizations is voluntary, and consequently they are not identified with village-wide activities. The second category of organizations is also voluntary and not coextensive with the village. This type differs from the first in that it is a part of a supra-village organization and the coordination of its activities is often directed from outside the village. This type may extend either vertically or horizontally. That is to say, it may be part of a nested hierarchy that may or may not follow the marketing system, or it may be linked loosely but directly to a number of other similar organizations, but not through a coordinating center. Good examples of this type of organization are the sectarian groups described by Susan Naquin in her studies of the White Lotus rebels.

The scale of the third type of organization is exactly coextensive with the village. In fact, in late imperial times, many villages had no village-wide organizations other than religious ones focused on the village temple. All members of the village were automatically included in the organization, and all those who were not from the village were excluded. Thus, the principle of affiliation was ascriptive, and in this sense, the organization marked the village as a distinct entity. A number of corollary features flowed from this primary identification. First, the temple and its property were seen as belonging to the village as a whole, and contributions for temple repair and maintenance were solicited from the entire village. Moreover, the leaders of this type of religious organization often took on the management of other village-wide activities.

The claims of such leaders that this type of organization defined the "public" arena were tested from at least the 1860s when Christian converts in northern villages refused to contribute toward, or participate in, village-wide temple ceremonies and festivities. Charles Litzinger, who has studied a large number of such conflicts in the villages of Zhili (Hebei) between 1860 and 1895, noted that village leaders and Qing officials argued that these activities and properties were for the good of all village residents as a whole and thus no group had the right to secede from this ascriptive community. After all, village leaders argued, "when the rains come, all profit from it and all should give thanks."[1] These claims were tested still more sharply around the turn of the century when certain groups attempted to stake a claim on temple property. As we shall see, apart from one exceptional case, the claim of the village that this property was its collective property prevailed universally.

The fourth type of religious organization is a combination of types two and three. Like type two, a supra-village religious organization defines and orchestrates the activities of a religious group in the village. However, like type three, the entire village as a collective entity is involved in these activities. Furthermore, the village government manages these activities in the village, which is now seen as a unit of the organization. It directs the affairs of the unit and handles all relations with the larger organization. The Red Spears studied by Elizabeth Perry fit this type.

Type One: Village-bound Voluntary Associations

The best examples of the first type of religious organization, involving only a segment of the village population, were to be found in Shunyi county in a village called Henancun. Each of the four temples in the village had various associations (*hui*) established either for the worship of a particular deity or for the management of a particular festival. Temple stelae of the 19th century list seventeen associations, some of which continued their activities into the 20th century. Among these associations were the Association to Offer Fruit (the members of which offered fruit, among other things, to Guandi, the god of loyalty); associations devoted to the insect god, the god of medicine, and the rain god, all of whom were worshipped on particular dates; and the Drama Association and the Lantern Association, which organized temple festivities.

These associations were restricted to people who contributed money or land for the particular activity. Those who donated the largest amounts became the managers of the association and were called the *xiangshou* or *huishou*. These associations often owned land that they leased out. We know this from the appearance of the word for rent (*zu*) appended by the side of certain sums of money in the stelae. In the late 1930s, only the Drama Association continued to possess some land, and it had only six or seven mou. The fact that these associations possessed considerable land in the 18th century is suggested by a temple stele from 1772 that records the total lands belonging to the Guandi temple association as 72.4 mou.[2]

The proliferation of this type of religious association seems to have occurred more often in large villages. There was a similar variety of temple associations in Nijing village in Changli county and Zhaicheng village in Ding county, Hebei. In Zhaicheng, some of the associations had over 100 mou of land. Both of these villages had populations of over 250 households. Sidney Gamble cites a village of 307 households located in Wanping county near Beijing that had fifteen temples in the village and several temple associations, which together owned more than 300 mou. These associations were often, but by no means always, formed by village elites.[3]

Smaller villages had far fewer village bound voluntary associations, and they were not particularly well endowed. For example, Xia Walled Village had an association formed to worship the goddess of Taishan for the security of the members' homes. Although there were similar associations in the area, there were apparently no links between them. The members held a banquet every three years for which they contributed money. Interestingly enough, this money was used to form a credit association for the members, who were expected to return the loans in time for the banquet.[4]

In each of these cases, whether in large or small villages, the voluntary organization developed an economic interest, either in the form of land that it controlled or as a credit institution. This would suggest that voluntary religious organizations in the village often became the means of specifying a narrower group within the community and creating a coalition of interest within it. Such organizations could, of course, serve as a political pressure group or a constituency for elite groups, but I believe that apart from their religious aspects, they functioned principally as economic coalitions.

Type Two: Supra-village Voluntary Associations

One example of an association in which membership was voluntary but the ties of the association extended beyond the village comes from Luancheng county in Hebei. This organization was organized not hierarchically but rather along what Philip Kuhn has called the "tinker-peddler network": horizontal networks linking villages directly to each other. According to an official in Luancheng county, there were "mountain associations" (*shanhui*) throughout the region formed by residents of two or three villages to organize pilgrimages and worship the spirit of Mt. Cangyan.[5] The largest temple fair in the area was held near the mountain every year on the 15th day of the third month.

This organization conforms to what Steven Sangren has called an "inclusive" type of association, which tended to encourage solidarity cutting across ties to kin groups and local communities and was traditionally associated with Buddhist and female and, we may add, local deities. He contrasts this with the hierarchy of territorial cults (resembling my type three), whose deities were often conceived as imperial officials and were thus linked to the officially sanctioned state cult. The pilgrimage association counted among its members both the poor and the rich, as well as large numbers of women, who were often managers as well. By supplying free food and tea to pilgrims from neighboring counties on the way to the mountain, the association widened the cultural community organized around principles that were an alternative to those of popular orthodoxy.[6]

However, religious organizations of this type were often organized hierarchically, even when they were not territorial or orthodox. This was the case in three associations from different parts of Hebei that all belonged to the same sectarian order—the Zailijiao, a branch of the White Lotus sect that survived in North China until the Liberation. The organization of all three associations followed the marketing hierarchy, and the coordinating center was located in the market town.[7] Other associations organized hierarchically were based not on the marketing system but quite probably on the *fenxiang* (division of incense) model discussed by Stephan Feucht-wang for Taiwan.[8] Hou Lineage Camp had two organizations of this type, both of which were referred to by the villagers as "incense associations" (*xianghuohui*). One was connected with the temple of the rain god in Qiaoshang, a village in the area that was not a marketing center. The other was linked with a Buddhist temple in the county seat. This was the largest marketing center in the county but not the closest one or the one most frequented by the residents of Hou Lineage Camp.[9]

Some sectarians in the second type of association were involved not in millenarian rebellion but in everyday local politics. In North Brushwood village, among the several village headmen who served in rapid succession within the space of a few years in the early 1930s was an unsavory type by the name of Li Yanlin, whom an inform-ant described as a local bully (*tuhao*). One year when the village headman was away, Li allegedly reported to the county author-ities that the villagers had elected him headman; apparently no such election had taken place. Being an influential member of the Zailijiao sect, whose members were particularly numerous in the county capital, which also served as the marketing center, he was able to do as he pleased and forced the villagers to pay unreasonable taxes. When they did not comply, he arrested them and took them to the county courts. In exasperation, the remaining leaders of the village filed a suit against him in court, and he was suspended from his job.[10]

The last example comes from Sand Well village. With the spread of banditry in the late 1930s, an organization called the Xiantian-dao emerged in Shunyi county and began to recruit members in increasing numbers. Their avowed purpose was self-defense of the community, and they claimed invulnerability from bullets for the virtuous among themselves. The county authorities viewed the organization with suspicion but were unable to do much about it. In 1939, the county authorities prohibited the planting of gaoliang. The Xiantiandao urged the villagers of Sand Well, where there were ten members of the sect drawn mainly from small property holders, to plant the crop. The group said that it would guarantee the harvest, and it did so.[11] As in the previous case, ties with such religious organizations, which traditionally had a militant side, could provide important, extra-village leverage to otherwise powerless villagers. This resource could then be used to contest power in the village, to defend the community, or even to challenge the authority of the state.

An intriguing and mildly anomalous case in this typology is that of Christian converts. The nominal organizational focus of the community of converts was often the village (and where it existed, the village church). Nonetheless, under the umbrella of extraterritoriality granted to missionaries, converts were frequently able to mobilize enormous power resources both to protect and to aggrandize themselves against the larger village community (with whom conflicts were quite numerous).[12] Thus, a village-bound group was, because of its special position, able to act much like the sectarian groups of this second type and decisively affect the internal structure of power in the village.

Type Three: Ascriptive Village Associations

The third category of religious organization is distinguished from the first two in that it was theoretically not voluntary but included everybody who could be defined as a village member. That is to say, every village member possessed a right to participate, although, practically speaking, he might not always have been able to realize this right. Nonetheless, given that the right to inclusion in the religious group was exactly identical to the right of village membership and that often these religious organizations were the only village-wide organizations, they were the agencies that responded to the collective needs of the village.

These villages were communities whose residents supported the worship of a god whom they considered to be their tutelary deity. In many cases, this was Tudigong, the earth god, but two other deities, Wudao and Dizang, were also found in this role. Though the name of the god varied from place to place, as tutelary deity, his role and the beliefs associated with him were everywhere the same. As in other parts of China, this deity was a kind of policeman of the underworld and a minion of superior gods. Upon the death of a villager, the family reported the death to this deity, who in turn reported the matter to Chenghuang, the city god. The city god decided whether the spirit of the dead one could be admitted to the "sphere of the shadows." In this way, ascriptive, territorial communities were symbolically linked to the state cult, in which officials performed rites to the city god at all levels along the bureaucracy culminating in the imperial sacrifices to heaven and earth on behalf of all China.[13]

Identification of the village with the tutelary deity was a primary, not an exhaustive, identification. Most villages also worshiped several other gods at regular intervals or during community crises. Some of the important gods were Guandi, the female bodhisattva Guan Yin, and Longwang. Sand Well village represents the classic statement of this identification. The village had two temples, a large one originally dedicated to Guan Yin but in which Guandi had become the principal god, and a smaller one to the tutelary deity. The temples and the 40 mou of temple property were the collective property of the village.[14]

Like the other villages in the county, Sand Well held five ceremonies during the year to which all villagers had originally been invited to participate. The festivals were held on the 15th day of the first lunar month for all the gods; on the 19th day of the second month for the goddess Guan Yin; on the 8th day of the fourth month for the Buddha; on the twenty-fourth day of the 6th month, celebrated as Guandi's birthday (many places held it on his official birthday, on the 13th day of the fifth month); and on the 13th day of the seventh month for the tutelary deity. During the ceremony, which was performed by a priest called in from the county seat, the worshippers gathered together, and a ritual council known as the *xiangtou* burnt incense to the gods. After the ceremony, the worshipers feasted together.[15]

The ceremonies were strictly affairs of the village. Following the definition of village membership, only one representative from a family or a courtyard was permitted to attend.[16] Outsiders residing in the village, such as the Lis, were not permitted to attend because they were not considered villagers.[17] Similarly, the village teacher, who was not of the village, was invited to eat separately from the gathering and did not join the group as they assembled to light incense.[18] Conversely, the members of the Xing family, who did not reside in the village but were considered to be villagers because they owned a house and land in the village, were invited to join the ceremonies.[19] The same community was involved in rituals marking crises that affected the village.[20]

A word of caution is in order about the meaning of "territorial" communities guarded by the tutelary deity. As we have seen, the jurisdiction of the diety included village members who were not resident in the village and excluded the numerous nonmembers who were resident in the village (see Chapter 7). The ascriptive community mirrored in this organizational type is territorial only in the very loose sense that most people living within a territory also happen to fit the ascriptive criterion being applied. This sense of "territoriality" is to be distinguished from its more strict usage to define the territorially *bounded* area that developed in the villages in the mid-1930s as a means of coping with revenue pressures (again see Chapter 7).

The striking fact about the five regular ceremonies is that although all village members were in theory expected to participate (and during an earlier period had allegedly participated), by the 1930s only about 30 families, or about half the village, took part. Apparently the other families—the poorer members of the community—could afford neither the dues for the banquet nor the time to participate.[21] The village functionary claimed that he used to invite all the member-households in the village, but since some people regularly did not attend, he had stopped inviting them.[22]

In Cold Water Ditch, where religious life flourished in the early 20th century, there were temples to Yuhuang (the Jade Emperor), Guandi, Guan Yin, and the tutelary deity. Although by the late 1930s, the village had only 2 mou of temple lands, informants claimed that there had been much more land before 1911, which had been sold off. The claim is highly credible because a large number of temple stelae, 25 to be precise, mention grants and the purchase of land after the beginning of the Qing dynasty. Most of these grants and purchases were made for the Guandi temple, which accords with the growing imperial patronage of this god throughout the Qing.[23]

Ceremonies were held on the birthdays of Tudi, the Jade Emperor, Guandi, but by far the most important ceremony in the village was the collective prayer to the rain god. The god to whom the supplication was made was not the Dragon God, but the Jade Emperor, the highest god in the Chinese folk pantheon. Several committees, involving over 50 people, were set up to manage the ceremony in its various stages and aspects. These committees ranged from those that were assigned to buy firecrackers to those that handled the finances and drafted the prayer. For three whole days, all the villagers participated in the elaborate rites and festivities, and before the inflation of the late 1930s they also staged plays if the prayers brought rain. The entire event was financed by levying a flat rate on each household, although very poor villagers and resident nonvillagers were exempted from this levy.[24] The identification of the religious group with the village is also suggested by the fact that funds for temple repairs and upkeep were solicited from all the households in the village.[25]

Wu's Shop, a small village of about 50 households, had two temples: one to Guandi and one to Wudao, alternatively known as the Tudi temple. The temples owned a little property, about six mou of land bought by the villagers. The purchase deed of this property cites the village collectivity as the owner (*Wudiancun cundajia gonggong*).[26] Temple ceremonies, financed by a levy on each household, were held on the first and fifteenth day of each year, during agricultural crises, and on Guandi's birthday. The last was a bustling affair, and despite the impoverished state of the village, all the participants ate a meal of noodles together following the rites. This was also the occasion for the village to discuss collective matters relating to crop watching and the like.[27]

Hou Lineage Camp had two temples: one to the tutelary deity and one to Caishen, the god of wealth, which had been established by contributions from all households in the village. This temple was also known as the Guandi temple. Even though separate temple festivals were held on the birthdays of Guandi on the 24th day of the sixth month and of Caishen on the 17th day of the ninth month, it is not at all clear that the villagers always distinguished sharply between the two deities. During these festivals, villagers lit lanterns, burned incense, and made offerings to the gods.[28] Informants claimed that these festivals had once been collective affairs when villagers ate together, but by the 1930s they had lost this collective character. By this time, only the leadership council in the village feasted together and performed the rites—in place of the village, as it were.[29]

The two remaining *CN* villages evidenced a somewhat weaker identification of religious organizations with a village-bound public realm. The four temples in North Brushwood were all extremely small and had never possessed any property.[30] The major religious festival in this village was the birthday of Guan Yin on the fifteenth day of the tenth month. However, the celebrations were conducted mainly in individual homes by lighting lamps and chanting mantras.[31] The absence of a major collective congregation may suggest a somewhat weaker identification of the religious with the public sphere. Nonetheless, this identification was not completely absent. A wooden stele in the Guandi temple from 1869 records the contribution of all the villagers for its repair.[32]

Lastly, although Xia Walled Village had four temples and as much as 49 mou of temple property,[33] the two most important religious festivals lie outside the category under study. The festival to honor the goddess of Taishan mountain is discussed above. The other major religious festival was part of the activities of the supra-village organization of the Red Spears, which falls into the fourth type of religious association.

Type Four: Supra-village Ascriptive Associations

As mentioned earlier, the category of supra-village ascriptive organizations is a combination of the second and third categories. Although the association's major organizational center was beyond the village, the entire village belonged to it. Moreover, given the involvement of the entire village, the village government managed its affairs and handled its links with the larger organization. This type was often organized hierarchically and proliferated particularly during the 1920s as community self-defense organizations organized around religious beliefs.

In Xia Walled Village, for example, the village community built a temple to Zhenwu, the military god known for protecting communities from banditry and crime. The temple was built in 1921, in response no doubt to the growing insecurity accompanying the warlord battles of the time. On the third day of the third month, all the men of the village, led by the village headman, worshiped at the temple. In the early 1920s, plays were also held to mark the event, and each household in the village contributed to it, with the richer households paying somewhat more than the poorer ones.[34]

The temple and the religious association were part of a larger organization of Red Spears in the area that had been started around the same time to fight banditry. Forged by a Red Spear leader from a neighboring county, the larger organization derived its strength by aggregating several identical village organizations in the area.[35] Although principally militaristic in function, these organizations were unintelligible apart from their religosity. Membership involved not just training, but belief in the founding spirit of the organization (*zushenye*), manifested in ritual exercises and the fervent pursuit of invulnerability in battle.[36] Religious beliefs were vital in sustaining the conviction of the members and the cohesion of the organization.

Sidney Gamble mentions another Red Spear organization in Shandong formed in 1925 by a teacher from Henan province. In the particular village he describes, the village head became the leader of the local chapter of the Red Spears, and since almost all the villagers joined it, the organization became virtually identical with the village. Gamble's example also reveals that this kind of symbolically mediated mobilization and aggregation of village-level resources was not always successful against the enemy because the bandits were also quick to match this strength by banding with others and aggregating their own resources.[37]

In the northern and western parts of Luancheng county in Hebei, there were religious societies extending across several villages and committed to spreading Buddhism and defending the local area.[38] In several cases, an entire village, led by the village government, formed a chapter of the society. These organizations were apparently absorbed by the baojia system in the early 1940s since the county government did not approve of their unsupervised existence.[39] Similarly, the two Red Spear organizations discussed above were officially disbanded by the Nationalists in the 1930s and reorganized into the multi-village militia organizations known as the *lianzhuanghui*, under the formal supervision of ward authorities.[40]

Not all religious organizations of this type were associated with self-defense. In certain irrigation associations, temples to the Dragon God were sometimes identified with the village, and the village headman led the ceremonies in the temple. Moreover, outsiders were not permitted to become ritual councillors of this temple.[41] At the same time, such organizations were able to combine with similar ritual communities to pursue practical goals.[42]

In his study of Christian converts and temple communities, Charles Litzinger discusses a case from Lingshou county in west-central Hebei that richly illustrates how this type of religious organization was articulated in the cultural nexus of power. Jishan temple, located in Zhangfuan village, was maintained jointly by the six villages in Fuan pai in the 1860s. This pai formed the kind of protective-brokerage arrangement designed to deal with the government through rural agents—the xiangbao, in this case—discussed in Chapter 2. But what in Chapter 2 are purely political intervillage organizations are here suffused with a religious identity. Apart from maintaining the Jishan temple, Litzinger writes, "the gentry and people (*shen-min*) of the whole *p'ai* went [to a Guandi temple] . . . to burn incense and pray for a fruitful year."[43]

The leaders of this community picked up cudgels against the Catholic converts in the villages. I will not repeat the specifics of the case, except to note that the Catholic version of the conflict alleged that the "instigators of the conflict were the head runners and the *sheng-yuan* [lowest-level degree holders] of the various villages in Fu-an P'ai who had formed a group of several hundred people called the One Heart Society (*I-hsin Hui*) and allied with the Mo-mo Sect in Shui-nien Village, P'ing-shan county."[44] Although official investigations did not support the complaints of complicity with sectarian groups, Litzinger believes that they may well have been valid.[45]

What we see in Lingshou, then, is the interplay of three analytically separate organizational forms in the cultural nexus: a type-four religious organization completely identified with a protective-brokerage scheme and possibly, or potentially, allied with a type-two sectarian organization. Each of these forms brought into play its own symbolic and material resources: the lower-level gentry–agent linkage in the protective-brokerage scheme; the mobilization, through the type-four religious organization, of affective symbols in the One Heart Society; and the power of alternative networks of sectarian societies. The intersection of these forms defined the arena within which the temple community of Fuan pai was most prepared to do battle. What they were entirely unprepared to deal with was the ability of the Catholic community to appeal to sources of power not only outside this particular arena but also beyond the cultural nexus itself.

This study of the four types of religious organizations is designed to bring out the different role of religious organizations in the cultural nexus of power in rural society. The first type of organization was perhaps the least powerful, consisting as it did of voluntary groups within the village with no ties to organizations outside it. Socially, such organizations specified groups within the village and created new interests among the villagers. But politically, as we shall see in the final section of this chapter, they were unable to resist the expropriation of their property by more powerful groups. A possible exception to this was the Christian converts, whose unique position put them between type one and type two of this typology. Example of the second type of organization show how links with extra-village religious organizations, particularly with sectarians, could decisively affect the structure of power in the village. As with the fourth type of organization, villagers utilized these outside resources to enhance their power to defend their communities and, on occasion, even to challenge the rulings of the state. Despite the strengthening of village government around the turn of the century, by and large they were unable to contain the power of groups in the village with these external sources of power.

The ambit of religious organizations in the last two categories more or less constituted the public sphere in the village. However, whereas in the ascriptive village cults of type three the community was linked symbolically to the imperial order through the tutelary deities, in the supra-village associations of type four, villages were linked to other villages in a mode that the imperial state might consider heterodox. Nonetheless, as we shall soon see, control in both types of organizations was wielded by village elites, who sought to express their leadership aspirations through them.

Another conclusion of the study of village ascriptive associations concerns the identification of the religious group with the public domain. In this context, the expression "public domain" is perhaps preferable to "community" because the community existed in a virtual rather than an actual sense since all village members possessed the right to participate in the ceremonies and outsiders did not. Yet in practice, many villagers did not participate, or did not participate equally, because their circumstances limited them. If "community" also denotes the transcendence of specific interests, then these ceremonies did not necessarily manifest that fact.

The inner structure of ceremonies in, for example, Sand Well, shows that these ceremonies reflected the differentiation within the village. Although earlier all villagers had been permitted to attend, those who could not afford to pay the fee were later excluded from participation. In Hou Lineage Camp, whereas earlier the entire village had feasted together on the birthdays of Guandi and Caishen, by the 1930s only the leadership did so. Gamble also notes that association leaders were accorded preferential treatment during ceremonies and feasts in several villages.[46]

In part, this had to do with the decline of religious institutions at the village level in the 20th century (see below). But I believe it would be inaccurate to view the ceremonies as essentially symbolizing the solidarity of the community. The religious domain expressed a layered framework of meaning. Although the scope of tutelary deities and others incorporated the territorial community as a whole, there was considerable variation in the inclusiveness of these associations. Whether because of historical or other circumstances, religious forms mapped out a range of social distinctions from village-bound exclusive groups to a public domain dominated by the elite.

The Cosmic Bureaucracy and Village Religious Leadership

The identification of religious activity with the public domain provided an arena for the village elite to express its leadership aspirations in local society. Involvement in religious activities, such as worshiping the gods or engaging in temple building and repair, was a legitimate area of elite responsibility in Confucian China. The practice of officials' revering the gods as part of their duties has been recorded in detail by various writers.[47] The biographical sections in several gazetteers from Hebei and Shandong that I have studied record frequent contributions to temple construction and repair not only by officials but by the gentry and nongentry elite as well.

The normative responsibilities of the local elite sanctioned by Confucian society can be seen in the biographical section of the 1905 gazetteer of Wangdu county, Hebei. This section registers the virtuous deeds of the non-office-holding gentry and the nongentry elite, many of whom lived in the villages. Of the 41 biographies (and

45 virtuous deeds) for the Qing period, 10 refer to degree holders. The following is a breakdown of the 45 virtuous deeds recorded:[48]

Temple building or repair	9
Dispute mediation	8
Distribution of food during crises	6
Building of bridges and roads	5
Establishing schools	4
Paramilitary defense activities	4
Medical service to the community	3
Other	6

From these figures, temple-related activities emerge as being among the more important activities of the elite. By the early twentieth century, however, the references to temple repair cease; instead, there are more references to activities associated with the modernization measures like school building. This fits in with the campaign to de-emphasize religion in the last years of Qing rule, a phenomenon discussed in the last section of this chapter. These figures do not tell us about the actual extent of elite involvement in religion at the local level. They tell us only that it had the sanction of both officialdom and elite culture.

Arthur Wolf and Maurice Freedman once debated whether there was one religion or two religions in China;[49] that is, whether the Confucian elite believed in a religion that was radically different from that of the common people. There is reason to doubt whether this remains a valid question, but my contention that religious ideology was an important element integrating the village with the Confucian polity obliges me to take a stand on the issue.

It is difficult to entertain the notion of two religions seriously any more. It is little more than a sociology-of-religion version of the gentry-society model. Late imperial society was far too complex to be explained by a simple division between the degree-holding Confucian elite and the masses, and we would be confining ourselves within Confucian categories if we did. There is, nonetheless, a great deal of truth to the idea of the "magnetic" role of the imperial state and the ambient Confucian culture that sustained it. People at all levels of Chinese society with a modicum of wealth and education aspired for the degrees and status of the Confucian elite. At the same time, their continuing links to their many different local communities no doubt enabled them to transmit cultural codes in both directions. This nongentry elite was probably to a large extent responsible for what C. K. Yang calls "the steady interflow of religious ideas between the Confucians and the general populace."[50]

If there is a question of the number of religions in China, it would be "Is there one religion or many religions?" The resolution of this issue necessarily hinges on one's definition of "religion." We might, for instance, get one picture if we defined religion according to the structural rules of Chinese rituals, and another if we defined it according to the practical functions of these same rituals. Similarly, we can define it in terms of overt beliefs and come out with many religions or as a single set of underlying cosmological categories generating many dissimilar beliefs.

For the moment, I will focus on a category defining the relationship between the supernatural world and the corporeal world underlying many religious beliefs in China. I refer not to the concept of "immanence," which is closely related to it, but to the idea that the system of authority regulating the universe derived not from one or the other world, but from a conception of power emanating from a universal bureaucracy. How else can we understand such phenomena as that repeatedly emphasized by C. K. Yang that apart from Heaven and some of the heavenly deities, the emperor assumed superiority over all worldly and supernatural beings.[51] Furthermore, although, as is well-known, relationships between the gods were cast in a hierarchy patterned after the structure of temporal government, a fairly universal phenomenon in the villages of North China as well,[52] a living official had power over the gods and spirits of a rank lower than his and performed rites only to gods at or above his rank.[53] The interpenetration of the two bureaucracies at all levels suggests that the relationship between them is best explained not by the concept of parallel bureaucracies but by the notion of a universal or cosmic bureaucracy.

This hierarchically ordered interpenetration of the two worlds produced a certain anthropomorphization of the gods, to be seen equally in the public thrashing of an uncooperative city god by the magistrate[54] as in the deliberate neglect of the image of the Dragon God by angry villagers when he failed to answer prayers for rain.[55] Conversely, this underlying category also permitted the apotheosization of local and national heroes, a phenomenon found at all levels of society. Indeed, according to Gary Seaman, the gods of spirit-writing cults were only bureaucratic offices—to be filled by deserving departed souls.[56] This interpretation of a common underlying fount of authority in Chinese religion is not incompatible with significant differences in meanings and beliefs, and we will soon see how the various interpretations of a particular myth reflected as many different social interests.

But this view does urge that the justly famous celestial bureaucracy of popular religion in Chinese history need not be seen as a monumental hoax perpetrated over the centuries by a supremely rational mandarinate, even if some among them did occasionally express doubts about gods and ghosts. The cosmology in which authority emanated from a universal bureaucracy structured the way in which the world was experienced by all classes in traditional Chinese society (even if it was itself structured by the encompassing character of the political in Chinese life) and defined a realm in which leadership exercised its responsibilities and represented its authority. Exemplary leaders at all levels of society sought to locate themselves in proximate relation to this hierarchy of cosmic authority, much as the paradigmatic emperor and bureaucrat served as intermediaries between the two worlds.

We should, of course, heed Stephan Feutchwang's warning that the ritual practices of the imperial and scholar elite and of popular temple communities differed. As he notes, "To the people, then, temple ritual is performed either by officials or priests, both of whom have ritual knowledge that they, the people, lack."[57] Although this may well be so, it is instructive to observe the extent to which the ritual procedures of Cold Water Ditch imitated the procedures of imperial official rites, even in the 1920s.

For three days before the ceremonial prayer for rain to the Jade Emperor in Cold Water Ditch, the villagers ate no meat, fish, garlic, leeks, or onions and abstained from all sexual contact. The ceremony began with four men leading a procession carrying the image of the Jade Emperor to a nearby spring, where he was reconsecrated and brought back to the village. Thereafter, a committee of five in charge of drafting the supplication, consisting of the most literate and prestigious people, performed their ceremonial duty. With "pure" (*jie*) bodies clothed in ceremonial robes, they knelt in front of the altar and drafted the prayer (the actual writing was done by the school principal) in the form of a petition to the Jade Emperor. They wrote about the depth of suffering of the people as a result of the drought and asked for rain to relieve it. The village headman then offered up the petition (*sheng biao*) to the god three times by burning it together with other ritual objects, to the chanting of a resident Daoist priest. The villagers, who were all witness to the events, then paid their respects and drew lots from bamboo slips that forecast the weather.[58]

Compare Feuchtwang's description of an official rain ceremony in mid-19th-century Taiwan, which I quote selectively in order to focus on the similarities:

The ceremony was to be the same as that of the regular rites, with the addition of a petition prayer for rain. . . . The officials wore court dress to the altars, but after the plea for rain had been read, they changed into plain linen. . . . In addition to the usual fast, there was a general taboo on the slaughter of animals, and thus the common people were involved. . . . If the plea was still not successful, Taoist and Buddhist priests were ordered to plead in their own ways.[59]

Note also the striking similarities with the ritual preparations for imperial sacrifices. "Each sacrifice to imperial ancestors required a three-day period of sexual abstinence preceded by ritual bathing. During this period, the whole court abstained from wine, meat and strong-smelling vegetables like garlic."[60]

Despite these similarities, it was not necessary for local leaders to follow a prescribed ritual procedure in order to participate in the cosmological representation of authority. The management of temple activities, a function usually undertaken by temple councillors, who contributed a larger share for expenses, was often sufficient involvement. In Sand Well, for instance, temple councillors acquired special blessings by their closer proximity to the gods.[61] The village elite no doubt undertook the management of religious ceremonies for a variety of expedient reasons, but the bureaucrat's patronage of officially sanctioned gods and the gentry's patronage of official and nonofficial gods sounded a clear message about both the style and the responsibilities of political leadership. The cosmology described above offered a framework within which the rural elite could articulate a political vocation that was not based on education and degrees.

Once again, Sand Well in Shunyi county illustrates most clearly the relationship between leadership in the religious sphere and leadership in the village in general. Collective religious ceremonies and temple properties were managed by a group of temple councillors called the *xiangtou* (literally, incense heads) who lit the incense sticks and led the villagers in the five annual religious ceremonies. One became a temple councillor—a desirable status in the village for the reasons just considered—by contributing more money to the ceremonies or to temple repair than did others.[62]

Before 1900, temple councillors also dealt with the other public matters that came up in the village, but they do not seem to have acted as a formally constituted group in these cases.[63] Moreover, since collective village expenses were paid from the income of temple lands, the temple councillors managed village finances as well.[64] After the Qing instituted modernization measures in 1900, a smaller circle from the temple councillors formed themselves into a more formal governing council called the *huishou* in order to handle these tasks and the accompanying taxation that the leadership were now obliged to undertake.[65]

The rapidity with which the functions of the leadership were transformed while the core personnel remained substantially the same or were succeeded by their progeny is noteworthy. Five of the nine village councillors (huishou) in Sand Well in the 1930s had direct ancestors among those named in an 1886 stele listing the names of temple councillors. Several of the temple councillors owned over 100 mou of land, and one family owned over 500 mou.[66] The association of wealth with leadership, particularly in type-three religious organizations, was a persistent one at all levels of rural society. At the county seat, for instance, the councillors who supervised temple property and religious ceremonies attained their status by making greater contributions to the temple than did the rest of the community.[67]

In Wu's Shop Village, the leadership underwent the same process of transformation as in Sand Well. Before 1901, only the temple council (xiangtou) existed, and there was no secular association encompassing the entire village. The council organized the temple festivals held on the birthdays of Guandi and Tudi, the only village-wide activities.[68] In the 1930s, these festivals continued to be organized by the leadership of the village, but now it was just one of their functions.[69] The 25 stelae in Cold Water Ditch provide ample evidence of the association of the village elite with religious matters in the Qing. Even in the 1930s, despite the considerable impairment of religious life in the village, village leaders continued to solicit funds for temple repairs, and the most important "accounts committee" (*guanli neizhang fang*)—that managing the elaborate ceremony to the rain god—consisted of the wealthiest and most important people in the village.[70]

The village temple was also seen as the ultimate authority in the dispensation of justice, providing another clue to the association of leadership with religious authority. In Wu's Shop, a temple plaque starkly records the words, written afresh every year, "So you, too, have come!" (*Ni ye laile.*) Residents felt that the words suggested the ultimate impossibility of escaping retribution since they would have to confront the gods in the end.[71] In Hou Lineage Camp, an offender apprehended in the village could be beaten by anyone belonging to the village, after which he was taken into the temple. Once in the presence of the gods, only the village leaders were permitted to thrash him, while villagers looked on at this mini-spectacle of the everyday ritualization of temporal authority.[72]

Thus an important way in which the village elite was integrated with the imperial polity was through its participation in a cosmological framework that generated a shared mode of expressing political leadership among elites at all levels of society. Involvement in community religious tasks may have been only one means of expressing the leadership aspirations of the elite at the higher reaches of local society. At the lower levels, as in many villages in North China, it was often the most important means because here elites had fewer resources and opportunities to realize these aspirations.

The assimilation of the village elite within a common mode of representing authority did not, of course, entail that all who engaged in such activities held exactly the same beliefs about the gods they revered. Nor did they actually do so. Nonetheless, there was no lack of effort on the part of the Qing state to impose a unitary interpretation of popular religion by superscribing its hegemony over the symbolism of the great gods of this religion. I deal with one such effort, and its consequences and implications, in the next section.

Patrons of the Guandi Cult in North China

Guan Yu (A.D. 162–220), as he was originally known, was an apotheosized hero of the Three Kingdoms period, and in the last thousand years his myth became increasingly popular through a variety of media—literature, drama, official and popular cults, and the lore of secret societies. He was probably the most popular god in the villages of North China. The numerous temples and stelae for him in all the villages in the survey are eloquent testimony to that fact.

According to Arthur Smith, the two deities found most commonly in North China were Guandi and Tudi, the earth god.[73] The coupling of the two deities is particularly apposite because villagers often spoke of them as paired but distinctly contrasting symbols. Thus, Tudi was seen as a subordinate god uniquely in charge of the affairs of a particular village, whereas Guandi was seen as a great being, symbolic of the nation, and worthy of being worshiped by everybody. The following exchange was recorded in Shunyi county:

Q: What is the difference between the Tudi temple and the Guandi temple?
A: Tudi is concerned with only one village, but Guandi is concerned not merely with one village but with the affairs of the entire nation.
Q: Do outsiders [*waicunren*] worship at the Tudi temple?
A: They do not. Even if they do, nothing will come of it.
Q: What about Guandi?
A: People can come from anywhere. Anyone may visit a Guandi temple anywhere.[74]

In Wu's Shop Village, an informant was asked:

Q: Which is superior, the Tudi temple or the Guandi temple?
A: The Guandi temple is superior. Tudi looks after the affairs of only this village. But Guandi is a great being and does not handle the affairs of this village only. He is not merely a god of this village.[75]

Unlike the sectarian and other inclusive associations discussed by Sangren, community-based religious cults were indirectly linked to the state cult and official religion and formed an important part of the sprawling infrastructure of popular orthodoxy. But even popular religious orthodoxy mirrored a complex political consciousness.

Tutelary deities, such as Tudi and Chenghuang (the city god), had been assimilated into the official religion in the bureaucratic mode. The tutelary deity symbolized the village as a discrete entity, but one that was encapsulated by the bureaucracy. Guandi, however, appears to have borne a relationship to the bureaucratic order similar to that of the emperor, with whom he came to share the title *di*. As such, he transcended a particular territorial identity and symbolized the relationship of the village with the outside, with wider categories such as the state and the empire. Although by Qing times he had attained the highest positions in the cosmic bureaucracy, his role in rural society can by no means be fully comprehended in terms of official religion. Rather, the process whereby he came to symbolize these wider categories in the villages was a dialectical one that can only be understood historically.

The most striking fact about the myth is the bewildering variety of meanings that were derived from the simple story of Guan Yu. His biography appears in the *History of the Three Kingdoms*, written about 50 years after his death.[76] Although originally an outlaw, he later became a bodyguard to Liu Bei of the royal house of the Later Han, and together with the butcher Zhang Fei, they took the famous "oath in the Peach Orchard" binding them to protect each other until death. Still later, he became a general and a governor of a province under the Later Han. Even though he was tempted by Cao Cao, the enemy of his lord, with a marquisate, Guan Yu remained faithful to his oath. In 220, he was captured by the enemy and put to death.

Over the centuries, this story has been elaborated, and Guan Yu's achievements have been magnified to mythic proportions in storytelling and drama. Apart from his well-known role as the god of loyalty, he became the god of wealth, the god of literature, the protector god of temples, and the patron god of actors, secret societies, and many others.[77] A historical sociology of the Guan Yu myth reveals a process whereby the mythic power of the god derived precisely and increasingly from the spiritual pursuit of this figure over a millennium by many different social groups. Although the interpretations of the myth by some of these groups, most particularly that of the imperial Qing state, were sometimes at odds with others, the conative power, or luminosity, of the myth radiated from the deeply sedimented symbolic values that each particular social interest brought to the myth and left within it.

The earliest temples dedicated to Guan Yu date from the early 8th century, where he appeared in the role of a protector god of Buddhist deities; during the next 200 years it was in this role that his worship spread through the empire.[78] It is really from the Song onward that we can trace the enormous popularity of the cult and the multiple meanings that it developed in the culture. A Song story demonstrates his divine powers (*ling*). At Salt Lake in Jie county, Shanxi, a Daoist temple was established to Guan Yu in the Song. According to the founding myth, the spirit of Chiyou, legendary leader of the Miao tribes defeated by the Yellow Emperor, menaced the area during this time, and Guan Yu dispatched *yin* (shadow) soldiers to fight and vanquish him. Inoue Ichii believes that Guan Yu's popular deification (Daoist deification, he insists) is specifically communicated through the elaboration of this story in Yuan plays.[79]

More generally, Huang Huajie has argued that it was the growth of vernacular novels and plays during the Song-Yuan transition, particularly the *Sanguo zhi pinghua* (The story of the Three Kingdoms) and later the *Sanguo zhi yanyi* (Romance of the Three Kingdoms) that contributed to the spread of Guan Yu as a folk deity. Huang associates his growing popularity throughout the Qing with the gradual breakdown of self-sufficient, kin based communities and the emergence of multi-surname settlements, sojourning merchants, and marginalized vagrants. None of these new social groups was able to avail itself of the primordial bonds of kinship to hold its members and their interests together. As a symbol of righteousness, loyalty, and trust, the image of Guan Yu provided an ethic of camaraderie (*jiaoyou*) to hold together "a society of strangers."[80]

Whatever the reasons for the immense growth in his popularity, it was doubtless in response to it that the imperial state showered Guan Yu and his lineage with successive ducal and princely titles from the Song period onward and revered him as a military god. In 1614, he was awarded the imperial title, *di*, and was declared the supporter of heaven and protector of the empire.[81] His worship was particularly intense during periods of war and rebellion. Although it is clear that the imperial state patronized the cult of Guandi from the Song until the late Ming, it is less clear that it employed any systematic means to monopolize all the symbols Guandi embodied. As we shall see, this was a trend distinctive of the Qing period. Rather, wittingly or unwittingly, the earlier dynasties may even have promoted his worship in his different aspects and encouraged the different interpretations.

This is evident even under the centralizing Ming. The Ming made large contributions to a temple in Dangyang county, Hubei, which was the site of the first Buddhist temple to adopt Guandi as its protector god. Both the temple and the cult of Guandi as protector god had been revived by the Mongols, who favored Buddhism. In addition, the Ming patronized two other Guandi temples in the Beijing area. One was the Baima temple, which was the highest-ranking official temple to Guandi. In the other temple, called Yuecheng, he was worshiped as a god of wealth, a cult that spread rapidly during the Ming. Indeed, it became so important that when the imperial rank was bestowed on him in 1614, it was to the Guan Yu of this particular temple that it was given.[82]

A myth such as that of Guandi, already full of meaning but still pregnant with potential, could scarcely escape the attention of a centralizing imperial state. The Ming state, however, sought to secure its control not by ridding the myth of those symbols that did not directly support its own characterization of Guandi as a warrior loyal to constituted authority but by bringing all his various aspects under the umbrella of imperial patronage. It thus became the patron of patrons. No doubt this contributed to the composite image of Guandi found in the popular imagination down to the 20th century: a hero who was a protector and a provider, and a warrior who was loyal to constituted authority but also to his oath.

The Qing followed a much more systematic policy of bringing the cult of Guandi under direct imperial control and evinced an intolerance of the nonofficial interpretations and miracle stories that were part of the myth. Evidence of this trend can be found in the official histories of the dynasty. Guandi was promoted successively to ever higher status, as was his worship in the official cult. By 1853, during the Taiping Rebellion, his worship was raised to the same level as that of Confucius in the official sacrifices (*sidian*).[83] But it was really in 1725, guided by the rationalizing impulse of the

Yongzheng reign, that the Guandi cult was brought under systematic imperial control. The best endowed of the hundreds of popular Guandi temples in every county was selected as the official Guandi temple by the local authorities. These temples were then brought under the control of the highest official Guandi temple, the Baima temple in the capital.[84]

Of equal consequence was the effort to Confucianize Guandi, as exemplified in his hagiography, the *Guanshengdijun shengji tuzhi quanji* (A complete collection of writings and illustrations concerning the holy deeds of the saintly sovereign Guan). There were elements in the story of Guan Yu's life that did not cast him in a favorable light from the point of view of Confucian orthodoxy: his obscure origins, his record as an outlaw. Even the solidity of his much-flaunted loyalty was questionable; he had, after all, released Cao Cao, the archenemy of the prince he served, making it possible for Cao Cao to continue to menace the state. Moreover, the spread of his worship as the god of wealth and as a patron god of various sectional interests was probably not particularly congenial to the Confucian mode of regarding its heroes. At any event, the above-mentioned compilation, which was first published in 1693 and re-edited four times after that, represents a massive effort to make him into a truly Confucian hero.

The occasion for the compilation was provided by the alleged discovery of his genealogy among some bricks in a well in the county of his birth. Because of his obscure origins, one of the projects was to root him firmly as a respectable practitioner of filial piety. The fourth preface to the text begins with a literary exegesis on the complementarity of the values of loyalty and filial piety: "It is by relocating filial piety that one gets loyalty. It is also said: if you seek loyal sons, seek them at the gate of the filial son."[85] After recording the events of Guandi's life that clearly reveal his loyalty, the author laments the fact that until the discovery of the genealogy, there had been no way of verifying Guandi's parentage or whether, in fact, he had been filial. The genealogy reveals how Guandi "deeply understands the great principles of the *Spring and Autumn Annals* . . . his fine spirit, which resides in heaven, must necessarily be unable to forget the benevolence and grace of his ancestors. He recalls these virtues to transmit them to later generations. Thus, his heart of pure filiality is greater than loyalty and righteousness, which are of but one lifetime."[86] In 1725, three generations of his ancestors were awarded the ducal rank, and sacrifices were ordered to be performed to them twice a year in all official Guandi temples in the empire.[87]

Other passages speak of his mastery of the Confucian classics. "People have always spoken of his courage and have not known of his knowledge of *li* [principle]. Guandi like to read the *Spring and Autumn Annals*. When on horseback, his one free hand would always hold a volume."[88] Indeed, his loyalty is attributed to his understanding of the subtle meaning of the *Annals*. In contrast to the historian Sima Qian, who represents the scholarly ideal, Guandi is depicted as representing the activist ideal, the Confucian sage who "protects the principles and perfects the exercise of power [*shoujing daquan*]."[89] Finally, his divinity is linked to the greatness of the empire. "Guandi's divinity [*ling*] resides in heaven. Sacrifices to him in the temple are held on an elevated plane in order to manifest his awesome dignity. He has silently assisted in the well-being and long peace of the empire. Herein lies his merit of protecting the state and harboring the people. Is this not great?"[90]

These efforts to Confucianize Guandi did not, of course, succeed entirely in reversing his popularity in his other roles, particularly as a god of wealth or as a protector of local communities. Nonetheless, the measures employed by the Qing were not without impact in local society. The stelae dedicated to Guandi in villages throughout the Qing period show that of all the possible interpretations of Guandi—as a god of wealth, as a protector of temples, as a hero loyal to his vow—the most common was the one that invested him with Confucian virtues and loyalty to established authority.

There were five stelae dedicated to Guandi in Cold Water Ditch. The earliest, dated in the Kangxi period (1662–1723), begins:

It is said that in ancient times sacrifices were made and temples were built to honor those who had brought merit [*gong*] to the dynasty, who had been virtuous among the people, who had glorified honor and integrity [*mingjie*]. . . . At a time when above and below were confused and the proper principles [*gangji*] disintegrated, there arose a special person who was loyal and acted appropriately to his status [*erjie buqu yiming bugou*]. He caused evil ministers and sons of robbers to know their position. He was granted the heavy responsibility of seeing that they did not confound righteousness [*dayi*] and create disorder. . . .

He [Guandi] did not accept a fief from the robber Cao Cao and remained loyal to the house of Han. Is this not merit to the dynasty! He eliminated the danger of the Yellow Turbans and executed the disorderly soldiers. . . . Is this not virtue for the people! He searched a thousand li for his [sworn] brother. Finally, he died the death of a martyr [*er zu shashen cheng ren*]. Is this not to bring glory to honor and integrity?[91]

The text of the stele was drafted by a degree holder from the county seat, but that was not always the case. Some texts were drafted by lower-degree holders belonging to the village, and others mentioned no gentry titles at all. The last usually had a brief text and recorded the names of the village leaders and contributors. In any event, the stelae almost invariably referred to Guandi's loyalty to the state or his Confucian virtues. One such stele, which records a grant of land to the temple, had no gentry signatories but recounts Guandi's successive honoring by the state.[92] Another text composed by a lower-degree holder of the village in 1819 and bearing the names of village leaders reads:

A chapter in the *Book of History* says: "There are times when a good man is afraid that there are not enough days; and when an evil man is also afraid that there are not enough days." Thus we know that the godly way [*shendao*] establishes religious teachings in order to bring happiness to the good man and harm to the evil man.

Now, the Lord Guansheng of Shanxi despises the nine evils with extreme severity. On the 15th day of the 9th month of 1813, the White Lotus invaded the precincts of the capital, and the imperial court was put in danger. In very little time, the blessed god of the armies, with the brilliance of his divine powers, pushed back the White Lotus. He caused them to submit to the law and executed every single one of them. . . .

The leaders of our village and others have saved their humble possessions and put together some money to build a new temple and a new image.[93]

A stele from Hou Lineage Camp was erected in 1864 on the occasion of the repair of the temple to the god of wealth and the establishment of an image of Guandi:

To Reconstruct the Temple and Mold an Image of Guansheng

His face is painted to create awe of his divine authority. By so doing, it will attach importance to his teachings and his favors, which have been the same in the past as now.

Our village of the Hou banners has of old had a temple to the god of wealth. Alas, it had become covered with brambles and smoke. . . . In the past we had repeatedly improved the temple, but for three years the yield of the land had been very poor. Now Taisui [the star god presiding over the yearly cycle] is aligned to the sun. As a tribute of thanks, we gathered to discuss the expansion of the temple. In this way, we enhance our admiration of Guandi's protection of righteousness [*yi*] and his preservation of the institutions of the empire [*gang*]. We wish to burn incense and make offerings to him.[94]

This stele, which bore the names of the village leaders and two degree holders, was emplaced in the presence of the county magistrate himself. What is going on here is the process of imperial superscription: the official image of Guandi is being written over an older cult of the god of wealth, a god who is often confused with Guandi in *his* aspect as the god of wealth. For instance, when merchants in Ding county were asked why they worshipped Guandi, they replied that it was because Guandi was Caishen.[95] This process was probably not uncommon in the 1860s when the imperial order was briefly reinvigorated during the Tongzhi Restoration. Even the poor and gentryless village of North Brushwood set up a stele in 1869 to commemorate the rebuilding of the Guandi temple and record his "great virtues."[96] What is remarkable about the Hou Lineage Camp case is the continued importance of Guandi in the village, as evidenced by the celebration of his birthday, in addition to that of the god of wealth, through the 1930s.

I have studied the myths and symbols reproduced in the stelae in the context of the larger, historical background of the multivocal myth of Guandi. A first conclusion is that, for the elite, involvement in the building or repair of temples to Guandi, whatever else it meant, appeared to symbolize a reorientation away from parochial identities and toward more abstract ones, such as the empire, state, and orthodoxy. The participation of the gentry, whether from the village or from outside, underscores this point. Moreover, it also suggests that, in some of the larger villages, belonging to temple committees may have allowed the nongentry elite in the village to come into contact with the gentry. This would suggest that cults like those of Guandi were responsible for integrating the village with the larger society not only symbolically but also organizationally.[97]

Second, the attempts of local leaders to identify with the culture of a national elite probably set them apart from the rest of the villagers to some extent. To what degree this really happened depends on the extent to which the symbols of Guandi had the same meaning for the ordinary villager as they did for the elite.

A clear statement favoring the view that Guandi had different meanings for different segments of the community comes from Sand Well, where it was said that the rich patronized Guandi and the poor prayed mostly to Nanhailao, a variant of Guan Yin.[98] In Wu's Shop, the ordinary villagers prayed to Guandi for all kinds of benefits, including medical ones.[99] This seems to have been the case for ordinary peasants all over North China, where he was worshiped in his generalized aspect as a provider and protector of communities. Li Jinghan, in his massive survey of Ding county, writes that common rural folk worshiped Guandi to "seek fortune and avoid disaster [*qiufu mianhuo*]."[100] Although this characterization of Guandi is not the least incompatible with the imperial and Confucian characterization, it does not invoke the state and Confucian culture symbolically in the same manner as do the myths in the stelae.

In a study of the Tian Hou (Empress of Heaven) myth, James Watson has argued for a separation of symbol and belief in the interpretation of myths. The outwardly unitary *symbolic* character of the goddess Tian Hou concealed differences in what different social groups *believed* about her. To an outside observer, Tian Hou was a state-sponsored deity symbolizing respectability and "civilization," but this did not prevent the various levels of the social hierarchy from constructing their own rather different representations of this deity.[101] This stimulating formulation can be used to understand the Guandi myth—to a point. Although Guandi meant different things to different people, I would urge that symbol and belief are not separate but closely intertwined. What Guandi symbolized to one person also communicated itself in some degree to another. Significantly, his different aspects are linked in a semantic chain: a warrior loyal to his oath, and loyal to constituted authority; a hero protecting state and communities, turned provider of health and wealth. A particular interpretation lay within the semantic chain and derived its conative strength from its participation in this chain.

The semantic chain that constituted the Guandi myth developed historically, reflecting the changing needs of the state and social groups even as they built on earlier symbolic constructions. Much as a word in poetry draws its power from its many hidden associations, any particular version of the Guandi myth necessarily drew its power from this vast historical background of associated meanings. Thus, in the last analysis, the efficacy of the Confucian characterization of Guandi depended on the popularity of his many aspects. And the source of his appeal among the village elite was to be found in the multiple significances that simultaneously rooted him both as a popular and as an imperial god.

Transformation of the Religious Domain

So far I have reached three related conclusions regarding how religious institutions provided the framework for organizing authority in rural communities. First, the religious sphere constituted the public domain through which the village elite was able to express its leadership responsibilities. However, because of economic differentiation, the elite often performed ritual activities in the name of the community, thereby simultaneously marking its exclusive status in this community. Finally, through the patronage of cults such as that of Guandi, the elite was able to express its identification with the values of the state and the gentry.

In this section, I examine the attack directed against religious institutions during the late Qing modernizing reforms, which prefigures several such attacks during the Republic: in the period immediately following the establishment of the Republic; during the May Fourth era; and during the antisuperstition drive of the Nationalists in the late 1920s.[102] Understanding the process of transformation of the religious domain during the first phase in the early 1900s is particularly important because the historical significance of the political component in village religion is brought out most sharply at this moment when community religion ceased to embody this component. The rapidity with which the village elite withdrew its active patronage of religious organizations and refocused its energies on the new projects testifies to its past interest in the political within religion.

In villages where most public activities had been embedded in the religious sphere, this sphere provided the foundation for the new and more purely secular realm of the public known as the *gonghui*. Wherever the elite had expressed its leadership in village-wide activities through religious organizations, these leadership structures automatically took over the new functions.[103] Indeed, the new activities were so important that the very basis of religious life in the village was threatened, as temples were converted into public offices and schools and temple property was taken over to fund the new activities.

Evidence of this process comes not only from the *CN* villages but also from gazetteer and other reports from various parts of Hebei and Shandong. In the 62 villages surveyed intensively by Li Jinghan and others in Ding county, Hebei, the number of temples declined by 316 between the years 1900–1901 and 1915, from 432 to 116. Some of these temples had fallen into disuse, but most had either been destroyed or been converted into public buildings. One period of intense appropriation came around 1900, when the order was given to build schools and public offices. Another came around 1914 and 1915, when the zealous modernizer of Ding county, Sun Faxu, ordered the destruction or conversion of 245 temples.[104]

The subcounty gazetteer of Wangdu county in central Hebei has the most detailed report on the conversion of temple lands. The report was drawn up in 1905 in response to the modernization measures being promoted in the region. In order to acquire accurate information on the resources available for schools in the villages, the authors surveyed the public properties of every village. A total of 59 of the 150 villages listed had some temple lands. Of these 59, villagers took over these lands for schools in 30 cases; they took them over to pay for taxes and other expenses in 23 cases. In the remaining cases, they continued to support religious functions in the village, maintaining priests, caretakers, and ceremonies.[105]

In 1899, the Zhili provincial government ordered Shunyi county to organize modern-style schools. The county magistrate instructed the gentry, as well as the leaders of the subcounty division, the lu, to mobilize resources for new schools throughout the county. The 1933 edition of the county gazetteer records 203 modern-style schools, of which 160 were lodged in what were previously temples.[106] The gazetteer for Changli county, Hebei, where Hou Lineage Camp is located, provides selective information on the fate of temples in every bao, not including the county capital. Of the 42 villages with temple lands, in 17 the plots became the property of the village government, in another 17 they became the property of the new schools, and in 8 they remained attached to the temple.[107] Although the gazetteer distinguishes school land from village government land, in fact most schools and their finances were controlled by the village government.

In Liangxiang county, Hebei, the gazetteer records that temples were converted into schools continuously from 1908 until 1923. According to the finance officer of the county, in 1911 all temple property in the county became the property of the public association.[108] The head of the finance department of Luancheng county recalled that in 1908 temples were destroyed and their lands converted into school lands:

Q: Did this happen throughout the nation?
A: Yes, it did.
Q: Was there a feeling that temples were unnecessary?
A: There was an order from the government to disregard temples and construct schools. It was just like the Meiji Restoration.[109]

We find the same process repeated in the *CN* villages. However, the dates provided by the informants are not reliable, and we would do better to rely on the dates cited in the gazetteers. In Cold Water Ditch, some of the temple lands were converted into school lands, and another part was pawned to finance the construction of the new schools. All three large temples were converted to public use: two became the offices of the village and the administrative village councils (*cungongsuo, xianggongsuo*), and the third became a primary school.[110] In Xia Walled Village, a portion of the temple lands was sold to pay for the school.[111]

In Sand Well, the income from the temple lands, which until the turn of the century had been used mainly to maintain a priest and finance temple ceremonies, was taken over by the village councillors, and the lands were designated as belonging to the public association. The income from these lands went mainly to finance the schools and to pay the taxes levied by the new police departments.[112] Gamble mentions three villages where temple lands were taken over in the early part of this century in order to finance the new demands on the village.[113]

The conversion of temple property to nonreligious uses seriously undermined religious life in the village and produced a great deal of disaffection. Rarely was the transition handled smoothly. One such instance came to light in an exchange between the *CN* interviewers and a village leader from Hou Lineage Camp:

Q: Would the people oppose any attempt to destroy the temple?
A: They would.
Q: When they set up the school in the temple and had to relocate the temple, did the villagers discuss the matter?
A: The village headman, Hou Quanwu, assembled all the villagers and spoke to them. He said, "Since the village is small, it is not good to have a temple that is too large. The reason we no longer have success when we go to Manchuria is because the temple does not harmonize with the small size of the village. So we will convert the temple into a school and build another, smaller temple."[114]

The informant attributed the success of the transfer largely to the persuasive skills of the headman. In addition, the plan was rather moderate, and no temple lands were involved because Hou Lineage Camp did not have any. In most cases, however, the conversion of these properties from religious to nonreligious uses was not an easy one. Dissent and resistance came, of course, from ordinary villagers to whom modernization and religious belief did not seem incompatible. But other groups were also affected by the conversions.

Most directly and completely affected were the priests and monks attached to these temples, who had managed to eke out a living or supplement their incomes from these lands. Although the monks had usufructuary rights to the temple land, there was no record of the actual proprietary rights in many villages since these lands were often tax exempt. Villagers stoutly defended the position that the lands belonged to the village, but where there were no proper records, a monk with influence in the county seat could even sell these lands. Legally speaking, the matter was not really clarified until a Nationalist proclamation in 1931 required all temple lands to be registered as public property and permitted their use for educational and official purposes.[115]

Once temple property was transferred to the public association, most leadership councils in the villages were able to get rid of their priests and monks. A finance officer in Liangxiang county reported: "In 1911, all temple property became a part of the public association. Since 1911, the power of the monks and the priests has dwindled. Because the villagers wanted the temple lands to set up educational facilities, they fought with the monks and priests."[116] In Luancheng county, the priests and monks reportedly opposed the move but were cowed by the police.[117] In Cold Water Ditch, although there is no evidence of opposition by priests, it is noteworthy that some temple lands were pawned to the priest attached to the temple.[118] Presumably, he could continue to make a living by cultivating them. Gamble also cites instances from Hebei of struggles—sometimes, legal struggles—between village leaders and priests over control of temple lands that ended in victory for the village leaders.[119]

The most interesting case of a struggle with a priest comes from Shimen, a village neighboring Sand Well in Shunyi county. Both Shimen and Sand Well got rid of their monks around the end of the 19th century. The village leaders then approached the priest at the city-god temple in the county seat to perform religious services in the village when needed, in return for some kind of compensation. But it was not clear whether he was to receive a share of the rental income from the temple lands or the entire amount in compensation. The villagers claimed that since he had never performed any services, the rents had ceased to go to him.[120]

Forty years later, the matter came up again. A local bully in Shimen by the name of Fan Baoshan claimed to be descended from a line of respectable and propertied temple councillors. He was himself, however, a pettifogger with intimate links to yamen underlings and the priests of the official temple. He was particularly close to the head priest of the temple of the city god, a successor to the priest with whom the villagers had entered into an agreement. According to the villagers, the priests in the city were debauched opium addicts. They reserved a special hatred for the head priest, who they claimed was a criminal who had acquired his position through his links with government functionaries.[121]

In 1938, Fan Baoshan contrived to become village headman of Shimen. In collusion with him, the head priest from the city claimed a right to the temple lands, which by now had become the property of the public association. According to the priest, the temple lands had actually been given over to the city-god temple, and he had orders from the temple authorities in Beijing to manage these lands. The villagers were afraid to take the case to the county courts because they were convinced that they would be no match for these crafty and influential types. The councillors of Sand Well were also closely involved in the dispute because they feared the same thing would happen to their village. Finally, in an unexpected move, the Sand Well councillors asked the *CN* interviewers to intercede on behalf of their neighbors, and the matter was finally settled to Shimen's advantage.[122]

The case is significant for several reasons. First, it reveals the extent of entrepreneurial brokerage even in the unlikely area of state religion. More important, it reveals the degree to which the system of authority organized around the cultural nexus had been rendered impotent and meaningless by the penetration of a lethal coalition into the power structure of the village: a coalition between a village power broker and yamen entrepreneurial brokers. Although this kind of case might just as well have occurred during an earlier period, the issue in this case was a direct result of the state policy of appropriating temple property. It strengthens the argument that the unprecedented degree of state intrusion during the modernizing era, by increasing the opportunities for profit in various ways, also increased the likelihood of intervention by such coalitions.

I now turn to the study of the effects of the appropriation of temple property on ordinary villagers and how they opposed it. The extent of this opposition is indicated by a statement made by the same finance officer of Luancheng county who compared these changes to the Meiji Restoration.

Q: Did the priests and monks oppose this move?
A: Not only did they oppose it, but the common people opposed it as well. The police had to be sent to the villages to forcibly remove the image of the Buddha and convert the temples into classrooms.[123]

We have already seen how in Hou Lineage Camp opposition was carefully circumvented by the deft maneuvers of the village headman. In Sand Well, the loss of temple property led to the gradual decline of religious activities, and by the 1920s the five annual ceremonies were virtually abandoned. At that time, about 15 families who were not councillors but belonged to the middle or poor peasant bracket decided to work for their restitution. When asked why they did it, the informant replied quite simply, "Because it was an association of our Buddha."[124]

Apart from the community religious institutions, the organizations that were most seriously affected by the appropriation were the voluntary religious association within the village. These groups conformed to type one in the typology of religious organizations, and they often controlled some property in common. Village-bound and relatively powerless, the properties of these associations were too tempting for village governments not to absorb. The formalization of village governments also legitimated their efforts to appropriate the properties and curb the powers of these groups.

An example from Gamble's work shows how the formalization of the village government adversely affected the power of other groups in the village. In Village B, there were several temple associations and one crop-watching association in the period before 1900.[125] In that year, when orders arrived from the county government to create the new organizations, since none of the temple associations was powerful enough to take over these functions, the crop-watching association responded to these orders. Its leaders appointed two of its members to the new positions, and the name of the organization was changed to Village Public Assembly.

One of the temple associations, the Association of the Fair of the Fourth Month, was managed by an independent group of leaders belonging to landless families. It hosted the temple fair by soliciting contributions, principally from the richer families, who found them extremely irksome. The richer families controlled the newly developed public association, and hostility developed between the two organizations. In 1929, the village authorities of the public association sought to bring a suit against the fair association. Although the authorities were ultimately persuaded to drop the suit, they were successful in preventing the fair association from collecting contributions.

The powers of a voluntary temple group in Nijing, a market town close to Hou Lineage Camp, were similarly usurped.[126] The market in this village was held in the temple grounds. One of the several temple groups in charge of this particular temple leased the space to vendors to set up stalls there. In the early 20th century, the formally constituted government of the village took over the right to lease the lands, as well as the income from the levy on the vendors.

Opposition by villagers to the appropriation of the properties of their voluntary religious organizations was most dramatic in Zhaicheng, the original model village in the model county, Ding county. The following information is drawn from the history of the modernization efforts in the village led by the elite and from the biography of its moving spirit, Mi Digang.[127]

By the first decade of the 20th century, the village had set up schools, defense organizations, and hygiene and welfare institutions. After having used all the public sources of income in the village for these efforts, the reformers still lacked funds. Therefore, in 1905 the village government expropriated the land and income of the various voluntary religious groups, such as the Lantern Festival Association, the Association for the God of Horses, the Drama Association, and others. Some of these associations had as much as 120 mou of land.

The village leaders argued that these funds were being unproductively employed and that the festivals promoted gambling and drinking in the village. The villagers, however, were outraged and rose up in defense of their property and festivals. They were joined by other villages in the area. A protracted legal suit of an unprecedented nature ensued and exhausted all parties. Later on, the biographer explains, as the villagers saw the benefits of the modernization efforts, the movement subsided of itself.[128]

Conclusions

The utility of the fourfold typology of religious organizations becomes readily evident when studying the changes that religious organizations underwent in the 20th century. The process of appropriation of religious property and the transformation of the religious sphere affected all organizations in the first and third categories. Religious organizations in the third category were affected most because they were *the* communal institutions in the village. Since the elites who had controlled these organizations seemed to respond eagerly to the state's drive to transform religious properties, organizations in this category felt the impact of these changes most deeply. Organizations in the first category, which included property-owning, voluntary associations within the village, also suffered because the need for greater resources tempted village governments to absorb their properties.

Associations in categories two and four, which had links with religious organizations outside the village, were not adversely affected by the transformation. In fact, they probably became a much more powerful influence in the countryside during the unsettled years of the 20th century. This was especially true for those religious groups with a militant side. These associations proliferated, especially during and after the 1920s,[129] because they provided villagers with a measure of security in the extremely anarchic circumstances of the period. Presumably, at the village level, these groups also gained sufficient power from their links with the parent organization to defy the transformative drive of the state. What this suggests is that although it may be true that villages tended to close themselves off economically during difficult times, their political connections with other communities almost certainly intensified during the same periods. Like affinal networks that bypassed the market town, these trans-village ties reveal ways in which several channels within the cultural nexus were kept open, or even developed, while others were being closed off by the involutionary state and the disruptions of the 20th century.

Resistance to the expropriation of religious property and to the generally diminishing role of religion in the village was by no means absent. Yet, for better or worse, the transformation was swift and, by and large, successful. How can we account for this? I believe the key to understanding lies in what C. K. Yang has called the "diffused" character of Chinese religion.[130] In China, control of religious life by a religious authority organized separately from temporal authority, as in the case of the Brahmin castes or the Catholic church, was very weakly developed. Rather, religion was "diffused" in the various sectors of society, such as the state and the village community, and its control by a secular leadership was ensured by a cosmology in which elites with leadership aspirations interposed themselves as mediators in a universal bureaucracy. This cosmology not only permitted the social elite to control local communities through religious forms but also enabled them to participate in a style of exercising power that was prestigious and pan-Chinese in scope.

This participation also oriented the leadership of rural communities toward the imperial order, particularly through their patronage of figures such as Guandi. The extension of state power in rural society in the initial stages made it possible, and even necessary, for the elite to develop alternative bases for the organization of its power in village society. The political element in their involvement in religion made it easier for them to transfer the focus of their activities. The outward-looking and integrating functions of the Guandi cult that had enabled the village elite to locate themselves in a national hierarchy were initially served by the new political arrangements of the 20th century.

It is important to note that the new political relations between the village and the state took place in a national context. Even throughout the early Republic, the titles and programs that came down to the village emanated from a national authority. Surely it is for this reason that the elite responded with such remarkable alacrity to the initial modernizing measures. The new schools, in particular, presented them with opportunities for upward mobility that they were quick to recognize and seize. My discussion of modern education as a novel type of "symbolic capital" has been rather desultory, and it deserves a much fuller treatment. At any rate, the symbolic linkages of the elite with the old empire were being transformed into an incipient identification with the goals of an emerging nation-state. How this early identification was systematically destroyed during the course of the Republican period is the subject of the subsequent chapters.

Six

Networks, Patrons, and Leaders in Village Government

Who were the actual leaders of village government? How important were such factors as wealth, status, and influence as sources of their personal authority, and hence as sources of the strength of village government, especially through the trying circumstances of the 20th century? These questions are taken up in this chapter; in Chapter 8, I examine the extent to which state penetration was responsible for the changing relationship between these sources of authority and those of village government leadership.

Wealth and influence were often translated into political resources through patronage networks held together by the status or "face" of the patron. Networks in the cultural nexus of power were formed by functionally diffuse and informal small groups, and these features distinguished them from hierarchical organizations. As a consequence, the codes of authority in these networks were largely interpersonal and did not necessarily reproduce institutionalized, orthodox values in rural society. Sometimes, as among sectarian religious networks, they may even have been subversive of the orthodox order.

However, the networks surrounding village leaders often served *indirectly* to reinforce the predominantly orthodox character of the cultural nexus—the characteristic that linked it to the higher orders of imperial society. Through these networks, village leaders or patrons performed various services for clients in the village, and the patronage bond reinforced their status as leaders in the more formal institutions of religion, kinship, and, in the early part of the 20th century, village government. Through interpersonal ties, these networks also linked the resources of different hierarchies, such as those of the higher levels of administration and lineages in the village, thereby assimilating these hierarchies into a continuous nexus of culture and power.

When, between 1900 and 1912, the institutions of formal government took definite shape in the villages studied here, village offices were dominated by the elite who had traditionally articulated their leadership aspirations through religious or lineage organizations. Although their religious and kin-based functions in the community gradually lost their original salience, many among this leadership elite continued to discharge certain social duties as patrons in order to maintain their status and influence among their clientele in the community.

By the 1920s and 1930s, however, the demands of an intrusive state, together with those of battling armies, had become so onerous that the patron type of leader increasingly began to abandon village offices, which were then filled by men of another sort. Although from diverse social backgrounds, these men shared a basic perception of the rewards of politics and village office. Office was no longer pursued as a way of expressing leadership aspirations or gaining prestige because these goals could no longer be realized through these means. Rather, like clerks, tax farmers, and other entrepreneurial state brokers at higher administrative levels, men began to seek office for immediate gain, often at the expense of the community's interests.

Perhaps the most important task of village government leaders in the 20th century was the allocation of tankuan dues (periodic levies). This was done by the village headman and the leadership council, with whom he conferred on all matters. Village leaders were also expected to manage the allocation of labor service dues for construction projects ordered by the ward or the military. Another of their tacit responsibilities was to make advance payments personally, when necessary, on the frequent irregular levies imposed by the government and the military.[1] They were forced to make these payments because villagers did not always have cash on hand. Later, while collecting the regular levy, they also collected these sums from the villagers. This was, incidentally, one reason why village leaders were expected to be wealthy.

A second set of activities related to the various community tasks started mostly between 1900 and 1912. These included crop watching, management of the village school, and village self-defense. Naturally, village leaders also handled the income of the village and records of village finances, which they guarded jealously. After 1930, the village headman in Hebei carried the additional responsibility of being the official middleman in land transactions. Just as significantly, around the same time, the village government was made the tax farmer for commercial taxes (yashui) in some villages.[2]

Although not on a strictly formal basis, the governing council determined who held power in village government. It chose the village headman and his assistant and recruited new council members. Toward the beginning of the period, this council was made up of well-to-do members of the village, and they often recruited new members from their own circle of the elite. In some villages, even after elections were instituted in 1929, the council continued to determine the candidates for the jobs of village head and his assistant. As a group, they were distinctly collegial, and their decisions were overtly consensual in character.[3]

The xiangzhen (township and municipality) and the numerical lülin systems that the Nationalists instituted in 1929 after capturing power were to constitute the apparatus not only of administration but also of local self-government under the county. Officers were to be elected by representatives of the next lower unit, down to the lin where all five households elected a representative.[4] In practice, however, these elections affected the political structure in only a few villages during the 1930s, and the lülin system increasingly resembled the baojia system of surveillance. The size and functions of the township (xiang) changed frequently during the 1930s, but the large township of 1,000 households (daxiang) replaced the natural village only after the Japanese-backed administration rigorously enforced it in 1941.

Profiles of Village Leadership

The following profiles combine data on property ownership with biographical materials to see how landed and nonlanded property, kinship, and patronage ties worked to define leadership in the village. I also examine the extent to which these resources became less important in village politics as the 20th century drew on.

Sand Well

Sand Well was considered by the *CN* interviewers to be an average North Chinese village. In the late 1930s, there were 70 households in the village. There were no large landlords with many tenants, but there were several managerial landlords who owned over 70 mou and employed wage labor. The distribution of land was unequal, with 60 percent of the households owning 14 percent of the land and 15 percent owning 52 percent.[5]

Leadership in Sand Well was in the hands of the wealthier 15 percent, and unlike in many other *CN* villages, they continued to hold on to it from at least 1900 until the late 1930s. The principal tasks of village leaders shifted from religious ones to those connected with the crop-watching association instituted by an order from the county in 1900.[6] Before this, crop watching had been done mainly on an individual basis. With the formation of the association and the village council (huishou), the state created both a protective community institution and an organizational format through which levies could be allocated in the village at any further point.

What was the nature of the village council? Scattered information on the property owned by village councillors before the 1930s makes it clear that wealth was the most important attribute of village leadership—more so in the earlier period than in 1940. The average landholding among the nine councillors was 50 mou, a figure that was considerably higher than the village average of under 15 mou.[7] From historical information, it is immediately apparent that the councillors of the early 20th century were even wealthier than those of 1940 (see Table 7).

Two of the councillors in 1940 whose immediate ancestors had also been councillors had had much greater holdings earlier. Seven of the councillors had ancestors who had been councillors, and from the interview data on the appearance of their names in temple stelae, it is clear that these ancestors had been wealthier than most of their successors.[8] Other villagers (and their ancestors) who had been councillors when they were wealthy were eased out when they ceased to be so.[9] However, when the baojia system was reintro-

TABLE 7
Information on Landholding in Sand Well Village, 1940
(mou)

Council members	Land in registers	Con-cealed land	Total	Historical information
Zhao Tingkui	18	1	19	From a line of temple councillors. Father had 130 mou. Originally had 70 mou himself.
Li Ruyuan	68	4	72	From a long line of village headmen.
Zhang Yongren	46	2	48	Not from a councillor family. Made his money 20 years before.
Zhang Rui	130	2	132	Became rich in his own lifetime. Not from a councillor family.
Du Xiang	12	0	12	From a councillor family. Had 54 mou in early Republic.
Li Xinfang	35	16	51	From a long line of councillors.
Yang Yuan	34	8	42	Village headman. Nonlanded source of wealth. His ancestors were wealthy councillors and village heads.
Yang Ze	31	5	36	Brother of Yang Yuan.
Yang Zheng	29	13	42	Brother of Yang Yuan.

SOURCES: *Chūgoku nōson* 1981, 2: 524–36, 1: 124–25, 174.

duced into the village in 1940, two new members were inducted into the ranks of the councillors as *jiazhang*, or decimal headmen. Neither was particularly wealthy, and this fact may reflect the tendency of village rich to shun official administrative positions in the later Republican period.[10]

Seven of the nine councillors in 1940 had fathers or grandfathers who had been village councillors. An analysis of successive village headmen shows that from late Qing times, this post was occupied by Li Zhen, his son Li Zhenying, and his grandsons Li Hangyuan and Li Hongyuan. Li Zhenying's brother was a councillor, and this brother's son was the Li Ruyuan listed in Table 7. According to Li

Zhenying's son, the family had owned 200 mou before his grand-father's time and 100 mou in his father's time, but this had dwindled to 20 mou in his own time.[11] With the decline in their fortunes, members of the family ceased to occupy the position of village head or even councillor. Thus it appears that a village officer was succeeded by his son only if the son met some property qualification. Lack of education was no bar to village office, and many councillors and headmen were illiterate.

A brief look at the biographical materials of the three most important councillors reveals the kinds of patronage networks that formed the less tangible bases of their prestige and authority in the village. The headman, Yang Yuan, was descended from a line of wealthy councillors. Two of his brothers were also councillors. His wealth was concentrated less in land than in a handicraft store that he owned in the county seat. Yang Yuan's store was too small to be included in the Shunyi Chamber of Commerce, but for the villagers it was an important opening through which they made contact with the commercial world of the city. Yang himself loaned money to needy villagers or, when he was unable to do so, took them along to the store and introduced them to a prospective moneylender from his wide circle of acquaintances. He also introduced prospective tenants of the village to their landlords.[12]

By some standards, Yang's public behavior was not spotless. He and his brothers jointly concealed more land than other villagers, and he had sold some of his swampy land to the village government.[13] This did not seem to affect his standing in the village. As an indication of this standing, he was an important mediator in disputes both between villagers and between villages. By 1940, when he had tired of his post and was eager to give it up, he had served as the village headman for eight years. He clearly remained interested in a public career, as evidenced by his recent appointment as principal of a school jointly set up by four villages. In short, Yang Yuan was a typical patron and leader in a small community, weaving networks with favors and obligations, materials spun from his links to the world outside the village.

Li Ruyuan was perhaps the most respected man in the village. He had been a councillor for longer than anyone else, and although he was from a long line of village leaders, he was a self-made man. In the early Republican period, he had only 20 mou of land, but by the 1930s he had accumulated over 70 mou. He built his capital, reputation, and clientele on his chosen profession as a practitioner of traditional medicine. He boasted that there was nobody within a radius of 50 li who did not know of his skill. Like Yang Yuan, he was an important mediator in village and intervillage disputes—a fact that was perhaps more a mark of his status than a cause.[14]

The ancestors of Zhang Rui, the assistant village headman, were poor and had not been councillors. An aggressive entrepreneur, he was rumored to have accumulated 130 mou in his own lifetime. Zhang was not particularly interested in a political career in the village, and he was a councillor because he was wealthy and could advance payments on tankuan levies.[15] Nonetheless, he organized a group of villagers to work in a shop in Beijing every winter during the slack season, and they were doubtless grateful to him for their extra earnings and probably expressed their loyalty to him in village politics.

Hou Lineage Camp

As mentioned earlier, Hou Lineage Camp became increasingly prosperous over the first third of the 20th century as a result of the increased incomes of workers and traders who went to Manchuria. In 1940, of the approximately 110 households in the village, about 22 percent held between 0 and 10 mou of land, 47 percent held between 10 and 30 mou, a little less than 20 percent owned between 30 and 60 mou, 5.5 percent owned between 60 and 100 mou, and 6 households, or about 5.5 percent, owned over 100 mou. Of these 6 households, 3 owned over 150 mou. Despite the relative prosperity of the village, the 70 percent of the households owning less than 30 mou had to supplement their income by leasing part of the land belonging to the some 12 households with surplus lands.[16]

I have already discussed at some length the political system of this village (see Chapter 4). In brief, the councillors (huitou) represented lineages and their segments, but at the same time they also represented the village elite. The recruitment process exemplified the intertwining of the two principles, economic and kinship, in the constitution of the leadership: the councillor was chosen from, or rather for, the appropriate lineage, but he was chosen by the remaining councillors and not by his lineage. As in the other villages, a son often succeeded his father, but only if he had adequate property and competence.

The 1928–29 data in Table 8 are from the time of the abolition of the councillor system and its replacement by the numerical lülin system. Of the eight councillors, two owned over 100 mou each, one owned 80, another 50, and the remaining four owned approximately 20 mou each. The fathers of three of the poor councillors had not been councillors. The modest wealth and the lack of background of half the councillors seem to have been a recent development. Hou Yintang, the leader of the Hous, said that when he had been village headman in the early Republic, people who were not wealthy had not been tolerated as councillors.[17]

The data on the councillors, however, do not tell us the entire story about the domination of village government by the elite. This elite also occupied the positions of village headman and assistant (see Table 8, data for 1914–42), positions not included among the list of councillors. Before the Republic, there was no single leader of the councillors, and all decisions were taken collectively. The positions of village headman and his assistant were instituted after 1911 by government order. The first two village headmen were wealthy men from the list of councillors. However, the next six, from 1921 to 1940 were not from this list, but all were extremely wealthy. Three of the five assistant headmen were also landowners of substance.

Thus, even though four of the eight councillors in 1928 were poor, most of the village elite seemed to be involved in running the village government either as councillors or village headmen in the Republican period. The village elite had not quite begun to avoid village office as their counterparts had in many other places. Indeed, when the problems of running the village were not quite so acute, there were distinct advantages to occupying a position in village government.

Q: Is it advantageous for people owning a lot of land to try to become a councillor or village headman?

A: Yes.

Q: Why?

A: Because if somebody else takes up the job, it may happen that they have to pay excessive amounts in taxes. If they are in charge, they will try and minimize expenses so as to keep their share low.[18]

TABLE 8

Property Held by Councillors (1928–1929) and Headmen and Assistant Headmen (1914–1942), Hou Lineage Camp

Name	Property (mou)	Name	Property (mou)
	COUNCILLORS, 1928–1929		
Father was councillor			
Hou Yintang	80	Hou Baochen	50–60
Liu Wanquan	100+	Hou Fengchang	20
Hou Xianyang	100+		
Father was not councillor			
Hou Zhuoran	20	Hou Xinyi	20
Wang Zhisheng	20		
	HEADMEN/ASSISTANTS, 1914–1942		
Headmen			
Hou Yintang (1914–17)	80	Hou Baochen (1928–32)	60
Hou Xianyang		Hou Dasheng (1932–36)	80
(1917–21)	150	Hou Quanwu (1936–39)	160
Liu Zixing (1921?)[a]	170	Liu Zixing (1939–41)	170
Hou Enrong (1921–26?)	70–80	Hou Yuanguang (1942–)	150
Hou Baotian (1926–28)	70		
Assistants			
Hou Erzhen	30	Kong Ziming	31
Hou Enrong	70–80	Xiao Huisheng	60
Hou Yonghe	70		

SOURCES: *Chūgoku nōson*, 1981, 5: 8–9, 41–42, 56–57.

[a]For the uncertainty regarding Liu Zixing's first term as headman, see *CN*5 41, 42–43, 56–57.

The role of patron as exemplary leader was particularly well developed in this village. There were three plaques in Hou Lineage Camp that had been presented by the villagers to their patrons. One of them, a wooden tablet dedicated to the first headman of the village, hung on the outer wall of his son's home and was a token of the villagers' gratitude for his various services to the village, such as mediating disputes, giving aid to the poor, and assisting people entangled in legal suits. Another recipient of such a plaque worked as a functionary in the county tax office. The plaque, dated 1870, noted that he often advanced money to villagers unable to pay taxes or requested the magistrate to grant extensions.[19]

The third plaque was granted in 1937 to Xiao Huisheng, perhaps the most influential village leader at the time of the survey. The words "ardent in public service" (*rexin gongyi*) were inscribed on it, and although the move was initiated by the leaders of Hou Lineage Camp, the plaque was presented to him by the residents of 38 villages within the ward. They were grateful to him for successfully mediating disputes that would have become legal suits, an eventuality feared by the villagers as bringing ruin to all parties. He was most often approached by villagers when he was director of the telephone bureau in the county from 1934 to 1937. He was also responsible for raising contributions for the village school in Hou Lineage Camp when it was in need of money, and for this and other services performed specifically for Hou Lineage Camp, he was granted another plaque by his fellow villagers. Apparently, plaques were granted to benefactors during their lifetime in order to enhance their "face."[20]

Although Xiao had not been born in Hou Lineage Camp, he grew up there. His father had been in business in Manchuria with a sojourning trader from Hou Lineage Camp. When the business failed, the father, having nowhere to go, came to Hou Lineage Camp with his partner. After acquiring a basic education in the county, Xiao graduated from a university in Manchuria and subsequently became the head of an office in the county. He was said to be well versed in the law and was therefore able to arbitrate disputes before they became legal suits, but it was also said that once a dispute became a legal case, he never tried to influence the decision. He had many friends and extensive contacts, which he appeared to use generously for the villagers. For instance, he could get loans for villagers without collateral, and he often acted as a middleman in contracts. He had 60 mou of land when he returned to the village in 1937. At that time, he served as the assistant village headman and on the board of trustees of the school. He was the most powerful man in the village and perhaps the only man feared by the headman of the enlarged township, a local bully we shall encounter later.[21]

In Chapter 4, we saw how cleavages along kinship lines structured much of the politics in this village. Xiao had no lineage in the village, and given his status in the community, he did not need the support of one. The other village leaders, who were not quite so influential, combined kinship bonds and patronage to form bases of support for their exercise of power. Liu Zixing (sometimes known as

Liu Zixin) had served as village headman twice, once in the early 1920s and again in the late 1930s. He had attended normal school and had been a teacher in a county school. Liu owned 170 mou and was among the richest men in the village. He also lent money, and in the late 1930s he began to accumulate more and more land by foreclosing mortgages. At the same time, however, he was often the guarantor in contracts requiring no collateral, thereby undertaking to pay for a peasant should he become bankrupt.[22]

Liu Zixing was the undisputed leader of the Lius and had been centrally involved in the crossfire of lineage politics. In 1921, when he was village headman, the village undertook a survey of all village lands for tankuan purposes, and Liu was found to be one of those with concealed land. His enemies among the councillors belonging to the Hou lineage threatened to take him to court. The matter was ultimately dropped because most people concealed only a few mou of land, and nobody in the village really cared. Liu, however, was made to resign from office, and from then on he devoted his time to teaching at a county school. He quit the job in 1929 but then served on the education board of the county even while he lived in the village.[23]

Liu was soon presented with an opportunity to avenge himself and re-establish his reputation. When Hou Dasheng became the village headman in the early 1930s, he began to ignore the councillors in decisionmaking and to misuse public monies, following a pattern that was to become increasingly common in the late Republic. Finally, in the mid-1930s, a group of ten influential villagers reported the matter to the county magistrate, and Hou Dasheng was made to resign.

Q: Who were the ten people who discussed the matter?
A: They were large landowners with ability and power. Whenever there was some expense, they had to pay a great deal because they owned a lot of land. They resented that, so they got rid of him.
Q: Did the poor think he was bad too?
A: Yes, they disliked him too.
Q: Why?
A: Because he spent money needlessly. Although they had to pay comparatively less, they finally ended up paying a lot, and they resented him for that. . . . Hou wasted money by feasting ten times a month.[24]

The principal leaders of the opposition included Liu Zixing, who in all probability took the matter to the magistrate himself. Since he was a member of the board of education, he had access to the authorities at the county seat. In 1939, some years after the incident, he became the headman of the village and remained in the post until 1941.[25] Through these biographies and eulogies, we see how leaders often developed their status and power by their simultaneous affiliation with two or more organizational hierarchies. By converting their administrative connections into political capital in village or lineage politics, leaders such as Liu Zixing or Xiao Huisheng brought together discrete organizational systems into an interlocking nexus that served as the arena of elite politics in rural society.

Until the late 1930s, village patrons continued to hold office in Hou Lineage Camp. Although the number of poor councillors was growing, the elite continued to dominate most important village government positions. Moreover, the case of Xiao Huisheng reminds us that patrons could still be found in village politics. But even his influence was unable to stem the tide of changing politics that came with increasing state penetration. After 1939, most of the new decimal headmen in the baojia system were not of the same class as the prestigious leaders who had occupied village posts earlier; they were merely representatives of a ten-household unit.[26] According to Liu Zixing, who was the bao headman at the time, not one of them had the ability to be a middleman in rural contracts. They were young, had little education, and were unable to bear any financial responsibility. Liu's successor was wealthy, but he was viewed by the old councillors as entirely subservient to the new township authorities.[27] The reasons for the eclipse of the old type of leaders had to do with the relations between the village and the new political center, the township, a theme I pursue in Chapter 8.

Cold Water Ditch

Distribution of the 4,200 mou of land (these were large-sized mou, approximately 2.5 times the size of an ordinary mou) among the 370 households of Cold Water Ditch was relatively equal. One household owned over 100 mou, 10 households owned between 50 and 100 mou, the majority—340 households—owned 10 mou (i.e., equal to 25 ordinary mou), and about 20 households were landless.

Although ten absentee landlords living in Jinan had acquired land in Cold Water Ditch through usury, the proportion of this land to the total land in the village was very small. The village's proximity to Jinan enabled most households to supplement their incomes with subsidiary occupations like straw making and coolie labor. Thus, despite the relatively equal distribution of wealth and the weak outside control, the village could hardly be considered an insular community.[28]

Until the Nationalists instituted the lülin system in 1929, the village was divided into eight neighborhoods (*duan*), each of which had a councillor called a *shoushiren* ("leader"). Informants claimed that the councillor came first and that the neighborhood was determined on the basis of his sphere of influence. The councillors were wealthy and prestigious members of the community who mediated disputes, managed the temple property and ceremonies, and organized crop watching. As in other places, the office was hereditary if the successor was also wealthy.[29] Perhaps more than in the other *CN* villages, Cold Water Ditch had the most dramatic transformation of leadership patterns in the 20th century.

For the late Qing, we have information on the property owned by only one leader, and he owned as much as 80 mou. However, from interview data and stele information and by extrapolating back from property data on the last group of councillors in 1928, we can conclude that councillors were substantial and prestigious.[30] The interesting point is the change that occurred in 1928–29. Table 9 shows the names and property of the councillors just before the institution of the lülin system in 1928–29 and those of the headmen of the lü (*lüzhang*) from 1928 until 1939.

As Table 9 suggests, the most noticeable change in the leadership during the 20th century was the decline in the wealth of the village councillors. Around 1928, the average amount of land owned by a councillor was 52.5 mou. From 1929 until 1939, the average landholding among the lü headmen was 24.1 mou. Even if we take just the eight largest property holders among them, the average landholding was 35 mou. What is even more remarkable is that not a single one of the pre-1929 councillors served as lü headmen. In some of the other villages, such as North Brushwood, the relative decline in the wealth of village councillors was at least partly attributable to the impoverishment of the same elite in the 20th century.

TABLE 9
Property Owned by Village Leaders in Cold Water Ditch Before and After 1928

Pre-1928 shoushiren	Land owned (large mou)	Post-1928 lüzhang	Land owned (large mou)
Li Xiangling	80	Wang Chigui	60
Yang Hanqing	80	Ren Fuzeng	40
Li Fengqie	70	Li Xiye	40
Li Wenhan	50	Li Xingzhang	40
Ren Dexuan	50	Zhang Zengxi	35
Wang Weixi	40	Li Yongxiang	26
Yang Lide	30	Du Yannian	20
Li Fenggui	20	Li Zhongpu	20
Total for 8 shoushiren	420	7 other lüzhang	80
		Total for 15 lüzhang	361

SOURCE: *Chūgoku nōson* 1981, 4:25. Cf. Myers's (1970) analysis of the data. Myers arrives at a figure of 28 mou as the average landholding for the lüzhang (p. 99), whereas I have found it to be 24.1 mou.

The information given above suggests that this was not the case in Cold Water Ditch, where the top landholders were replaced by middle and poor peasants. Instead, we have to assume that the village elite were deliberately avoiding these positions. The consequences of this change were plain from the villagers' point of view.

Q: What is the difference between the neighborhood (duan) and the baojia systems [introduced in 1940 and not very different from the lülin system]?
A: The baojia was imposed from above. The neighborhood emerged spontaneously.
Q: Were the households in the neighborhood closer to each other than to outsiders?
A: A little more. Certainly they were closer than the present jia.
Q: Did the councillors [shoushiren] of the neighborhood mediate quarrels between two fellow members of the neighborhood?
A: Certainly they did.
Q: What about the present head of the jia?
A: Not necessarily. It depends on his ability.[31]

Clearly, the relationship between the leader and his constituency had changed. The councillor had possessed a measure of traditional authority in his neighborhood, which, as we have seen, conformed to his sphere of influence. This was not always the case with the representatives of the numerical units. Moreover, the two figures had different relationships to the village headman. Whereas earlier the councillors selected the village headman, the lü and jia headmen were appointed by him.[32]

Just before the change in the system in 1929, Zhang Zongchang, one of the most terrible warlords of North China, had ravaged Shandong province with his excessive demands for taxes and provisions. Partly as a result of his depradations, the rural elite vanished from village leadership positions. Also around 1929, the village headman who was in office in the late 1930s assumed his post. In earlier times, the post of village headman was said to have been occupied by wealthy villagers, but as a result of Zhang's excessive demands, the headman in 1928 left his post, and there were no candidates for the office.[33]

Du Fengshan was selected as village headman by the village councillors in 1928. Du claimed that he had not wanted to become headman and had thrice attempted to resign, but the councillors had not permitted him. Du owned only two mou of land, and although he owned a couple of hundred ducks, he was not considered wealthy—a view I confirmed during my 1986 visit to the village. Since it had become difficult to keep anybody in the post of village headman, the village decided to give him a salary of 100 yuan for his services.[34]

In Du, the village found a happy compromise that most villages could not. As the village elite slipped out of official positions, a political vacuum was created in the official administration of the village. Nobody wished to take up these posts. That is, nobody but a certain unscrupulous type of villager who saw opportunities for profit in the allocation and collection of tankuan dues. In the words of one informant, people who wanted to become village headmen in the 1930s were those who did not have a fixed occupation, those who smoked opium and liked to gamble. In two words, they were *tuhao* and *wulai*, or local bullies.[35]

Du Fengshan was not wealthy, nor could he read or write, but he was not a local bully. Even though he wished to resign from the job, he was very proud of it throughout his term of office. He took some pride in the fact that two-thirds of the voters had elected him to the position after 1929. He appeared to be extremely competent at his job and derived a measure of prestige from handling it as best as could be done under the circumstances. He was clearly the most respected mediator in village and intervillage disputes. Not only did he help settle personal quarrels, but disputes between landlords and tenants were repeatedly brought to him. It was also said that in redeeming mortgaged lands, in asking for loans, and even in negotiating a price for grain in the market, Du's "face" was extremely helpful in acquiring favorable terms.[36] Du was a rare case of a competent man acquiring village office and building a reputation around it even in these difficult times. Thus, when the elite evacuated village office, an ordinary villager could use this office to enhance his status in the community, but such a villager was an unusual person indeed.

North Brushwood

North Brushwood and the remaining two villages of the *CN* survey reveal a pattern of leadership very different from the first three mainly because of the material circumstances of the villagers. By the late 1920s, these villages had become so impoverished that there were no patrons or substantial and prestigious leaders left in the village, in or out of office.

North Brushwood was predominantly a cotton-growing village. As in other villages in the area, cotton cultivation in North Brushwood began to outstrip millet sometime between 1910 and 1930. The county gazetteer of 1872 registers the land owned by the villagers of North Brushwood as being between 2,400 and 2,500 mou.[37] A number of bad harvest during the early 1920s and early 1930s had rapidly impoverished the village. By the early 1930s, over 1,600 mou of this land had shifted to the hands of big absentee landlords in the county seat. However, 627 mou of this land had been mortgaged and could still be redeemed. Indeed, with the rise in prices of agricultural commodities in the late 1930s, many peasants were in a position to redeem this land.[38]

Nonetheless, North Brushwood was among the two poorest villages in the survey. The average family owned less than 10 mou and cultivated less than 15 mou in any economy in which a family of five needed 25 mou to make ends meet.[39] Within the village, stratification was not very sharp, and only three households had as much as 30 to 40 mou. Even the one large landowner, Zhang Yuejing, had mortgaged 48 of his 80 mou to landlords in the county seat. Only about ten families in the village were able to manage without taking loans in a normal year.[40]

The three landlords in the county seat who controlled most of the land mortgaged by the villagers kept the villagers on as tenant-cultivators on their mortgaged land. Together the three controlled 723 mou of the total of 1,372 mou of land leased by the villagers.[41] Relations between the mortgagor-tenants and the moneylending landlords were far from smooth, especially after the Japanese invasion. Even before 1937, landlords frequently had tenants who delayed payments arrested. Tenants retaliated by burning the houses of the landlords. The turmoil following the Japanese invasion made it impossible for tenants to harvest their crops and pay their rents, as bandits and soldiers pillaged their fields. In 1940, when the Japanese army "pacified" the region, the landlords began to demand these rent arrears. From an extended interview by *CN* interviewer Andō Shizumasa with the moneylending landlords, it is clear that not only did the landlords refuse to allow tenants to redeem their lands unless the arrears were paid, but they insisted on having the arrears paid in current prices, which were much higher as a result of the wartime inflation. They justified this as legitimate interest on the capital. Moreover, they appeared to have the full backing of the county government. Without many possibilities of recourse, the tenants of a landlord sometimes banded together and collectively demanded reductions.[42]

Earlier I examined the political system of North Brushwood in terms of its relations with the kinship system (see Chapter 4). In order to complete the picture of the political system, I study it here within the framework of dependency that characterized the relations of the village with the outside. The most striking fact about village leadership was that by the late 1930s no person occupying a leadership position could be considered a community leader of standing. In fact, there was hardly a single figure in the village with the wealth and connections capable of generating a clientele of support of the kind seen in the villages studied so far.

Scattered evidence suggests that in earlier periods the village leadership may have been composed of more substantial individuals. Before 1908, there were 12 councillors called *dongshi* (managers) in the village who represented the various lineages or their segments. Some of these councillors had 200–300 mou of land.[43]

An 1869 temple stele to Guandi mentions that the grandfather of Zhang Yuejing, a former village headman, had made a monetary contribution to the temple that was equivalent to 3 mou.[44] Moreover, villagers maintained that the position of the councillor was usually hereditary.

From the figures on stratification, it is clear that the number of wealthy villagers had declined as had their number among the village leadership. Moreover, as an extremely poor village, the difficulties of collecting the inflexible tankuan demands were particularly acute for its leadership (see below). As tankuan demands began to accelerate in the 1930s, village leadership posts—especially that of the village headman—began to turn over rapidly. For instance, there were three village headmen from 1930 to 1934, and four from 1939 to 1941.[45]

The single exception to the characterization of the village as lacking patrons capable of generating a basis of support among a clientele was Zhang Yuejing, a village headman for 14 years and a descendant of wealthy councillors. But by the late 1930s, even his standing in the community had declined considerably. At some point before 1930, Zhang owned 80 mou of land. He claimed to have had to mortgage 48 mou of this land because he had lost some capital in a liquor store mismanaged by his brother and because the heavy tax demands of the Nationalists in the late 1920s had cost him a great deal of money. He had advanced money for these irregular taxes, but the villagers were so miserably poor that they had not been able to pay him back. He resigned from village office soon after. In 1934, he became the village headman again. After the Japanese invasion in 1937, the countryside became infested with bandits. One of their tactics was to kidnap a wealthy villager or the village headman and demand a ransom from the family or from the village as a whole. After Zhang had been robbed and almost killed, he gave up the post for good.[46]

Despite his reduced circumstances, Zhang strove to retain his status as a community leader. He claimed that he was about the only person who was invited to every marriage and funeral in the village. He also claimed that he used to be the most effective middleman in negotiating loans because of his "face"—as he put it. As testimony to his tremendous energy for public work, even while he was village headman, he worked as a traditional doctor in the village, dispensing his services free of charge. After 1931, he ran a school in his home, where he taught the *Analects* and the *Mencius*. Moreover, he was an expert at measuring land.[47] Judging from all these activities, it seems unlikely that, even if we discount his tendency to exaggerate, there was anyone else in the village who could match his status.

Nonetheless, not only Zhang's fortune, but, as we will soon see, his reputation was on the decline. As the power of the moneylenders increased, he became less and less influential in the village. He himself had mortgaged 48 mou to the biggest moneylender, Wang Zanjou, and because he had incurred rent arrears in 1937, Wang refused to let him redeem his lands. Not surprisingly, he was the bitterest critic of these moneylenders in the village and a vocal champion of the rights of the mortgagor-tenants.[48]

Although Zhang's influence was declining, a new type of influential person—one connected with the absentee landlord—was emerging in the village. Not only did villagers mortgage their land to the absentee landlords, they depended on these landlords to allow them to cultivate these lands as tenants, to increase their mortgage value when the value of the land rose, and to give them additional loans, extensions on rent payments, and the like. As the hold of these landlords tightened, the influence of independent patrons who could provide access to the credit and labor markets on terms favorable to the villager declined. Instead, the villagers became entirely dependent on a different kind of person to communicate their needs to the landlords, a person who was not necessarily interested in seeking favorable terms for the villagers.

There were two such individuals in the village, Zhao Laoyou and Hao Laozhen. Neither of them owned more than a few mou of land, nor did they have prestige or authority in their lineages. But they were the middlemen in all negotiations with the three big landlords. Indeed, it was claimed that they were the agents of the landlords, receiving money secretly for each transaction and keeping an eye on each mortgagor-tenant to see that he did not sell off the land secretly. They certainly received excellent terms from the landlords themselves, leasing 80 mou and 60 mou, respectively, under the best conditions of tenure. They also got interest-free loans. Villagers often wined and dined them in order to obtain favorable terms from the landlords, but the evidence suggests that their function was to protect and promote the business of their patrons.[49]

Wu's Shop

Wu's Shop was another village with a similarly dependent status. In the late Qing period, Wu's Shop had 2,000 mou of land. By 1941, the village had only 1,100 mou, of which 600 mou were owned by landowners living outside of the village. Although some of the absentee landlordism represented landowning villagers who had left the village for the county capital in the 1920s and the 1930s, most of the decline represented the absolute sale of land by villagers to landlords living in the county seat. Cyclically poor harvests and the high incidence of disorder and excessive taxation after the early 1920s explain the phenomenon. Liangxiang county was located just south of Beijing and, as the county gazetteer notes, was thus subjected to all the depradations of the wars in the area.[50]

As a result, 77 percent of the 57 families in the village owned under 20 mou in an economy where 25 mou was the minimum required for a family to make ends meet.[51] Not surprisingly, most peasants in the village had to supplement their incomes by working as tenants or wage laborers. Even so, most of them were forced to borrow at the end of the year, leading to the familiar cycle of debt, alienation of land, and further debt. As for the absentee landowners, 200 mou were owned by 3 landlords in the county seat who owned between 1,000 and 3,000 mou of land each. The remaining 400 mou were owned by middle and small landlords in the city.[52]

As in North Brushwood, in late Qing times there was a group of village councillors (huishou or dongshi) drawn from the village elite. They managed temple festivities and other public activities, such as the crop-watching association, which was the prototype of the gonghui in its function of allocating tankuan dues. However, it was claimed that in Qing times, before the tax demands became excessive, the councillors often paid the tax and did not bother to collect the amount from the villagers.[53] In this context, the interviewer asked:

Q: Do such people still exist?
A: Nowadays we do not even have enough to live on, how can we have such people?

In Wu's Shop Village, the rich and powerful began to shun leadership positions earlier than in most other villages. The warlord battles began to ravage the area around Beijing as early as 1919; particularly damaging were the battles between Wu Peifu and Duan Qirui and the three successive battles between Zhang Zuolin and Wu Peifu in the early 1920s. The demands of the army were so intolerable that many of the rich leaders resigned their posts and fled the village. In 1937, the last two remaining village families of some substance also left the village.[54] From that time on, village offices, especially that of the village headman, were occupied mainly by reckless villagers who felt that they could squeeze some personal gain from an otherwise entirely unrewarding role. Wu's Shop Village demonstrates very clearly the changing bases of leadership power in the village.

Yu Xinsan was the village headman in the early 1920s and possessed over 100 mou of land. He was nearly ruined by the heavy tax demands during the warlord battles of the early 1920s. He died soon after, and his family never took up village office again.[55] Guo Kuan, who was village headman during the mid-1920s, was perhaps the richest man from the village. He gave up village office and moved to the county seat in the 1930s.[56] The wealthy, educated, and influential Zhao Quan was a classic patron type and was held in great regard by the villagers, who approached him to mediate their disputes. Although he held village office in the early Republic, he avoided it throughout the 1920s and 1930s and finally quit the village in 1937.[57]

The village headmen of the later period were distinguished from the earlier leaders not only in viewing office as an object of gain, but also in seeking to base their power on sources outside the cultural nexus, most typically among entrepreneurial state brokers in the yamen. Zhang Shilun, who became headman in 1942, had been a policeman earlier. Soon after he assumed his post, the county authorities discovered that he had embezzled public monies. He was summoned to the court but managed to pay the amount and return to the village. There was a village meeting to discuss the matter, but because no one else wished to take over the job, he was asked to apologize and was kept on the job. It was perhaps no accident that the village headman before Zhang had been arrested for embezzling tankuan funds, but would later serve as a county policeman.[58]

Xia Walled Village

Xia Walled Village was a relatively poor village of 130 households in 1942. In 1911, there had been about 100 households, but the village as a whole had owned much more land than it did in the late 1930s. The sale of land to outsiders and the increase in the population of the village led to an average landownership of 20 mou per household. Villagers claimed that a family of six required 30 mou to live on, and so most peasants had to supplement their income by leasing more land, hiring themselves out as wage laborers, or engaging in petty trade.[59]

Distribution of landownership within the village was not very unequal, and the three families with the largest landholdings scarcely had more than 50 mou. A little under half of the village families owned between 20 and 50 mou, and a little over half had less than 20 mou.[60] The political system of the village was based on representation of the three most important lineages in the village; this was replaced in 1937 by the baojia system. The change was rather dramatic; whereas earlier there had been only three councillors and the village headman, the baojia system involved 13 jia headmen, apart from the village headman and his assistant. The three councillors had been among the richest men in the village, and they were often succeeded by their sons. By 1937, all three had lost much of their wealth over the years.[61] It stands to reason that the average landholding among their successors was greatly reduced because the jia headmen were a much larger group. Unfortunately, there is not enough data on the jia headmen to tell whether they were from the upper or lower half of the village landowners.

There are some data on the village headmen. The post of village headman was fairly stable until the Japanese invasion. A relatively well-to-do villager served in the post between 1922 and 1929. He was succeeded for eight years by the biggest landlord in the village, Wang Baoyuan, who owned over 70 mou of land.[62] From 1937 on, nobody wished to become village headman, chiefly because of the vexatious nature of tankuan allocation. Four people served in the post in a period of six years; in order to halt this trend, the county authorities instituted a rule forcing village headmen to get permission from the county to resign.[63]

The study of the bases of leadership power in the village yields several conclusions. First, there was a clear tendency in the early part of the period for sons to succeed their fathers in village leadership posts. Other studies bear this out.[64] Succession was, however, conditional on the wealth of the successor. Consequently, the process by which leadership was constituted reflected the Chinese preference for combining kinship and economic criteria, the fusion of which formed the organizing principle of many social forms in the village. Second, village leaders with "face" based their authority on the performance of certain social responsibilities. Interview data reinforced the testimony from plaques that influence and standing in the community did not flow merely from the possession of wealth, although power per se may have. Wealth was more often than not a prerequisite, but to be a patron, a leader also needed to undertake such social responsibilities as providing traditional medical services, making contributions to community religious events, mediating disputes, and providing access to outside economic and political centers.[65]

Until the early 1920s, such elite patrons were common among village government leaders. After that time, there was a distinct change in the bases of leadership power and a very different type of villager took over village office. The timing of the change varies from village to village, but in three of the six *CN* villages it occurred before the Japanese invasion. More evidence comes from Sidney Gamble's study, conducted around 1932. He supplied information on the leaders of eight villages at two different points in time; in five of these, village government was no longer in the hands of the elite by the 1930s.[66] In the three remaining *CN* villages, this transformation began to occur after the Japanese-backed regime further expanded the role of the state. I consider how state penetration contributed to this situation in Chapter 8. For the moment, having considered the role of economically powerful men in village government, let us see the extent to which the state was able to elicit the participation in this government of men who commanded legitimate authority in the economic life of rural North China.

Patrons and Middlemen: The Structure of Authority in Customary Law

An area in which authoritative roles were necessary in the rural economy was customary law, or the local norms and conventions regulating the contracts into which Chinese villagers entered with great frequency. In order to be effective, all contracts required middlemen, a role often filled by village patrons. A patron could serve to link ordinary villagers, whether in the sale of land or the provision of credit, to people drawn from a circle of connections far wider than that of his client. The patron thereby sustained a network of relationships that facilitated the operation of an impersonal commercial process in a rural society principally equipped for face-to-face relationships. At the same time, he also developed a network of support that he could employ for politics or honor in the cultural nexus.

I focus on three kinds of contractual arrangements: those for taking out a loan, those for leasing land, and those for selling land. All three types of contracts were critical to the life of the commercialized agricultural society of North China, and the middleman was necessary to all of them. He played various roles in these contracts. First, he often brought together the two parties to the exchange. Second, he was the witness to the contract and was called to court in the event of a legal dispute. Third, in some contracts, such as those for certain types of loans, he guaranteed the repayment of the loan.

Moreover, the middlemen had the authority and the responsibility to mediate any dispute over, or violation of, the terms of the contract. It was here that the most interesting aspect of his role resided. The presence of a third party known to the two contracting partners, who were in all likelihood strangers, was itself a means of reducing the possibility of contract violation by personalizing an impersonal relationship. The burden on the would-be violator was heavier when ties of personal obligation to the middleman were reinforced by the high status or "face" of the middleman. Once a dispute occurred, the higher the status of the middleman, the more successfully was a disagreement likely to be mediated. Finally, the middleman played another significant role for the villager in contracts where the other party was in a considerably stronger bargaining position, such as when he was from the city. In such contracts, where the relations between the two parties were asymmetrical, the more face the middleman had, the greater his ability to secure favorable terms for the weaker party. Recursively, the middleman's face was considerably enhanced the more he became known for his ability to secure these terms.

From this description, it is clear that, except for those roles where a guarantor was required, the middleman did not necessarily have to be a man of substance or prestige. Nonetheless, for many villagers it was distinctly advantageous to employ a person with face as the middleman, particularly when dealing with outsiders. These advantages will become clearer in the course of the discussion. Here, it suffices to say that frequent recourse to prestigious figures by villagers indicates that they were not mere middlemen but patrons in the community.

Central to the structure of authority in customary law is the concept of face, an important cultural construct that has received little systematic attention in the literature. Martin Yang's analysis of the concept, appropriately included in his chapter on village conflict, brings it close to notions of honor and shame.[67] He demonstrates that face is a potential attribute of every individual, and gaining or losing it depends on the social context of an event. This context is defined not only by the relative statuses of those directly involved but also, transitively, by people variously related to the principal actors. Thus, for instance, when a younger man has offended an older man and the older man is about to retaliate, he may be dissuaded from doing so by pleas to consider the face of the boy's parents.

However, face is not only a latent psychological attribute of every person but also a manifest quality that endures with certain people. Usually people with wealth and influence had face; acquiring face was the culturally sanctioned means through which these people converted their resources into prestige, status, and trust. Trust was an extremely significant aspect of face; one *CN* informant used it as a virtual synonym of face. In economic matters, the trustworthiness of a person was not easily separable from his wealth and standing in the community. Indeed, in this usage, face could be a surprisingly tangible and instrumental construct, judged by its efficacy in obtaining a practical result.

When it became operative in economic contracts, the face of a middleman played two different types of roles. It could directly dictate many of the terms of a contract. In a loan contract, the size and duration of the loan and even the rate of interest were determined as much by the face of the middleman as by the market. The logic here could be a purely economic one. Take, for instance, the situation of a moneylender who makes a loan to a villager whose middleman is an ordinary fellow, not particularly known for his trustworthiness or standing in the community. In order to justify the higher risk involved, the lender may well feel inclined to loan a smaller sum for a shorter period and charge a higher rate of interest than he would if the middleman had the ability and reputation to ensure repayment.

The second role of face did not entail such a strict economic calculus. Here, the face of a middleman could operate to bring *social* pressure to bear on one of the parties—usually on the more powerful one. Thus the success of a villager needing to redeem his mortgaged land before the stipulated period of a contract was likely to depend entirely on the face of his middleman. Underlying both of these roles were two social premises: that the market did not regulate all aspects of economic exchange in this society, and that the state was not the best agency to guarantee the rights of the parties to a contract.

In a society where neither the market nor the state fully regulated economic relationships, the individual peasant (or village household) was often dependent on a powerful local figure, a patron, to ensure the fulfillment of a contract, to provide access to the market on terms that were not impossibly weighted against him, and to protect him from predatory local government functionaries.[68] In return, the patron received expressions of gratitude and loyalty on which he built a stock of political capital. Thus the relationship between the patron and his client was marked by reciprocity, but reciprocity should not be mistaken for equality.[69] Indeed, the patron exercised a considerable measure of domination over his client, and the attitude of the client toward his patron was correspondingly characterized by ambivalence.

In what follows, I examine the extent to which patrons were to be found in authoritative roles embedded in the economic life of rural North China and whether in this role they were also associated with village government. In other words, I probe the relationship between economic authority and political leadership in rural society.

Let us look first at middlemen in loan contracts in the *CN* villages. There were three ways of acquiring credit in rural society: by mortgaging property, by pledging land as collateral, and by providing a guarantor. The last of these was one where the middleman, who was always the guarantor, obviously ran the highest risks, and I consider it first.

It is difficult to assess the frequency or proportion of loans involving guarantors, but in at least Hou Lineage Camp, they were said to be the most common type of loan. They were often short-term loans made by merchants from outside the village. The responsibilities of the guarantor-middleman were heaviest in this type of loan, and in Hou Lineage Camp, five of the most prestigious and powerful village leaders were said to play this role frequently. Four of them, including Liu Zixing and Xiao Huisheng, were wealthy villagers with face and fitted the role of patrons in the village.[70] The fifth guarantor, Kong Ziming, was not a rich man. He owned less than 20 mou of land, but what he lacked in property, he made up in resourcefulness. In 1940, he leased 50 mou of rice land from a Japanese company and farmed it with two hired laborers. Kong was regarded highly in the village because he was educated—he often quoted the Confucian classics—and also because he was a smooth talker, a skill learned from his days in Fengtian, where he had worked as a shop assistant. Kong was obviously interested in building a public career. Not only was he a middleman for various contracts, but he was also a skillful mediator. It was he who mediated the conflict between the Lius and the Hous in the village and initiated the move to grant the plaque to Xiao Huisheng. In 1940 he became the assistant village headman.[71]

Kong's case shows that a guarantor need not be rich. He was clearly employed as a middleman because of his skill and reputation. This would suggest that it was probably rare for a guarantor to have to repay a bad debt in this village. In Sand Well, though, it was not so rare. Two villagers had actually lost some property as guarantors, and their careers are instructive. Du Xiang was a councillor.[72] His father had also been one, and his uncle was reputed to have owned 700 mou of land. In the early years of the Republic, Du Xiang owned 54 mou. During these years, he was active in arranging loans and tenancies for the villagers. Once, he acted as a guarantor for an affine who was unable to return the loan, and Du lost 10 mou of his own land. For various other reasons, he lost more and more land, and by the 1930s, though he still acted as a middleman, it was said that Du Xiang did not have the same face that he had had earlier. Zhao Tingkui's career followed a similar pattern. In his case, the person for whom he acted as guarantor died, and the family was unable to repay the loan.[73]

In several villages, grain loans requiring guarantors were made by the grain store or by speculators in the grain market. This was the case in Sand Well, where the highly regarded village headman Yang Yuan, who had extensive contacts in the market town, was often the guarantor.[74] In North Brushwood and Wu's Shop, the necessity of providing a guarantor often posed a problem because, by the 1930s at least, these villages had become so impoverished that it was difficult to find people with sufficient property to play the part. Given the precarious condition of the villagers, such an undertaking would have been truly risky. Nonetheless, life had to go on, and ordinary relatives and friends stood as guarantors for each other for loans of very low value. Needless to say, these guarantors were often unable to pay when called on to do so, and the case often ended up in the county courts. Apparently, the state often let both the borrower and the guarantor off the hook.[75]

In Cold Water Ditch and Xia Walled Village, the principle of payment by the guarantor was strictly enforced. Banks and merchants gave loans only with a guarantor because land pledged as collateral could be secretly sold off. If the guarantor died, his son inherited the responsibility. As a consequence of these strict conditions, only a close friend or relative performed this role. Nonetheless, it had to be someone with adequate property to cover the debt.[76]

In the case of loans made on the basis of collateral, the main function of the middleman was to act as a witness, to ascertain the contents of the contract—in particular, to investigate if there were any competing claims on the pledged or mortgaged property—and to mediate disputes. If the loan was not repaid or, more commonly, if the interest payments were not forthcoming, it was his duty either to arrange for an extension or to dun the debtor.

In order to perform these functions, it was enough for the

middleman to be competent and know both parties to the exchange. But from the point of view of the borrower, particularly if he was an indigent villager, it was important to get somebody with face. A prestigious figure was likely to have good relations (*ganqing*) with a wide circle of rich people outside the village and was able to secure favorable terms. He could negotiate a lower interest rate, obtain a loan for a longer period, arrange for its extension, or get the lender to forgo part of the interest. If the middleman was very powerful, it was said that there was no need for a contract.[77]

Thus there were distinct advantages to having a middleman with face, but not every villager was able to find such a patron, and not every prestigious person was willing to undertake this rather bothersome task. In Hou Lineage Camp, of the three men cited as middlemen in such loan contracts, two were wealthy, and all had been honored village officials. They were never paid for their services, but if they performed special favors for a client, as a token the client often gave a gift to their children.[78] In Sand Well, the village headman, Yang Yuan, and Du Xiang, the councillor, often became middlemen, especially in contracts with outsiders.[79] By the 1930s, however, another very different type of middleman had emerged on the scene.

Fu Ju came to the village in the early 1930s, a penniless peddler who also did odd jobs. Despite his poverty, he had acquired a wide range of contacts, probably as a result of his peripatetic occupation. In the late 1930s, he became a tenant of a powerful landlord living in the county seat, and he frequently used this and his other contacts to act as a middleman. In particular, he arranged mortgages for villagers with landlords in the county seat. Unlike the patrons and leaders in the village, and although he denied it, he charged a commission for his services.[80]

In North Brushwood, the principal means of acquiring credit was by mortgaging property, and as we have seen, a substantial portion of the village land had been mortgaged to city moneylenders. There were only two men in the village through whom villagers dealt with these moneylender-landlords. Like Fu Ju, they were poor, and they were rumored to be agents of the landlords and to receive special favors for their services. Because of the special relationship of such middlemen with powerful figures outside the village who dominated the credit market, the villagers were in good

measure dependent on their contacts. But they were not independent patrons who could employ their face to secure favorable terms
for the villagers. Rather, they performed their role of middlemen as
clients of the big landlords themselves or as quasi specialists who
charged a fee for their services. The former headman of North
Brushwood, Zhang Yuejing, whose fortunes, as we have seen, were
on the decline, captured the difference between the type of middleman we have characterized above and the patron: "If the mort-
gagee feels that he has already lent out too much money and does
not wish to raise the value of the loan, he tells that to the middleman,
who simply communicates that to the mortgagor. But as long as I
was the middleman, I would never simply communicate such a
decision because I would incur a loss of face."[81]

In Hebei, guarantors were not usually required for land tenure
contracts, probably because in many villages, such as Sand Well,
tenures were for a year or because, as in Wu's Shop, the tenure
period was unspecified.[82] Under these circumstances, nonpayment
of rent meant certain eviction and inability to find another tenure.

In Sand Well, most of the middleman services in land tenure
contracts were performed by Fu Ju, the landless peddler with
extensive contacts.[83] When the landlord was not from the county
seat but rather from a neighboring village, a relative, usually an
affine, was used.[84] In Wu's Shop and North Brushwood, where
absentee landlords leased out much of the land, these landlords
usually selected their own middlemen, who checked the productive
capacity of the prospective tenant before the land was leased out.
Only after ascertaining that the tenant had adequate productive
capacity in terms of labor, farm animals, and tools and that his
own property was not so much that it would absorb all of this
capacity did the landlord lease out the land. The middlemen also
dunned tenants in case of arrears and acted as witnesses when
actions were brought against them.[85] In these villages, there was
nobody sufficiently important to influence the opinions of the
powerful landlords, some of whom were officials in the county
government.

In the two villages in Shandong, where the duration of tenure was
longer, a guarantor was usually required to pay the rent in case of
default. In Cold Water Ditch, it was not village officials but friends
and relatives of some means who undertook this role. In Xia Walled

Village, city-based landlords had begun to demand that a village official undertake this role. But few village officers had much property, and many of the middlemen were no more than ordinary middle peasants.[86]

In a land transaction, the middleman had several functions. He was usually approached by the seller to seek out a buyer and negotiate a favorable price. He was responsible for ascertaining the quality and the size of the plot. More important, he had to determine, by inquiring of neighbors and the lineage, whether there were any competing claims on the land. He saw to it that payments were properly made and mediated all disputes.

Villagers claimed that it helped to have a middleman with face because such a person could fetch a good price for the property. Moreover, the middleman's face prevented violation of the contract, as an example from Hou Lineage Camp demonstrates.[87] A buyer wanted to buy a piece of land at a lower price than that demanded by the seller. There was a great deal of negotiation back and forth, and finally the buyer decided to settle for the seller's price. He said, "I agreed because it is difficult to do the job of the middleman. If I decided not to buy it, it would affect the middleman's face." In North Brushwood, an embittered Zhang Yuejing, who was no longer often asked to be a middleman, remarked:

If a seller wants to return a deposit [having changed his mind about the transaction] and the buyer refuses to accept it, there is no hope for the seller if his middleman is a poor man. On the other hand, if I were the middleman, I would use my face and ask him to accept the deposit. Even if he accepts the deposit, he will demand interest, and only if the middleman is skillful, can the seller get away without paying the interest.[88]

In Hou Lineage Camp, all the leading councillors undertook this role.[89] They had a large circle of friends and acquaintances and could negotiate a good price. In the other *CN* villages, however, the middleman in land transactions was seldom a prestigious person.[90] In Wu's Shop, there were said to be just as many middlemen from the ranks of ordinary villagers as there were from among the village councillors. In Sand Well, it was often a friend or the ubiquitous Fu Ju. In North Brushwood, most of the land was bought by the city landlords, and they could be approached only through their two agents in the village. Most villagers who wanted to sell their land approached someone from their lineage, and this man then approached one of the agents. In neither Xia Walled Village nor Cold Water Ditch were these middlemen notable figures.

The study above shows that there was a complex relation between middlemen, patrons, and leadership in North Chinese villages. Broadly speaking, three types of middlemen were employed in Chinese contracts. The first type was the patron with face. He was usually propertied and often had extensive contacts beyond the village, especially in the market town. More often than not he had been a village leader, undertaking community tasks as well as the tasks of village government. As a middleman, he could often secure a contract with favorable terms for the villager, and for this he did not expect a material reward.

The second type of middleman was often a friend or relative of one of the parties and was known to the other party to the contract. Because of the closeness of the middleman to one of the contracting parties, he would try to acquire favorable terms for him, but presumably, unless he was close to the second party as well, he would not be as successful in his efforts as the patron. This kind of contact was widely utilized when the parties were spread over different villages of the marketing region, and more often than not, the middleman was an affinal relative living in the other village. Networks woven around affinal links may have become even more useful when village ties to the marketing center weakened during the period of disruption in the late 1930s.

The third type of middleman was neither a patron with standing in the community nor a particularly close associate of the villager seeking a contract. He was sometimes the agent of an absentee landlord or some other powerful figure or a professional middleman who took a commission for his services. Since he had neither face nor a personally close relationship to the party seeking the contract, he usually did not acquire favorable terms for him.

Of course, these three categories were not watertight. They often overlapped, but analytically, I believe, the distinctions are useful because they enable us to observe historical trends in the various villages. To a certain extent, the type of contract determined the kind of middleman sought out. For loans requiring guarantors, a wealthy person with a close relationship to the borrower was usually necessary. By contrast, when a prospective tenant sought a tenure in another village, he approached an affine living in that village; when he sought it from a landlord in the city, he might have to approach a substantial patron with extensive contacts.

More commonly, however, the kind of middleman available to a villager differed according to the circumstances of the village. In other words, the villager may not have had access to the preferred type. The time period under consideration is, of course, critical because villages that had no wealthy patrons in the 1930s did have them in an earlier period. Therefore an analysis of the kinds of middlemen found in the different villages has to be made in conjunction with the historical information on leadership discussed in the previous section.

In Hou Lineage Camp, where substantial and prestigious landowners continued to hold village office until 1940 when the baojia system was reintroduced, these figures were frequently employed as middlemen for every type of contract. Even after 1940, they continued to perform these services because they had only left office, not the village. At the same time, however, this meant that village government leaders had now become divorced from the legitimacy-conferring functions embedded in the patron's role.

In Sand Well, too, substantial landowners continued to hold office until the end of the period. Here, however, these figures did not always fulfill middleman roles. The three most active middlemen in the village were Yang Yuan, the respected village headman with extensive contacts in the market; Du Xiang, an active village leader whose fortune and face were on the decline; and Fu Ju, an indigent but resourceful peddler who had built up a network of contacts and a business as a middleman. Friends and relatives also served as middlemen for each other. Thus Sand Well evinced all three types of middlemen, but by the late 1930s, Fu Ju was handling most of the land tenure and mortgage contracts. Given the low degree of involvement of government leaders in middleman roles in this village by the 1930s, we may conjecture that relations between these leaders and the villagers were weakening.

In North Brushwood and Wu's Shop, the changes in leadership occurred relatively early. Here the shift in the nature of village officials clearly paralleled the change in the type of middleman. In North Brushwood, a weak leadership emerged partly as a result of the general impoverishment of the village that began in the 1920s but accelerated dramatically in the early 1930s. There were few villagers with the means to undertake the responsibilities of a patron. This economic decline was accompanied by the increasing domination of the village by absentee landlords. This process was dramatized in the career of the former village headman Zhang Yuejing, who recalled his role as a patron in earlier days and rued the fact that his services had been taken over by the two agents of the landlords. By the late 1930s, the villagers were almost entirely dependent on these two agents for all middleman services.

In Wu's Shop, rich village leaders either sold their land or fled the village during the early 1920s when the warlord battles and high tax demands began to ravage the area. Conditions never really stabilized sufficiently after the battles to warrant their return. Consequently, the village was left with almost no prestigious leaders who could perform the role of patron. Moreover, like North Brushwood, the economic resources of the village began to be increasingly controlled by absentee landlords. Under these circumstances, friends and relatives seemed to have performed the role of middleman as best they could.

Information on village personalities from the two Shandong villages is rather spotty, and I am thus unable to come to any firm conclusion about the types of middlemen found here. Nonetheless, the data show quite startling changes in the bases of leadership in both villages, but especially in Cold Water Ditch. By the late 1920s, powerful village leaders had either fled the village or were avoiding a public career, and there appeared to be only one prestigious figure who was repeatedly asked to serve as a middleman. Du Fengshan, headman of Cold Water Ditch, had so much face that he was even asked to negotiate the price of grain that villagers sold on the market. Otherwise, it appears, most middlemen were friends or relatives of the parties involved.

Conclusions

All types of middlemen and their networks facilitated the operation of customary law, which Ramon Myers and Fu-mei Chen have shown to be vital to the commercialized agriculture of China.[91]

Although middlemen did not directly reproduce the political values of the social order, they did reproduce the conditions necessary to maintain this order. Networks that developed around patrons and around affines and friends were more clearly a part of the cultural nexus of power. The role of the patron was particularly significant in this regard; in using his network of outside connections, he created not only new bonds across villages but also a web of internal support. The ties of gratitude and obligation accumulated by a patron, or to a lesser extent by an affine or friend, became symbolic resources that enhanced their authority in other organizational schemes.

The combined effect of state penetration, warfare, and economic dependency reduced the numbers of such patrons in several of the villages as the prestigious elite either fled the village or became impoverished. By the 1930s, wealthy and prestigious figures were no longer around to perform authoritative roles in the economic, much less the political, sphere.

How then did customary law operate in local communities without the regulating authority of a local patron? What did it cost these communities to function without such patrons? There is no doubt that people continued to enter into contractual arrangements and work through customary law. This was possible because of the nature of this law in China, which could, *on a minimal level*, function without the regulating authority of a powerful local figure. Violation of a contract made it difficult for the violator to obtain the services of a middleman in the future. Thus it was possible for whole villages to manage without the services of a patron—but at a cost. These villagers would rarely be able to obtain favorable terms in markets and political centers.

Other villages continued to have elite patrons among their residents till the end of the period. In such communities, authority in the economic relationships of the nexus remained relatively stable, but from the 1920s on, and certainly by the late 1930s, this authority became increasingly dissociated from village government, thereby robbing this government of much of its status and strength. The patron's desertion of political leadership was particularly unfortunate for the Republican regimes. Never had the Chinese state so desperately needed a political leadership both integrated with the community and committed to the goals of the state. Political leaders were indispensable not only for restoring stability in this war-ravaged region but, even more, for attaining the expansionary and modernizing goals of a state that sought to rebuild society from the top down.

Seven

The State and the Redefinition of Village Community

Rural society was transformed both by the conscious design of state policies and by state-involutionary forces that accompanied the implementation of these policies. In this chapter, I analyze how state policies intended to strengthen the state and consolidate the village as the most basic unit of governance wrought changes in the structure of control and the cohesion of the village community, but not always with the effects intended.

Eric Wolf has described a process of village evolution under the colonial state in Mesoamerica and Java that is relevant to 20th-century developments in China.[1] In these societies, the impact of colonialism and the colonial state culminated in the transformation of relatively open peasant societies into closed corporate communities with a strong collective identity. The fact that the state charged the villages with tax responsibilities was an important factor behind this transformation. These villages evolved from political insignificance through the acquisition of taxing powers to the development of a distinct territorial jurisdiction, climaxing finally in a powerful sense of corporate identity.

In the emergence of formal village governments with taxing powers, we have already seen the early stages of a similar evolutionary pattern in North China. Here, I study how rationalizing agencies in the state sought to create a territorial jurisdiction of village control in order both to strengthen the village as an administrative unit and to stabilize the sources of the state's own revenues. In the process, the boundaries of the village community were transformed, but the rural society of North China in the early 20th century was much too complex to permit the easy flowering of a corporate village identity.*

Tankuan and the Village

Although the village in late imperial society was not the sole, or perhaps even the dominant, node of coordination in the cultural nexus, it was an important one. Traditionally, the village managed various community activities, the most prominent of which were collective religious ceremonies in which, as we have seen, outsiders were not entitled to participate.[2] Only village members were permitted to lease or buy the public lands of the village.[3] The village also managed certain public areas to be used for graveyards for the poor, for threshing grain, for aging nightsoil, and for making bricks and using the earth for construction purposes. Only village members could use these areas.[4] There were also various voluntary organizations in the village, such as credit societies or mutual-aid groups, in which outsiders customarily did not participate.[5]

With the advent of the late Qing reforms, the village became still more important as the coordinating center of the activities detailed above. At the same time, the question of which village one belonged to became extremely important when village public associations (gonghui) were created. Membership in these associations was expressed most clearly during the election of officers: only village members were allowed to vote and run for office.[6] The public associations were instituted to manage such modernization projects as the village school, but they became more important as a taxing and taxable unit. The tankuan burden that villages had to bear was not only onerous but arbitrary. These impositions varied considerably from village to village and demonstrate the importance to the villager of belonging to a village where the rates and the methods of levying were reasonable. A survey conducted in 1935 of four villages in three counties in Hebei shows the following variation:[7]

---

*"Village community" refers to a social settlement in the same way as "urban community" or "market community." I do not presume that the village was characterized by the deep bonds of solidarity and affect that Wolf writes about and that are associated with the concept of gemeinschaft or kyōdōtai in Japanese—a concept addressed below.

County	Village	Total tankuan (yuan)	Total land cultivated (mou)	Total households	Avg. tax/ households (yuan)
Pinggu	Xiaoxinzhai	650	2,820	170	3.80
Pinggu	Huzhuang	574	2,400	218	2.60
Miyun	Xiaoyingcun	1,168	3,025	100	11.70
Zunhua	Lujiazhai	726	2,442	92	7.90

I have deliberately chosen data from this period to suggest that the arbitrariness of tax demands was not necessarily connected with the wars of the Republican period. The mid-1930s were an era of relative tranquillity, coming as they did after the major warlord battles and the establishment of Guomindang power in the north and before the Japanese invasion of 1937.

The full impact of the new tankuan rates on the village polity is discussed in Chapter 8. Here I discuss how the different rates and the mechanisms of implementation devised by each village could make the particular village in which one lived important. Variations occurred, first, because the levies were charged whenever the need arose and not according to any fixed schedule.[8] Second, although a particular village had to pay a fixed percentage of the total demanded from the county or the ward, this percentage was quite arbitrary because there was no way of assessing the actual taxpaying capacity of a village. Land tax assessments, for instance, did not always provide an adequate idea of the taxing capacity of a village because the land tax registers were based on the holdings of households and did not reveal the actual taxable land that all the inhabitants of a particular village owned. In many areas, according to the head of a county police department, the ward based the tax share of the villages on the baojia population registers.[9] The fact that these shares bore no relationship to the wealth of the village is amply borne out by Amano Motonosuke's study of a ward in Zhuo county, Hebei, in the mid-1930s. In this ward, the villages were grouped into eight categories according to population. Each of the eight categories was assigned a share of the tankuan burden, without regard for the land resources of the village. Thus, two of the villages in the top paying category (ten shares) had less land than two villages in the second lowest category (four shares). Amano felt that in general villages with more land paid less in taxes than did smaller ones.[10]

The demand from above was one factor determining the rate of taxation in a particular village. Two other factors were extremely important: the village's own expenditures, which usually depended on the scale of its modernization activities; and the ratio of land from which the village could obtain taxes to the size of its taxpaying populace. This ratio could vary considerably because tankuan rates could be based either on a fixed territory or on a variable one, and either on the number of landowners or on the number of cultivators. Consider, for example, Village A. Its taxable area is not fixed but varies according to the land owned by its residents. The sale or loss of land by a villager to an outsider automatically reduces the taxable area without decreasing the tax demand, which was mostly quite inelastic. Consequently, the same number of taxpaying residents of Village A have to pay the same amount from a smaller tax base. Another village that began with a comparable tax base and a similar tax burden but whose inhabitants have not sold any land to outsiders now pays lower tax rates per unit of land.

Contrast Village A with Village B, where the taxable area is fixed and the village continues to obtain its tax from either the owners or the cultivators of the land, no matter where they live. In this case, if there is no external increase in the tax demand, the tax rate per unit of land should not change because the ratio between the land controlled by the village and the taxpayers controlled by the village is fixed. That is, a taxpayer who alienates his land is, from the point of view of the village, immediately replaced as a taxpayer by the new owner of the land.

Next consider a second pair of variables. In Village X tankuan rates are paid only by the landowners, and in Village Z they are paid only by the cultivators. Even though the taxable area is fixed, the two systems of payment make an obvious difference to the taxpayers. A large landowner who has leased a great deal of land to tenants in Village X would wish that his land belonged to the taxable area of Village Z. He might even try to sell his lands and buy elsewhere where either the rates were lower or where tenants paid the tax.

Thus, state penetration forced the village not only to develop a fiscal system, thereby making it an important managerial center, but also to devise distinctive methods of assessment, making the particular village in which one lived a matter of some moment. In time, the logic of these developments had the further effect of transforming relations within the community, as well as among neighboring villages.

Crop Watching, Village Territoriality, and the Village Community

Curiously, the organization through which the impact of the state on the village community is best understood is the crop-watching association. These associations were of great interest to observers like Sidney Gamble and the *CN* researchers. The crop watch provided the framework for intense intervillage transactions conducted entirely outside the marketing system. Their significance lies less in their role as a protective organization than in their role in village finances. In many villages these associations provided the format for the assessment not only of crop-watching dues but of the tankuan. Moreover, in order to demarcate the financial powers and jurisdiction of the village vis-à-vis its neighbors, the crop-watching boundaries of the village came to function as the village boundaries in a general sense, making it a territorially bounded entity for perhaps the first time in recent history.

Documentary evidence on the establishment of these associations is hard to come by, but informants from Shunyi county suggested that crop-watching associations were set up between 1900 and 1907 on the order of the county government.[11] Another source indicates that they were started by a provincial order to the counties in order to facilitate the collection of new taxes for the police and education.[12] In other parts of Hebei and Shandong, crop-watching associations were in existence before 1900.[13] But even where their origins cannot be traced to state policy, their organizational structure suited them to respond to state fiscal demands in the early 1900s. Incidentally, crop-watching associations were designed to protect the fields and villages, not from marauding armies and bandits, but from petty thieves. Indeed, in many places the crop thieves were the poor and derelict from the village itself.[14] The crop guard was usually a poor "tough" from the village,[15] and potentially, perhaps, the most dangerous thief. Employing him in such a capacity was a device designed as much to neutralize him as to protect the crops from others. Thus, the crop-watching association was a community institution for internal surveillance.

The crop-watching associations were significant because they necessitated the creation of a rudimentary budget for the village as a whole and the demarcation of the boundary of the lands guarded by the crop watch. Much of the land within this boundary belonged to the guard's fellow villagers but it also included land belonging to nonresidents. At the same time, it excluded land owned by village residents whose property was at some distance because it was inefficient, and perhaps impossible, for the watch to guard distant, scattered pieces of property. These pieces of land were guarded by the crop watch of the village near which the land was located.

No small proportion of the land within the crop guard's area—or "green circle" (*qingquan, bencundi*), as Gamble has translated the various terms used for this area—belonged to outsiders, revealing a highly active land market in North China. In Wu's Shop Village, for instance, outsiders owned over half the land within its green circle.[16] According to the registers of the crop-watching associations of seven villages collected by Gamble's team, 6 percent to 46 percent of the families in the crop-watching associations were nonresident. In another group of eight villages, nonresident families made up 36 percent to 90 percent of the associations.[17]

In order to ensure that all dues were ultimately paid, an elaborate system of negotiations and transfers of payments was set up by the crop guards. A crop guard arranged a system of exchange of crop-watching responsibilities and dues with the crop guards of several villages within the radius of which the land of most of his fellow villagers was located. He transferred the amounts paid to him by nonresidents to the crop guard of their village and, in turn, received the amounts paid by his fellow villagers to the other crop watch. Since most of the land of the villagers was within a radius of one or two li, this system took care of the lands of the majority of the villagers. In several places, this system was called the "linked circle" (*lianquan*) system, and this system was often the basis on which other tax rates were exchanged.

Not all crop-watching systems and their boundaries became the boundaries of the village and the basis for apportioning other village taxes. Particularly in Shandong, the crop-watching system worked only to assess and exchange crop-watching dues and nothing else.[18] But even here, a tendency to base village tax rates on this system emerged in the late 1930s. Originally, for example, the village of Lujiazhuang in Licheng county, like other villages in Shandong, had a green circle only for the wages of the crop watch. All other dues were paid by landowners to their village of residence. But by the time of *CN* interviews, a new system had developed: a resident of Village X who owned land traditionally within Lujiazhuang's green circle continued to pay his tankuan rates to Village X, but henceforth he had to pay not only crop-watching dues but also the tankuan for any new land he acquired within Lujiazhuang's green circle.[19] This village was attempting to cope with a fluctuating and probably diminishing tax base. Defining the borders absolutely and demanding that taxpayers pay a different rate to Lujiazhuang would have amounted to flouting the customary practice of the area. The new system appears to represent a compromise that left the old arrangement unaffected but stabilized the future taxable income of the village by defining its tax boundary. Cold Water Ditch, too, faced a similar problem of a diminishing tax base. However, its response was to require villagers to sell land to their fellow villagers as much as possible.[20]

Where tax rates were based on the crop-watching system, the entire system became an extremely important aspect of village government. All the examples of this type are from Hebei, and except for the southern cotton-growing regions, where crop thieves were unlikely to benefit from stealing petty amounts of cotton,[21] there is no reason to believe that this was not a general phenomenon in the province.

The crop-watching associations followed two different levying procedures, corresponding to the difference between villages with variable and with fixed taxable areas. In some cases, the one type preceded the other, and in others they coexisted. The transformation of one type into the other represented an effort to deal with one of the more important sources of friction between villages in the period. In both types, the crop watch dues and the tankuan were paid into the village within whose green circle the land was located, and at the rate determined by the village. But whereas in one type these dues were ultimately transferred to the village in which *the landowner or cultivator resided* through the process of negotiation and exchange of the linked circle system, in the other type, the village within whose green circle *the land was located* received all the dues paid to it as its income. Since many villagers owned land outside their village, the difference was a very real and important one. In the first case, the crop-watching system provided the mechanism of assessment and payment; in the second, the village controlling the green circle possessed a right to the taxes of the area.

Sidney Gamble, who sensed the importance of the crop-watching association, did not seem to be aware of this distinction. He did note that one village in his survey, Village H, located near the Grand Canal, had two rates of assessment: one for residents and one for nonresidents cultivating land within its green circle. Since the crop-watching dues were used to finance so many other projects in the village, the nonresidents began to pay at only half the rate that residents paid. Gamble writes, "This differentiation in crop rates between resident and nonresident cultivators was very unusual. In fact, village H was the only village where we found it. Ordinarily, the village charged all cultivators, resident and non-resident, the same rate per *mu*."[22] As a matter of fact, Gamble has information on whether the tankuan was received for all lands within the green circle only for one village. For the rest, he merely assumes that this must have also been the case because he does not make a distinction between villages where the payments received were exchanged and those where they were not.

Evidence from the *CN* villages in Hebei (excepting the southern Hebei examples) suggests that until 1936 these villages followed the system in which a crop-watching association with a fixed boundary existed and nonresidents paid the regular rates to it, and the association then transferred the funds to the villages in which the cultivator or owner resided. This was the case in Sand Well and Hou Lineage Camp until 1936, when they began to follow the other system.[23] In North Brushwood, where there was no crop-watching boundary, an official document states that in 1936 an order was passed for villages in the county to develop firm boundaries and retain all taxes paid on the land within these boundaries.[24] The reasons for this change and the process of its implementation had important implications.

In Shunyi county the crop-watching association was utilized to collect both the dues of the crop guard and other village expenses. However, it is clear that at least after 1915, the funds collected from nonresidents who lived in the linked circle of villages ultimately made their way to their village of residence.[25] Not all villages, however, belonged to a linked circle. Some, like Beifaxin near Sand Well, were not part of one because their residents were so numerous and the land they owned so extensive that they did not need the extra funds from their residents who may have held land outside their village area. Beifaxin did not levy any taxes on the lands that villagers of Sand Well owned around Beifaxin. The government of Sand Well entered into an agreement directly with the crop guard of Beifaxin to pay him for guarding the crops belonging to its residents. If the crops on these lands were robbed, the government of Beifaxin was not held responsible, whereas the village governments within the linked circle did have to pay compensation.[26]

The frictions generated by this system of assessing and transferring funds are brought out most clearly by the case of Sand Well. Before 1936, Sand Well belonged to a linked circle that included Shimen, Nanfaxin, and Wangquansi. Within this circle, taxes were first paid to the village in whose green circle the land lay, and subsequently they were transferred to the village where the cultivator resided. For several reasons the system did not work smoothly. First, the rates of assessment differed from village to village even within the linked circle because the ratio of their revenue demands to the total taxable land varied. Consequently, there was bound to be some inequality in the process of exchanging payments. Sand Well, where the rates were lower than Shimen, transferred a lesser amount to Shimen than Shimen did to Sand Well for exactly the same plot size. This inequality tempted those with large landholdings to change their residence to a village in which the rates were lower. In 1936, a man named Jing Defu moved from Shimen to Sand Well for just this reason.[27] Sand Well welcomed the man because he was a large landowner and his entry would enlarge its tax base. However, the governing council of Shimen insisted that he continue to pay his rates to Shimen because in that very year the principle of payment had changed in the county. The case went to the police court in the ward, where it was decided that Jing would continue to pay his rates to Shimen but perform his labor services according to the schedules of Sand Well.[28]

Perhaps a weakness greater than the unequal exchanges was the fluctuating nature of the tax income of the village. Whenever a villager sold his land or left his village, the village suffered a diminution of its tax base without a corresponding reduction in its tax requirements. This was the basis of Shimen's opposition to Jing Defu's move to Sand Well and was the cause of fights and legal battles throughout the county and other parts of the province.[29] The difficulties generated by this diminution were not only unbearable for the poorer villages but also intolerable for the state because they affected its principal source of revenue. An order from the county magistrate of Shunyi in November 1936 declared:

It is an old custom of the crop-watching societies in the villages of this county to differentiate between a "live sphere" [*huoquan*] and a "dead sphere" [*siquan*]. This difference is the cause of many complications and law suits where people waste money. It constitutes a special problem in the ordering of village finances.

According to my detailed investigations, both the live and dead spheres exist, and the latter are greater. In view of the fact that we seek to bring village administration under a single law, we have determined the "principle of land belonging to a village" [or village territoriality, *shudi zhuyi*]. This is what the villagers call the dead sphere. Even if Village X's land has been sold to [a resident of] Village Y, all the tankuan, including crop-watching, education, police, and all other dues, are to be paid to Village X. Conversely, if Village Y sells land to Village X, all taxes will be paid to Village Y. This rule will be implemented from the day of the announcement. The villages whose finances have not yet been ordered according to this principle can now avoid disputes; those who have already implemented it naturally do not need to do so again. Merchants and people obey and do not violate this order.[30]

A village with a live sphere was one that determined and levied the rates on lands that lay within its green circle but ultimately transferred these payments to the village in which the landowner resided. The decree sought to transform these live spheres into dead spheres—to establish the principle of village territoriality in which the village retained all taxes from its green circle. The principle of village territoriality was adopted around this time in other counties as well, including Luancheng (the site of North Brushwood), where the crop-watching system was uncommon.

Implementing the principle of territoriality, however, brought discord and generated a fresh crop of litigation. One source of conflict was the definition or redefinition of village borders. Villages without crop-watching boundaries or with older territorial markers independent of the crop-watching boundary sought to claim larger areas than their neighbors cared to concede. Petitions by subordinate officials to the county magistrate complained that many villages continued to follow the principle of the live sphere because there were many complications and conflicting claims when it came to demarcating boundaries once and for all. In one such case, three villages that claimed to have a joint crop-watching organization agreed to submit the village land registers for investigation jointly. Suddenly, one of the villages turned on the other two. Maintaining that the three villages had had individual village territorial spheres all along, it staked out a largish area of the "joint territory" as its own. It is hardly surprising that the other two villages saw this as an insidious attempt by the first village to preempt them and lionize the territory.[31]

Other conflicts arose simply because in certain villages the income of residents from land they owned outside the territory of the village was greater than the tax income from outsiders owning land within its territory. A ward official reported that the officials of one village physically uprooted the trees marking the village boundaries and replanted them at more distant points because so much of the land of the village lay outside its current boundaries.[32] Another ward official sought advice on a problem involving three villages that had agreed to demarcate their borders amicably. One of the villages refused to accept the initial plan because whereas earlier this village had owed 9 yuan to another village, under the new arrangement it would owe 14 yuan.[33] Other cases suggest a fair amount of bullying by bigger and richer villages as smaller and poorer villages tried to claim the taxes on lands that had previously gone to the big ones.[34]

Perhaps the villages that were ill-inclined to accept territorial boundaries or the dead sphere for taxes were ones with landowners with substantial land outside the village area. Conversely, those that welcomed the territorial principle were villages whose residents were losing land from both inside and outside the territory. The 1936 boundary law was seemingly a progressive step taken to stabilize the diminishing income of poor villages. Yet, we cannot infer that the Nationalist state was acting solely from considerations of social justice. This is clear from the omission of policies that would have ameliorated the conditions of the poorer taxpayers in the village. The law left untouched the whole question of who was to pay the rates: the cultivator or the landowner. As it was, villages made this decision autonomously, and their choice depended on the balance of power between tenants and landowners in a village.

In some villages, landlords refused to lease land to tenants who suggested that the landlords share the tankuan rates; in other places, they simply raised rents if they were made to pay these rates.[35] When the tax demand became great, the tenants who had earlier been exempted from these taxes now found that they had to pay.[36] Sometimes the "rich" were just as badly squeezed by the tankuan rates. In one village dominated by landowners possessing under 5 mou of land, the few landlords owning 40–50 mou complained that they were rapidly being impoverished because a disproportionate share of the tax burden fell on them since those who held under 5 mou of land were exempt from tankuan payment.[37] In Changli county in northeastern Hebei, prosperous villagers with high-grade lands objected vigorously to a proposal to divide the land into three grades according to quality so as to make the rates more progressive.[38]

Thus the order to develop village territoriality was apparently designed to stabilize the state's own flow of revenues. Village territoriality was of first importance to the state both in terms of its short-range interest of ensuring tankuan payments, however these were collected, and in terms of its long-range, state-making interests. Receiving the revenues from all the land within its boundaries would reduce the tax pressures on populous but poor villages. It might even temper the consequences of levying taxes with little regard to the actual taxpaying capacity of a village.

Village territoriality could also enable statemakers to conduct an investigation of the ownership of all rural land. Land investigation, which is discussed at length in Chapter 8, not only was important for overcoming the historical problem of evasion but was widely considered to be the sine qua non of a just tax system.[39] Where the principle of territoriality did not exist or was violated, it was impossible to determine the lands belonging to the residents of a village if these lands were scattered over a wide area. Making sure that every plot of land was now the responsibility of one village or the other made this task much easier. In other words, from the point of view of the state, the order represented an effort to link village and land in a stable manner and to account for all the land in a highly fluid land market.

No doubt the state expected that the establishment of territorial boundaries would ultimately strengthen the village as an organizational center. The expectation was all the more reasonable because tankuan levies and other developments since the early 20th century had established the importance of the village as a fiscal entity. As a matter of fact, however, although the village was given more responsibilities, it was not necessarily strengthened. The fixing of village boundaries marked a subtle change in the nature of the taxing powers of the village. The tankuan levies had granted village authorities the power to tax the residents of the village. The establishment of territorial boundaries transformed this power of control over residents to one of control over a determinate area of land. From the point of view of the village authorities, a certain disjunction had been created between the residents of the village, who were under the customary ambit of their control but would now no longer necessarily pay their taxes to the village, and outsiders, who owned land within the newly defined territorial sphere of the village. Although the village had the right and the responsibility to tax the land of these outsiders, it did not necessarily have the ability to compel them to pay.

In some ways, village territoriality was a traditional response to a historical problem. But in the late Ming, which provides the closest parallel, the problem lay with the collection of the land tax, not the tankuan. During the late Ming, in response to the growing commercialization of the economy, labor exactions were increasingly commuted and merged with the land tax—in the well-known single-whip tax reforms. The lijia system, formed of the 110-household groups that had been collectively responsible for corvée labor dues to the government, also became responsible for the increasingly important land tax. The *li* of the lijia system gradually came to be identified as an area of taxable land rather than an aggregate of households liable for labor dues. At the same time, however, the growth of absentee landlordism in an active land market, among other factors, made it absurd to expect that the village-level lijia leadership, designed originally to be responsible for the labor dues of village residents, could compel these powerful outsiders to pay their taxes. Consequently, the lijia system became irrelevant to the real social structure of the late Ming.[40]

The process was repeated in North China with the tankuan during the 20th century, particularly where large absentee landlords living in county seats controlled much of the land, as in Luancheng and Liangxiang.[41] But during the turmoil of the 1920s, 1930s, and 1940s, when property owners fled in increasing numbers to the cities, the problem of absenteeism became widespread, and the burden of taxation fell more and more on those who were less and less able to pay. Therefore, although village territoriality may have been advantageous for villages that were losing land, by transforming the object of a village's taxing rights from the people over whom it had customary control to outsiders who held land in its territory, the new system often considerably weakened the powers of village authorities to collect these taxes.

A Corporate Village Community in North China?

What was the nature of village cohesion in North China? Did the new taxing powers of village government and the creation of a distinct sphere of control contribute to the development of a closed corporate identity as they did in other parts of the world? Although villages in North China in the first half of the 20th century were relatively egalitarian, villagers were, nonetheless, differentiated in terms of public participation, rights and obligations, and access to collective resources.

There were two modes of exclusion in the villages: certain individuals and families were denied access to the collective resources of the village, and individuals were denied the right to participate as formal equals in the public sphere. Let us consider the latter first. Accustomed as we are to thinking in individualistic categories, we assume that in a society such as that of China, which is basically nonascriptive, all individuals are equal participants in the public sphere. However, in the villages of North China, whether for community religious functions or public meetings, it was not the individual but the family, represented by its head, that possessed the right to participate in these activities. To be sure, the remaining family members were not denied access to the collective resources of the village. What they lacked was the right to participate in or influence public processes as individuals. This is consonant with the relations between the individual and the family in other areas as well. For example, with respect to property rights, Martin Yang and Fei Hsiao-t'ung have noted that it was the family head, not an individual member, who had the right to dispose of property in the family.[42] This principle of representation in public life persisted down through the 1940s, even in modern-style elections under the supervision of county authorities.[43]

Moreover, there was a category of people who were not only unrepresented in village community activities but were, in fact, not considered to be members of the village. Fei, who wrote about such outsiders in the lower Yangtze valley, noted that their assimilation into the life of the village was extremely slow.[44] In North China, these people were variously known as *fuhu* (supplementary households), *jiju* (temporary dwellers), *lohu* (outsider residents), and *fuzhu* (floating residents); the original residents of the village were known as *bencunren*, *laohu*, or *shiju*.[45] Some such families had lived in the villages for as long as ten years, but they were entered in the baojia records as supplementary households, or not at all, as in the case of people who rented their homes from village residents.[46] Typically, none of these people participated in community functions, and they were sometimes barred from owning certain types of property, such as a house or land.[47]

The relationship between villagers and outsiders over the period is believed to be a key to understanding the corporate character of northern villages. But before evaluating the degree to which these people were kept outside the community, we must examine the background of the concept of corporate village community.

There has been a persistent tendency to define a village community in strictly alternative terms. On the one hand, the village is depicted as a solidary group with a highly developed sense of collective identity. This position is best expressed in the notion of gemeinschaft or the Japanese concept of kyōdōtai. A recent reformulation of the basic elements of gemeinschaft appears in James

C. Scott's "moral economy" of the peasant. In this version, the right to subsistence of the entire peasant community takes precedence over individual interests, and village institutions typically protect the collective by redistributing the wealth of the rich.[48] The opposite point of view, identified most recently with Samuel Popkin's theory of the "rational peasant," views the village as a more open society where peasant families compete with each other to maximize their interests. Although Popkin grants that peasants may at times care about their friends and their village, he believes that they usually act in a self-interested manner, making choices that they believe will maximize their expected utility.[49]

In the field of Chinese history, Japanese scholars have developed the notion of the corporate village community, or kyōdōtai, as well as its refutation, most completely, and it is instructive to refer briefly to the history of this idea. As Hatada Takashi has shown, the idea was adapted from Karl Wittfogel and had acquired a certain currency among Japanese scholars even before the war. During the war, the idea came to be assimilated within the Japanese imperialist idea of the Greater East Asian Co-prosperity Sphere. Elements from the mythology of kyōdōtai were selected to formulate the idea that the pristine Asiatic values of cooperation and community were to be found in Chinese villages as yet incompletely sullied by the competitive urges of Western capitalism. It was the moral duty of the Japanese state to protect these values from the onslaught of the West since it was the only force in Asia with the capacity to do so.[50]

When liberal and leftist Japanese scholars did not find the idealized village community in their surveys of North China, they subjected the idea of kyōdōtai as applied to China to a scathing attack. The virulence of their rejection no doubt had something to do with the association of this idea with wartime politics, but it also made an objective appraisal of the importance of the village as a locus of coordination very difficult. Much of Japanese scholarship on rural China continues to be dominated by the paradigmatic opposition between the kyōdōtai idea and its complete rejection.[51]

In the West, the study of the Chinese village on the mainland came to be de-emphasized with the appearance of G. William Skinner's work on marketing systems, which located the basic unit of Chinese society not in the village but in the standard marketing area. Recently, however, there has been a cautious return to the study of the village as a focus of identity. Philip Huang, in his study of the *CN* villages, has argued that village insularity, identity, and solidarity were much more highly developed than Skinner's study of Sichuan villages would lead us to believe. This was generally true before the political disintegration of the 1920s, and after that time, for villages dominated by a stable community of middle peasants.[52] Although Huang's analysis is quite different, his conclusions are remarkably similar to those of Hatada Takashi regarding the degree of village corporateness in North China as expressed in his study of the conditions for gaining village membership.[53] Both invoke kinship and stratification in their characterization of the nature of village community.

Hatada and Huang discuss six villages each. Five of the six are the same, and all seven villages are drawn from the *CN* survey. Hatada argues that there were two types of villages.[54] In type A, which includes Sand Well and Wu's Shop, the corporate character of the village community had eroded considerably by the 1930s. These villages set relatively easy conditions for gaining village membership. All one needed was an introduction to the village headman by a village resident; after village leaders were convinced that the candidate had not been guilty of any serious misconduct, he was permitted to reside in the village.[55] Sand Well also required that the prospective village member set up a house in the village where his family could cook separately.[56]

These conditions suggest that any newcomer who clearly expressed his intention to reside in the village for some length of time was regarded as a village member. He needed to possess neither cultivable lands nor gravelands in order to participate in elections and religious ceremonies or even to be addressed by terms of fictive kinship.[57] Correspondingly, any villager who left the village with his family, thereby expressing his intention to be absent for some length of time, was no longer considered a village member.[58] However, even in Sand Well, there were people who rented houses or in some other way expressed their intention not to stay for a long period. One such person was the schoolteacher. These people continued to be regarded as outsiders and did not participate in village activities.[59]

The conditions that qualified an outsider to become a villager were much stricter in four other villages for which we have information. One of them is North Brushwood in southern Hebei; the remaining three are in Shandong. Hatada classifies them as type B. Cold Water Ditch in Licheng county, Shandong, required new-comers to own land and a house. There were many families, known as *jizhuanghu* (temporary dwellers), who possessed neither and rented their homes. These people were often tenants whose land-lords guaranteed their proper conduct in the village; whenever the outsiders committed an infraction, the guarantor suffered the penalty.[60] However, in certain cases in this village, one could become a village member by virtue of having lived in the village for about ten years despite having neither land nor house.[61]

The three other villages, Lujiazhuang in Licheng county and Xia Walled Village in En county in Shandong and North Brush-wood in Luancheng county in Hebei, had an additional require-ment: the possession of grave lands.[62] In North Brushwood, in fact, a person was not considered a full member of the village unless three past generations had lived in the village,[63] but it is doubtful that in actual practice those people whose ancestors had not lived quite so long in the village were seriously distinguished from the others.

Nonetheless, this condition points to the importance of belong-ing to a lineage, and the presence of ancestral graves was the surest indication of the existence of past generations in the village. Moreover, the condition stipulating *three* past generations is signifi-cant because it expressed the importance of the five mourning grades within the lineage. Similarly, precisely because his ancestral graves were still located there, a person who moved out of the village continued to be regarded as a member even though he may have lost his land and house. When he ceased to visit the graves on the proper ceremonial occasions, he was no longer so regarded.[64]

According to Hatada, the different conditions for membership reflect the different social structures of the villages. He contends that the two villages in type A were more sharply stratified than those in type B. The conditions of entry into type-A villages required neither land nor housing because this matched the cir-cumstances of type-A villages, where there were large numbers of people so destitute that they could not afford to own land or housing.

The more difficult conditions of entry for type-B villages reflect the more egalitarian social structure of these villages. Type-B villages, according to Hatada, were characterized by a mass of petty producers with more evenly distributed holdings than those of type-A villages. Moreover, kinship ties were also stronger in these villages, especially in North Brushwood. These factors made for a stronger sense of corporate identity, which is indicated by the relative inaccessibility of the status of village member. Finally, he posits a developmental scheme in which there is a historical transition from type B to type A based on the inability of type-B villages to prevent stratification.[65]

Although Hatada's analysis successfully explains some of the facts, it has important gaps. First, in North Brushwood, which he describes as a community of relatively equal landholders, more than half the land belonging to the villagers had been mortgaged or sold to merchants living in the county seat.[66] Judging from the violence of agrarian relations in North Brushwood, it can scarcely be said that the experience of class differentiation was much less here than in type-A villages such as Wu's Shop, where most of the land had been sold outright to outsiders.[67] Second, kinship ties in Cold Water Ditch resemble those in type-A villages closely. Third, though inequalities were not great, there were many landless households.[68] Finally, there is not sufficient evidence to demonstrate a process of historical transformation from one type to the other.

Huang proceeds by classifying the six villages into three categories. Xia Walled Village and Cold Water Ditch (both of which Hatada classes in type B) are solidary villages. Not only can their corporate character be understood by reference to the dominance of peasant proprietors and the strength of lineages (at least in Xia Walled Village), but it is also exemplified by their response in the form of "community closure" to the external threats of the 20th century. He sees in their resistance to outside forces through Red Spear and self-defense organizations a high degree of village community solidarity. Villages in his second category, such as Sand Well and North Brushwood, start out as solidary communities, but this identity gradually erodes as more and more land comes to be held by outsiders. Lineage and village associations also begin to weaken in these communities. Huang characterizes Wu's Shop and Hou Lineage Camp as atomized villages since he claims they were highly stratified and lacked meaningful lineage and other village associations.[69]

Huang's analysis is more finely nuanced than Hatada's, and there is much in it that is correct. But there are also several problems. The criticism regarding stratification in Cold Water Ditch that I applied to Hatada can also be applied to Huang. Furthermore, it is not at all clear that lineages were declining in strength in North Brushwood and that they were powerless in Hou Lineage Camp; Sand Well had a relatively strong village-wide organization in the crop-watching association. But most important, it is a mistake to see the Red Spears in Xia Walled Village and the self-defense organizations in Cold Water Ditch as expressions of community closure. Both were part of multi-village organizations,[70] and they were important modes through which villages were linked to wider organizations in the nexus.

The theses of these two studies, that villages composed mainly of peasant proprietors *tended* to have tougher conditions for assimilating outsiders and were able to sustain strong community institutions, is perhaps broadly true. Indeed, it is likely that the power structure in this type of village was enhanced by the creation of territorial jurisdictions if a higher proportion of the land within its territory was owned by its residents. Yet, to go on from there and make assertions about community closure and corporate identity would ignore the myriad organizational and interpersonal ties that linked villagers and villages to outsiders in the nexus. Moreover, it is not easy to generalize about the nature of collective consciousness from institutional data. The collective consciousness of a community is a highly contradictory phenomenon, and it is not any less so in the village. Sentiments of cooperation coexist with competitive urges, sometimes even within the same institution or practice. Consider the following information from the *CN* villages.

On first sight, kyōdōtai bonds appear to exist in the religious ceremonies of the village, in particular in the collective supplication to the Dragon God for rain.[71] They can also be seen in the fictive kinship terms by which villagers addressed their fellow village members in virtually all of the villages studied. One might observe them as well in the preferred sequence of priority in the sale of land—first to lineage members, then to village members, and finally to outsiders. They might also be expressed in the fact that

in many, if not most, villages, the knowledge of actual landholdings in the village was a closely guarded secret among the villagers.[72]

On a closer look, however, many of these practices can be seen to
reflect stratification and competition within the village. Collective
religious ceremonies functioned as much to map out social distinctions and generate political authority as to regenerate community
ties. Fictive kinship terms were used equally often to express distance, as when outsiders residing in the village were addressed by
terms junior to ego even when the person so addressed was of ego's
grandfather's generation.[73] Although land was indeed first offered
within the lineage in most villages, it was rare that, in practice, it
was offered to a fellow villager over an outsider. And possessing a
collective secret, as Feng Huade has pointed out, does not mean
that some could not gain more from it than others or that this secret
knowledge could not become the object of a bitter struggle within
the village.[74]

It is surely in the nature of most social institutions and practices
to embody both cooperative and competitive modes of behavior.
These practices merely reflect the dual impulses among participants to respond to the shifting circumstances of domination and
advantage by combining strategies of cooperation and competition. Indeed, there is *a priori* no reason why a community of peasant proprietors should be less competitive among themselves than
peasants in a more "feudalistic" social arrangement. I have often
alluded to the theme of the double meanings of social and ritual
practices. Characterizations of village identity as insular and
solidary can be quite misleading unless we look at the ironic
underside of these same phenomena.

Conclusion

It is important to distinguish the characterization of the village
as a corporate community with close solidary ties from that of the
village as a functionally significant entity that coordinated several
important activities. During the course of the 20th century, the
village became an increasingly important locus of coordination in
local society, and for very practical considerations, the matter of
which village one belonged to also became increasingly significant

in all the *CN* villages. But this growing importance was neither engendered nor accompanied by any deep bonds of community solidarity.

Aside from the conceptual problems regarding collective identity that I have just alluded to, strong social and historical factors inhibited the growth of this identity. In many cases, the active land market in North China made it difficult for villages to translate territorial control into enhanced village power because of their inability to control outside landholders. Thus, although the village became a distinct organizational node, it gradually lost its ability to make much of this status.

More crucially, the formalization of village political authority, its disarticulation from the cultural nexus in rural society, and the subsequent pressures of the involutionary state were transforming the domain of political power into the hunting grounds of political predators. To the extent that a cohesive communal identity required a center with moral authority, developments during the Republic led to an attenuation, rather than a strengthening, of such an identity. For instance, even where, in North China, it was relatively difficult to become a village member, it never became as difficult as in the societies Eric Wolf discusses. And there is no historical precedent to indicate that villages were successfully able to close themselves off during periods of disorder. Yamagata Kanki's work, in fact, suggests the reverse: that the chaos of the Ming-Qing transition saw instead the diversification of rural communities and the emergence of multi-surname villages in North China.[75]

Village territoriality might have strengthened protective-brokerage relations within the village by stabilizing its fiscal foundations. But we have seen that even where the leadership was rooted in the village community, it would not find it easy to get outsiders to pay their dues. How much less were community relations likely to be strengthened when the political system was dominated by entrepreneurial brokers. In such cases, the scope of village leadership, torn away from the fabric of social life, was not particularly enhanced by developing a territorial basis for its financial powers. Entrepreneurial brokers of state power at the village level were no more likely to be able to get absentee property owners and outsiders to pay their rates than were community leaders. Thus, it was perhaps as much because of the ineffectiveness of village-level leadership in the Republic, as for any other reason, that the village was once again relegated to a status of political insignificance when the large township was established in 1940–41. With this, a cycle of village political development was brought to a close.

Eight

The Modernizing State and Local Leadership

During the best of times in late imperial China, village leadership had involved a measure of tightrope walking in negotiating between the interests of the community and those of the state and its agents. But even when fiscal and administrative pressures were at their worst, village leaders could still identify with the orthodox order through the shared cultural nexus that bound their legitimacy as leaders in local society with that of the imperial state. The modernizing drive of the 20th-century state forced local leaders to dissociate their political vocation from the traditional cultural nexus and rearticulate it through more formal administrative arrangements with the state. But the combined pressures of formal and informal state penetration were such that the role of political leadership in the village became an increasingly unviable one for all except those who, like state brokers at higher levels, saw office as an object of entrepreneurial gain. In this chapter, I turn to the specifics of state expansion that led to this development.

Was it state penetration or war and unrest that was responsible for the traditional leader's desertion of politics at a time when the state needed a stable and committed political leadership? Undoubtedly, war and the banditry that it generated in the countryside played an important role in this alienating process. But by focusing on the ways in which the state encroached on the prerogatives of this leadership, I hope to show that the combined impact of state policies and state involution was far more enduring and historically the more significant force. The elite had survived war and disruption before and had shown great resilience in its ability to reconstitute itself and recapture community leadership. What made this nearly impossible in the 20th century was the everyday, continuing demands on village leaders to levy taxes and implement policies that could only alienate them from their constituencies. Moreover, state building and warfare are not necessarily contradictory; they were closely associated in European history. Warfare did not contribute to state strengthening in China because the structure and behavior of armies exhibited the same involutionary tendencies we have seen in civilian state structures. Chinese armies during the Republic increasingly used mercenary soldiers for whom warfare, and not service, was a source of livelihood and profit.[1]

The principal reason the elite relinquished its control of offices in so many villages was that the symbolic and material rewards of a career in public office were gradually being outweighed by the increasingly onerous nature of the tasks involved. Not the least of these tasks was allocating, levying, and collecting tankuan. As mentioned earlier, officially tankuan were levied twice a year, after the harvests (when the villagers possessed cash); however, irregular or provisional tankuan, levied by the county, the ward, the administrative district, or a passing army, could strike a village as often as ten times a year. (The largest item in the tankuan accounts of some villages was the payment of county and ward police despatched to the village, which was euphemistically entered in the account books as "entertainment charges.")

My chief concern here is to demonstrate the impact of tankuan on the relationship between village leaders and the community. As such, the absolute size of the tax burden is not as critical to my arguments as the question of how this burden was perceived. (Those interested in an analysis of the magnitude of this burden and its relation to other factors, such as the rate of growth of government income, the inflation rate, and the terms of trade can consult my article on state involution.)[2] Although it is impossible to ascribe precise or total values to these factors, the broad trends suggest that each worked to increase the tax burden of the peasantry at a rate perceptibly faster than the growth of per capita rural income.

Materials from two villages, not particularly known for a heavy tax burden, indicate the extent of this burden. Sidney Gamble provides the best estimate of village finances in North China before the Japanese invasion. His figures, which cover the period 1907 until 1932 for Xinjuang village in central Hebei, do not include levies made by the county or the ward or by their functionaries but do include village-level and military assessments. In terms of the increase in real expenses (deflated by Nankai price indices; 1926 = 100), village expenses during the early Republic, excluding the military component, were approximately 373 yuan, whereas during the early 1930s they were 670 yuan, an increase of 80 percent. If we include military expenses, the increase was over 200 percent. The increase in village expenses after 1905 or so was probably even more dramatic since it was around then that the modernization measures began; before that, public expenses in the village were low.[3] The other illustration comes from Hou Lineage Camp, where according to the calculations of one Mantetsu researcher, 60 percent of the cash expenses of the average villager in the early 1940s was paid as tankuan.[4]

To return to the role of village leaders in managing tankuan levies, the most noticeable problem was that wealthy village leaders were called on to pay provisional tankuan levies in advance since these levies were often imposed when peasants were without cash. The villagers were supposed to reimburse them during the regular collection. Needless to say, it was not always easy to recover these amounts from a completely impoverished villager. In Cold Water Ditch, the village head, Du Fengshan, claimed that he had had to suffer the loss personally during the rule of the warlord Zhang Zongchang (1923–28) when the rates were highest.[5] In North Brushwood, ex–village headman Zhang Yuejing blamed the loss of part of his wealth on the same cause.[6] In Wu's Shop, the village officers were beaten by the police if the levies were not delivered on time.[7]

The plight of village officials was particularly unenviable because not only were they held responsible by the state for the collection of the levy but their relations with ordinary villagers were severely tested whenever they had to collect these rates. This was especially so in the case of the village headman. The village headman of North Brushwood expressed the problem succinctly:

Q: Is it difficult to do the job of the village headman because of the county functionaries or the villagers?

A: Because of both. . . . I am very busy with the work related to government demands and unable to do any work of my own.

Q: What about relations with the villagers?

A: When I attempt to collect the levy from them, they are very reluctant to pay. They behave as if I wanted the money for myself.[8]

The village headman and the other officials responsible for collecting the levy were trapped in a situation in which no respectable patron could retain his status for long. The village headman of Cold Water Ditch, Du Fengshan, although himself a respected leader, claimed that no other influential villager cared to take village office because of the tankuan, which was by far the most bothersome of all the tasks in the village.[9] The alternative was for the village officer to throw in his lot with that of the state and stand against the community. In Xia Walled Village, for instance, the headman reported cases of nonpayment to the ward police, who would then beat up the villager in question.[10]

Opposition by the villagers to the village headman's and the councillors' decisions on tankuan was reported in every county of the *CN* survey. The severity of the opposition varied from case to case, but it led to resignations of village officials in Xia Walled Village and Hou Lineage Camp.[11] In Wu's Shop, wealthy village officers not only quit their jobs but also left the village over tankuan problems.[12] In Shunyi and Luancheng counties in Hebei, disputes over the tankuan between villagers and village leaders were arbitrated by the ward authorities, who usually upheld the decision of the village authorities.[13] Gamble mentions a village near Beijing where the villagers, led by opposition councillors, sued the headman and others for mishandling tankuan assessments. The power and position of the village headman were considerably weakened by the affair.[14]

There are several interesting cases from Luancheng county of tankuan disputes. Petitions to the county magistrate from ordinary villagers throughout the 1930s document complaints against village officials about injustices in the allocation of tankuan. One petitioner charged that the village council had arbitrarily violated the customary standards of assessment in the village. Traditionally, his village, like many others in North China, had had a highly differentiated and progressive system of assessment. Those who had mortgaged their land paid a lower rate than those who owned their lands. Tenants paid a still lower rate, and the landless paid nothing. The petitioner complained that the village council had suddenly decided to make mortgagors pay the same rate as landowners.[15]

Two other cases from this county are worth considering because they reached the highest provincial court. A village neighboring North Brushwood called Gangtou had two main streets with 70 households in one and 40 in the other. However, the village leaders levied tankuan on the traditionally accepted 50–50 basis. In the late 1920s when the rates began to accelerate, this division was opposed by the street with fewer households, and the case went to the high court. The court decided that the village would be split into two separate fiscal entities.[16] In another village, Famapu, the land held by one subdivision of the village had shrunk considerably, but village leaders maintained its original tankuan quota. Consequently the villagers of the subdivision in question took the village leaders to court.[17] The decision of the high court was not known at the time of the survey.

Increased tankuan dues, a phenomenon peculiar to the 20th century, were an important but not the only means whereby village leaders were put in a position of potential and actual opposition to villagers. Partially in order to circumvent or minimize the role of entrepreneurial state brokers, the formal agencies of the state in Republican times, especially under Nationalist and Japanese domination, attempted to implement their policies by enlisting the services of the village leaders, especially those of the village headman. But these policies tended to deepen the division between the leadership and community interests, particularly when popular practice in the village ran counter to the letter of the law, causing prestigious leaders to become even more wary of assuming office. This was demonstrated most clearly in the case of the deed tax, which introduced new dilemmas into the village headman's role.

Most land deeds in North China, as elsewhere from at least the late Qing, were unstamped deeds (*baiqi*) that did not have the red seal of state authorization. In order to acquire the red seal, or to transform the contract into a "red contract" (*hongqi*), the buyer had to pay the deed tax, a provincial tax. During the Republic, the tax was nominally 6 percent of the value of the transaction, but by the late Republic, it amounted to over 12 percent when all surcharges were included.[18] It is not surprising that villagers ignored the tax when they could. The red contract was not essential for paying the land tax because there appears to have been little coordination between the land tax department and the deed tax bureau. The red contract was, however, essential for claiming a legal title to the land in a court case, and villagers paid the deed tax only when such disputes seemed likely.

Before the Nationalist takeover of North China, there was, in many market towns, an officially designated overseer of the deed tax (*guanzhongren*), who sometimes also contracted to pay the tax. In 1930, the Nationalist government eliminated this broker and charged the village headman with responsibility for overseeing the payment of this tax. Henceforth, all land transactions were to be made on official forms called *caoqi*. The village headman purchased these forms from the county office and sold them at a slightly higher rate to any buyer of land in his village. The difference, which varied from county to county, was the headman's commission. The headman was called the official witness (*jianzhengren*), and he was expected to turn in the stubs of the official forms he had sold regularly to the county office. In this way, the county had evidence of all land sales.[19]

In getting rid of the earlier intermediary and replacing him with the village headman, the authorities were operating on the accurate supposition that the village headman had a surer knowledge of village land transactions than did the intermediary. Not only did he know village landholdings, he was also an active accomplice in the efforts of the entire village to keep this knowledge a well-concealed secret. We know from the reports of Feng Huade, Gamble, and the *CN* surveys that by the 1930s most villages in North China had two land registers.[20] One of them was for outside consumption and corresponded to the land records in the county seat. The other was for the village. As the land investigations of 1941 were to show, in some villages as much as half of the land was unregistered in any public account book. Much of this land was, however, recorded in the second register, which was meant strictly for the villagers and was used to calculate the allocation of the shares of individual households for tankuan and other village dues. In this one respect, the village was an insular community that shared a common secret.

An overly enthusiastic village headman who actually pursued and sought out every person who either did not report or underreported the value of land transactions was a threat to this community. (Incidentally, the existence of two registers suggests that those engaged in microeconomic studies of farm-family behavior in the 1930s should be cautious about using the reported data on actual farm size.)

Happily for the villagers and their leaders, in some counties the authorities rarely verified the reports of official witnesses from independent sources. This laxity can probably be explained by the fact that the deed tax was a provincial tax, not a county one. In Shunyi county, a clerk reported that although more people paid the deed tax after the village headmen had been made the official witnesses, most people still did not pay it, and the village headmen deliberately ignored these transgressions.[21] But in other villages, the pressure on the headman to report those who did not pay was considerable. In Lujiazhuang in Licheng county in Shandong, the potential for conflict inherent in the new system was realized when the police came to dun and beat offenders whom the village headman had reported.[22]

The new type of village official who began to emerge in the late Republic had to base his power on sources outside the cultural nexus. Occasionally, this type of leader relied on sheer brute strength, as in the case of some "local bullies," but more often than not his power derived from links with state brokers in the county and subcounty administrations. We saw this not only in examples in the previous chapter, but also in the discussion of religion in Chapter 5, for example, in the case of Fan Baoshan and the city-god temple priest in Shimen village in Shunyi county.

The enforcement of the large township (daxiang) in 1941, which replaced the administrative functions of the natural village, created a different scale and resource base for this new type of rural official. As mentioned before, the township was a 1,000 household administrative unit first introduced between 1931 and 1935. All village governmental activities were to be centralized at this level, and the old natural village was to become a subunit governed by a township assistant. In theory, the natural village was no longer empowered to levy tankuan, have a budget, or engage in any autonomous activities, such as self-defense or crop watching. In practice, however, during this early period many villages carried on as they had before. In some villages, self-defense and educational activities were relocated at the township, but the village continued to levy and collect taxes according to its own principles.[23]

It was only in 1941, when the Japanese provincial and county governments forced the strict implementation of the large township that it became a reality. They did so because they wanted to create a basic unit of control and development that was more amenable to the interests of the state—a unit that ultimately tore apart what was left of the nexus of interests linking elites with the power structures of local communities. An order from the county magistrate of Changli (where Hou Lineage Camp was located) publicizing its enforcement reveals the twin goals of concentrating authority and bureaucratizing it at this level.[24]

On the one hand, the order prescribed elaborate rules for the election of the headman of the township and his assistants and specified their responsibilities and salaries. It also quoted strict regulations for giving receipts for tankuan payments. On the other hand, all disputes over interpretation of rules, including those over tankuan allocation, could be arbitrated only by the headman. There was no mention of any officer to supervise his conduct, an office that appears in some Nationalist regulations.[25] This concentration of authority in one office was accompanied by pleas to the officeholder to develop a constructive attitude toward public affairs and to avoid using the office for private gain.

In many respects, the township represented a logical development of the efforts of the formalizing agencies of the state to solve the problem of tax evasion, such as the nonpayment of the deed tax by villagers or of tankuan by those living outside the village, which neither traditional leaders committed to village interests nor petty local bullies had achieved. Even more important, the township would enable the state to conduct land investigations with more success than other Republican-era regimes. But the forceful implementation of these measures required a leadership that not only was uncommitted to traditional roles and village interests but could combat the opposition that these measures would evoke from both elite and commoner.

Information on the actual operation of the township exists for two villages surveyed in 1942, Hou Lineage Camp and Wu's Shop.

From the point of view of the villagers, the township had, if anything, worsened the involutionary effects of state penetration. First, these villages had to pay for another level of salaried staff. Second, the townships were equipped with an efficient means of communication, the telephone, which the villagers simply interpreted as being a more effective means of enforcing compliance. When taxes were not paid on time, the county police were contacted by telephone and promptly came over to collect them.[26]

As a large unit, the township was also expected to be an appropriate unit for development projects. The only evidence available on this activity is from Wu's Shop. Several wells were constructed in the township by the villagers for irrigation purposes. However, all the wells were dug on lands belonging to the large absentee landlords living in the county seat, many of whom were county officials. Township officers claimed that the orders came directly from the magistrate.[27]

Hou Lineage Camp belonged to a township whose center was located in Nijing, its market town and also the ward headquarters. The township was headed by an unsavory character named Zhai Yangding, whose biography gives a fair idea of the background of a "big local bully." Zhai's father had supplied provisions for the army and, through this connection, had become very powerful in the Nijing village government, from which he made money. It was rumored that the father had killed his own elder son. Zhai Yangding, the remaining son, followed in his father's footsteps and was equally disreputable. Zhai was wealthy and had close connections with the county magistrate. When the township was formed, he allegedly bribed a number of bao headmen to vote him in as township headman.

After taking office, Zhai unleashed a reign of terror in the villages. He absorbed every single piece of collective property in the villages and abolished their various progressive systems of tax assessment. He terrorized the councillors and arbitrarily demanded taxes from them. The only person Zhai feared was the redoubtable Xiao Huisheng, whose services earned him a plaque from 38 villages, but each kept out of the other's way. His excesses became so intolerable that in 1941 three men representing three villages in the township took him to court for dishonest accounts and capricious conduct. But Zhai had powerful contacts in the county and won the case.

Fearful of reprisals, the three representatives fled the area. None-theless, Zhai immediately imposed an additional levy of 5,000 yuan to make up for the losses he had suffered in the litigation.[28]

Under the circumstances, no villager with prestige and standing in the village could be expected to remain in village office. The new bao headman of Hou Lineage Camp, not to speak of the baojia officials, was said to be a mere puppet of Zhai's. According to ex–village headman Liu Zixing, township headmen like Zhai were not uncommon. The unprecedented concentration of political power in the township headman, together with the enhanced resource base in the township, especially when it was a market, seemed to draw especially powerful "local tyrants" with links as high as the magistrate, who, it was alleged, depended on their "gifts" for much of his income.[29] The level of wealth and the connections of this "tyrant" distinguished him from the petty village political entrepreneur and were enough to drive community leaders from village office, even in villages like Hou Lineage Camp where such leaders had survived in office until the institution of the township.

Can the township be considered successful from the point of view of state making? It did succeed in achieving certain state goals, such as the prompt payment of taxes and the implementation of land investigation, goals that might ultimately have strengthened formal state agencies. Meanwhile, however, these very tasks often pitted leadership against community even more dramatically than before. Consequently, the propensity for these positions to be taken over by powerful local bullies in the involutionary mode of state expansion delegitimated the state more rapidly than it could devise new means of integrating leadership with community.

Ordering Revenues: The Registration Clerk and Land Investigation

One of the great tasks of state strengthening was the institution-alization of the means of acquiring and transmitting information about its revenues. Yet it was not until the 1940s, when the alien Japanese regime finally tore apart what remained of the nexus of interests linking elites with the power structures of local com-munities and eliminated such state brokers as the registration clerk, that the state was able to gain some idea of the actual taxable capacity of these communities. In this section, I analyze the fate of rural society in the three-way competition between the village and the formal and informal state agencies over control of this vital source of power.

Scholars and fiscal administrators of the various regimes saw the necessity of controlling this information early in the Republic. It was considered important in order not only to increase revenues by eliminating tax evasion and engrossment but also to introduce a measure of justice in the distribution of the tax burden. In a special issue devoted to tax reform of the *Journal of Land Economy* in 1936, Wan Guoding expressed the conviction that the rich often increased the burden of the poor by avoiding their tax responsibilities, and he advocated a differentiated tax based on land values. But he noted these measures presupposed the successful implementation of a land investigation, which had eluded every regime so far.[30]

An important factor behind the failure of some of these efforts was the continued reliance on the existing arrangements of information collection during the course of the investigation, in particular, on the registration clerk (sheshu, lishu). This clerk conducted his operations within the revenue division that we encountered earlier (she, li, tu). His most important function, from the point of view of the state, was to compile and update the registers on which the land tax and its surcharges were based. Although some sources trace his origins back to the Ming,[31] his role in the 20th century was associated with the breakdown of the Qing revenue system, which was well under way by the middle of the 19th century. In part, he undertook some of the functions that should have been performed by the lijia and baojia, such as updating registers, urging tax payments, and even collecting taxes. But, as we have seen, his indispensability derived from the Qing state's reliance on the registers made and updated by him after the loss of the fish-scale and yellow registers in the rebellions of the mid-19th century.

The registers were records of households like the yellow registers, but unlike the yellow registers they were not compiled anew every year. Indeed, they were notoriously unreliable since they were often based on the clerk's personal ability to find out the actual amount of land a household owned.[32] Despite this shortcoming, the institution of the registration clerk may have worked quite well for the state, given the breakdown of the older system of information gathering and the relatively slow increases in tax demands. The chief officer of the finance department of Luancheng county described the tax division as a voluntary organization and the registration clerk as a functional representative of the local community whose original role was to help peasants enter the exact amounts they owed to the state.[33]

It is possible that in the early stages the registration clerk was a state broker who played as much a protective as an entrepreneurial role in the community. Like the rural agent (difang), there were ambiguities built into his role since the desire to maximize the returns on his "franchise" was mitigated by his ties to, or control by, local communities. In the case of the rural agent, the trend was for local powerholders to keep his entrepreneurial instincts in check; in the case of the registration clerk, these same instincts tended to become less restrained in the late 19th century. This may have resulted from the registration clerk's greater indispensability to the state compared with the rural agent. Not only was the clerk an inexpensive means of updating tax registers, but, as a local, the state no doubt believed that he would be able to add hitherto unreported taxable land (*heidi*) to the registers better than anyone else available.[34]

Aside from his principal function of compiling tax registers for the state, the clerk also recorded all transfers of land titles, whether through sale or through division of family property. For this he charged a commission, usually paid by the receiver of the property. Most such transactions took place within the tax division, which did not raise any special problems since the clerk simply transferred the title to another name in his records. Occasionally, however, a plot was sold outside the division, and in order to keep track of the plot, the registration clerks of the various divisions in the county met from time to time to exchange information on the transfer of titles to their areas. Konuma Tadashi observed that it was not uncommon to see such a meeting of registration clerks in the market towns, with throngs of land purchasers waiting to register a transaction at the last moment.[35]

In many parts of North China, the registration clerk also undertook the responsibility of delivering the land taxes and surcharges. A seven-county survey of the Jidong region of Hebei found that 70 percent of the peasants paid their taxes through these clerks. The manner in which the clerks were organized to perform this function closely resembled the organization of the farming of excise taxes discussed in the next section. In Changli, the county authorities dealt with the chief registration clerk, who was appointed only after he was able to demonstrate financial backing by two merchant guarantors. Under him were the various registration clerks of the revenue divisions, to whom he provided cash advances. These clerks were expected to pay the unpaid taxes in their divisions once the date for payment by the taxpayer had passed. After the clerk had paid the tax, he would, of course, collect the amount from his "debtor" together with "reasonable interest."[36]

As an intermediary monopolizing the channels of revenue information, the registration clerks derived a measure of power by which they could both defraud the state and bully the villagers. As long as revenue increases remained within the traditional expectations of the patrimonial state, the authorities were not unduly perturbed by this monopoly. In the 20th century, however, when revenue needs accelerated dramatically, the monopolizing of such vital information by a private contractor became intolerable. It was at this time that the abuses associated with the job of registration clerk came to light.

By the 1930s, the office of registration clerk could be purchased for between 250 and 500 yuan on the average, a sum of money that a rich peasant might be able to accumulate in a few years. This was, of course, after the position had already come under considerable fire, and there is evidence that in earlier times, the clerk might have been able to accumulate more money at his post than its market value would suggest.[37] But even in the 1930s, there was no dearth of writings censuring the multifarious ills associated with the job.

First, the commission the clerk charged for transferring titles in his records was not subject to close supervision. Although the officially permitted rate was one-tenth of a yuan per mou, he was known to charge anywhere between one and three yuan. He also took advantage of the peasants' ignorance of the conversion rate between the Qing silver tael and the Republican yuan and made a considerable profit from this conversion. He often tampered with the accounts, sometimes entering sums greater than that owed by the taxpayer and sometimes entering taxes less than those due the state, pocketing the difference in each case. These are a few items in the long litany of abuses associated with this broker by contemporaries.[38]

From the late Qing to the 1930s, the extortionary practices of this clerk had become so intolerable that many legal suits were brought against him. In Cold Water Ditch, a temple plaque recorded an order from the county in 1873 responding to complaints about the rapaciousness of the clerk. The order regulated, in minute detail, the values and types of commissions that he was permitted to charge. Even in the 1930s, Cold Water Ditch villagers confronted this clerk through their headman, the redoubtable Du Fengshan, who entertained him and provided him with all the information and his dues, including several extra bushels of wheat. The amassing of this last "gift" was shared by the villagers as a form of tankuan.[39]

The registration clerk was violently opposed by reformers not only because he was seen to be oppressive but because he posed an obstacle to land investigation. There was a general awareness that vast amounts of land remained unreported in the countryside. Every administration from the early Republic on expressed a need for a complete survey of all taxable land. The registration clerk was seen as a problem partly because of his interest in falsifying accounts. But even where he was considered more amenable to the goals of the state, he was regarded as a hopelessly inadequate means of surveying land. The investigation campaigns sought to supplant the services of this state broker by a far more formal system of channeling tax information.[40]

As the successful investigations of the early 1940s were to show, the amount of unreported taxable land was considerable. The principal factor behind the high figures was the continued existence of large tracts of tax-exempt lands granted by the Qing to its military organizations and to religious and educational institutions in Hebei and Shandong. County and provincial governments had no records of these lands.[41]

The largest component of these lands were those granted to the military, or the Manchu banner lands. The history of these lands is a complex one, the details of which need not detain us here. In the 18th century, these lands comprised more than 20 million mou in Hebei, and 3 million mou in Shandong. Much of the land had been rented to Chinese tenants, and throughout the 19th century, because of the gradual impoverishment of the bannermen, a great many plots had been sold or mortgaged to Chinese proprietors, but remained untaxed. Nonetheless, large but unknown tracts of banner and other tax-free lands were still being cultivated by Chinese tenants at the end of the 19th century. These tenants paid their rents to a manager called the *zhuangtou*, who in turn paid the rents to the Imperial Household Department.[42]

With the fall of the empire in 1911, the tax-exempt status of these lands was rescinded. But in the confusion of the revolution, many of the managers disappeared, and whatever records existed became irretrievable. Tenants of these once tax-free lands found themselves the virtual owners of lands about which the state had no reliable knowledge. In 1914, the Yuan Shikai regime established a national Bureau of Land Investigation (Jingjieju), and in 1915 its first two branches were established, in Liangxiang and Zhuo counties near Beijing. Because of the political turmoil that followed those years, the investigation was discontinued. At the same time, the state sought to abolish the post of registration clerk, but only in Liangxiang was the administration able to manage without these clerks. Elsewhere, for instance in Changli county, the clerk was stopped from collecting unpaid taxes between 1914 and 1926, and the police were required to perform this task. But the new arrangement must not have worked very well because the clerk was called back to resume this task in 1926.[43]

In other places like Qinghai, the administration sought to bureaucratize this position. The chief registration clerk was made an official supervising the collection of taxes in 1917 and was given a small emolument. But the situation was not really altered because the tasks of transferring titles and issuing tax assessments and receipts still had to be performed. The chief registration clerk merely brought the registration clerks into his personal employ, and they continued to earn a living by transferring titles and supervising tax dues.[44] In most of the counties surveyed, the registration clerks, although more cautious than they had been before, persisted until the 1930s. The state was not yet able to institutionalize the system of making reliable tax registers and so continued to depend on the clerks.

Branches of the Bureau of Land Investigation were established sporadically throughout the early 1920s, but they did not have much success.[45] In some counties like Shunyi, an incentive was given the owners of unreported land to declare these lands voluntarily by the no-questions-asked, penalty-free granting of a legal title to the land.[46] In Hou Lineage Camp, several hundred mou were brought to light in 1922, but the investigations of the 1940s were to show that in most places these early efforts had barely scratched the surface.[47]

The establishment of Nationalist rule in 1928 marked a new phase in thinking about institutional means of gathering information and revenue. These functions were to be performed by the formal institutions of government—the county, ward, township, municipality—all of which ideally linked state to society in an unbroken chain of command. Thus, in the late 1920s, when the Nationalist party conducted its campaign against local bullies and "superstition" in its last radical phase, it also launched a severe attack on the post of the registration clerk.[48]

Between 1931 and 1936, the post was abolished in several counties, but we still find the clerks lurking about under different titles and guises. In parts of Hebei, they were known as "tax collection officers" (*zhengshouyuan* or *zongfang*) until 1940.[49] An instruction booklet from Huolu county in central Hebei on the calculation of the land tax lamented the sorry state of affairs the reform of the land tax system had reached. Although the responsibility for compiling new registers had been assigned the new townships and municipalities, they were still being compiled by private contractors. The instructions warned against the evils of using the registration clerks and admonished the county and wards to play a much more active role in supervising the compilation of these registers by lower levels. As it turned out, the movement to investigate land trailed off after the early 1930s because not much headway was being made.[50]

As Wan Guoding pointed out, the Nationalists were caught in a bind. A proper investigation would have necessitated making accurate maps and actually measuring the plots of land. Moreover, this would have to be done by outside specialists because the existing personnel were not disinterested agents. Yet the costs of this undertaking were such that most county governments were quickly discouraged and resorted to the existing arrangements of information collection to conduct the investigation. Wan himself proposed using aerial surveys, but there is no evidence to suggest that this was implemented until the Japanese took over.[51]

We know why it was futile to use the registration clerk, but why were the leaders of the township so sluggish about compiling new registers? As mentioned above, during the 1930s the actual working unit within the township was still the natural village, and village leaders, like the rest of the villagers, concealed great amounts of land. In fact, according to Feng Huade, the leaders concealed much more than the rest.[52] The pressure on the leadership to conduct the investigation threatened to reveal this community secret and to divide the leadership along the lines of suppressed traditional rivalries, as it did in Hou Lineage Camp in the early 1920s (see Chapter 4). Small wonder, then, that they were hesitant in going about this task.

Might not the dissociation of the village elite from leadership roles have helped the state achieve its goal of uncovering untaxed lands? Even where the structure of leadership no longer conformed to the traditional structure of power, as long as the configuration of interests in the township still paralleled that of the village, the common interests of the elite and the other villagers presented a challenge far too formidable for the mere village political entrepreneur. The enforcement of the large township under the Japanese in 1940, together with the baojia system, was designed precisely to develop an apparatus of administrative power sufficiently strong to break this community of interest in the natural village.

The relocation of the lowest, but unprecedentedly powerful, unit of political administration to the large township was the first condition for the success of the land investigation. The second was the establishment of specialized investigatory committees at the county level. The way in which these two measures worked can be seen in Changli county. The Japanese army in this area had conducted a preliminary land investigation in 1939. The smaller townships were instructed to make new registers of their landholdings (within their green circles) and submit them to the county. The county then assigned 50 trained investigators to check these registers randomly. The plan probably met the same fate as the Nationalist ones because it was dropped. In the next two years, after the creation of the large township, the land investigation plan was modified. The number of specialized investigators was reduced from 50 to 16. They were sent down to the ward and instructed to work closely with the headmen of both the ward and the enlarged township. In May 1940, this order was sent to all counties in the province.[53]

The results were phenomenal. In Hou Lineage Camp the total amount of taxable land went up by a thousand mou, and in Changli county as a whole by 7,700 mou.[54] In Luancheng, there was an increase of 3,000 mou. For the entire Jidong region, one source reported a doubling of taxable land after the investigation.[55]

The state was finally able to dispense with the registration clerk and obtain tax information through the formal channels of government. The Nationalists had aspired to this goal for more than a decade; ironically it was achieved by their enemy. As an alien power, the Japanese regime probably had less compunction about destroying the traditional structure of power and authority in the village in the process of establishing the township. The headman of the enlarged township was subject to more bureaucratic control than either the community leaders or the registration clerk had been. The source of the headman's power did not lie so much in an autonomous, private realm, such as the clerk's personal tax knowledge; to be effectively exercised, his power had to be coordinated with that of the county and the ward. But the very conditions that made him more amenable to state goals—his complete alienation from community institutions and interests—made him, under the circumstances of a still involuting state and high tax demands, perhaps the most powerful and oppressive state broker ever found at these levels.

State Building and Commercial Tax Farming

In the historical process of state building, the revenue base of the European state was transformed from a primarily agrarian one to a commercial one. Judging from the rapid increase of indirect taxes in Hebei and, to a lesser extent, Shandong from 1919 to 1935, the Chinese state was well on its way on a similar trajectory of expansion (see Chapter 3, Table 2). The impetus behind the accelerating rate of growth of commercial taxes, which were mostly introduced in the late Qing period, was related to the same state-making and nation-building concerns behind the more familiar tankuan levies.

As in other areas, the late Qing state collected these commercial taxes by subcontracting the rights of collection to private agencies; the mechanisms of control over these agencies were weakly developed. Thus the growth of provincial income from these commercial revenues was obtained at the cost of a corresponding increase in the take of the intermediaries in the collection process—a typical instance of state involution.[56] In this section, I study the efforts of the various 20th-century regimes to use and control these informal state-brokerage structures of collection and the way in which rural society was affected by these policies.

A significant component of the commercial taxes was the tax on the commercial middleman (yahang). The original role of these commercial middlemen can be seen in the general role of the middleman in Chinese customary law. The commercial middleman brought together two parties in an economic transaction, and in a market where there were no sure legal guarantees of rights, he provided this guarantee by bringing the relationship into the public sphere. He was also an expert measurer, possessing standard weights and measures. Finally, to the peasants a good middleman was one who was able to negotiate a fair price for their goods.[57]

At the same time, because these functions gave middlemen a certain power to manipulate market prices, the imperial state began to license commercial middlemen in an effort to regulate their activities and their numbers. Until the early 1900s, imperial licensing of commercial middlemen represented an attempt to maintain a relatively open market. With the greater need for revenues around the turn of the century, the purpose of state regulation changed drastically. The periodic sale of these licences now became an important means of increasing state income.[58]

It was not until 1915, however, that the character of this tax changed from a licence fee to an excise tax on commodities marketed in Hebei. This may have been the decisive point at which the service functions of the middleman became decidedly less important than his taxing function, a view not infrequently expressed in the *CN* interviews.[59] Also, at this time, the tax rate was set at 3 percent of the sale price, and the franchise to levy these taxes was auctioned off by the county authorities to the highest bidder in the market. The tax on licensed middlemen now came to resemble several other commercial taxes that had been farmed out since the early 20th century, such as the tax on domestic animals, the butcher tax, and the taxes on alcohol and tobacco. The early Republican state thus sought to extend its control over the market and its revenues through an avowed tax-farming system.[60]

During most of the Republican period, the county authorities nominally retained 10 percent of the returns from the auctioning off of these taxes and forwarded the rest to the provincial authorities. Before the beginning of every fiscal year, tax farmers were invited to bid for contracts. The tax farmer ultimately subcontracted his franchise to collectors for each item in each market, who further subcontracted or employed petty commercial middlemen in the markets or even in the villages.[61]

Although revenue farming increased the income of the state, it also generated many problems. For the provincial government, the problem arose from the system's operation at the county level. The method of selecting tax farmers was riddled with problems, and these people frequently did not fulfill their tax quotas. First, the auction was often a formality since the tax farmer had been pre-determined by the county authorities. These revenue farmers were powerful local bullies who bribed the county functionaries, not infrequently the magistrate himself, and threatened potential competitors with violence. Given the circumstances, merchants with the wealth necessary to make up deficits refused to act as guarantors. Although tax farmers were required to provide two guarantors and pay an initial quota, their collusion with county runners enabled them to get around these requirements. Second, the extensive network of subcontractors meant that a failure by any one of them to collect the contracted sum led to a deficit at the top, once again confronting county authorities with unfulfilled quotas.[62]

The burdens that a tax-farming system imposes on taxpayers are heavy. The reason lies in the logic of the system: the tax farmers attempt to collect as much tax as possible in order to garner a sizable surplus for themselves after fulfilling the quota. The size of a tax farmer's surplus can be expected to vary with the tenure of his contract. A longer tenure usually means that the tax farmer restrains his exactions in order to ensure future collections. Moreover, as Weber observed, the ability of the state to protect the long-term taxpaying capacity of its populace against the immediate interests of the tax farmer also made a difference.[63] In China, the yearlong contracts removed the first restraint, and collusion with county-level functionaries, the second. Given these circumstances, the litany of ills associated with revenue farming in the Republican period is understandable.

A few illustrations of the practices by which licensed middlemen and tax farmers increased their income beyond the prescribed amounts should suffice. For instance, they rarely respected the law that exempted small transactions from the tax. Moreover, instead of bringing together the parties to a transaction, these middlemen and tax farmers often kept them apart in order to levy the tax on both the buyer and the seller even though only one party was expected to pay.[64]

The system tended to discriminate against the weakest section of the market: the unorganized peasant. The larger grain stores in the market often had their own licensed middlemen who weighed the grain brought in by peasants and tipped the balance in favor of their employer. Large merchants could also resist the extortionary demands of the licensed middlemen by holding off and moving to another market, an option that small transactors did not possess.[65]

Competition among licensed middlemen and subcontractors, which might have held down their charges, was reduced by market-sharing arrangements. In Changli, they were organized into a group called a *bang*, which divided the market and pooled their incomes. Similar organizations also existed in Luancheng county.[66]

In response to the exactions of tax farmers, peasants devised various ways to avoid paying high rates. Where they could, they approached a licensed middleman from their own village. The assumption was that a licensed middleman who attempted to exploit a fellow villager would lose face—an assumption that was not always true. Peasants also attempted to sell commodities outside the market, but the revenue farmers had many spies, and the penalties, if they were caught, were high.[67]

Traditionally, the most effective response by villagers to the exactions of licensed middlemen was for an organization of the village itself to buy the license and undertake the payments of the villagers. Such organizations are another example of the self-protective associations designed to defend the interests of the community in its dealings with the state brokers discussed earlier. An example from Xingtai county brings out this role very well. A tablet from a village in this county mentions that from the 1850s on the villagers who sold their handicrafts in the market were increasingly subjected to the extortionate demands of licensed middlemen. Consequently, the village council set up an organization that collected money to acquire the license, and from that time until 1901, when the plaque was set up, no private person was permitted to levy the yashui.[68] The Changli case of 1895 in which the butchers of Nijing elected to pay their taxes through the rural agent falls into the same category (see Chapter 2). In both of these cases, community action had a clearly protective function.

In the circumstances of the 20th century, however, just as protective arrangements tended to develop into entrepreneurial ones in the field of tankuan collection, so, too, the purpose behind the undertaking of yashui seems to have changed similarly. In some places, as in Shunyi county, the village government seemed to have undertaken this activity voluntarily in order to increase its revenues. Ever since the village had become a fiscal entity in the early 1900s, its expenditures had frequently outstripped its revenues, and it was constantly on the lookout for new sources of income. The absorption of temple and other public properties was, of course, undertaken partly for this reason. Tax farming, of the butcher tax in this case, provided it with another opportunity to increase its income. However, one village discovered that tax farming for profit not only conflicted with any protective role it may have played toward the community but also eroded its popular base. Village leaders did not want to report relatives and friends who did not declare every animal they slaughtered. In the late 1930s, the village government handed this franchise over to a villager. But he, too, complained that spying on his fellow villagers was causing him to lose a great deal of face.[69]

In other places like Licheng county in Shandong and Luancheng county in Hebei, the state ordered villages to undertake the levying of some of these taxes in the 1930s. In Luancheng, the excise tax on cotton was farmed out to the village headman since most of the crop was marketed and no one could be expected to know the amount of cotton harvested by the villagers better than the village authorities. Rather than add another burden to his already heavy responsibilities, both here and in Licheng, the headman promptly subcontracted these taxes to private persons.[70] No protective function was being served in any of these cases.

Despite some superficial differences, the evolution of village brokerage in the collection of commercial taxes was quite similar to the collection of tankuan. Tankuan collection was first undertaken by the village authorities in the 20th century. An entrepreneurial element became most evident when the nature of village leaders changed during the 20th century and the tasks of tankuan allocation and collection became a source of personal profit. With commercial taxes, villages undertook this activity as a protective function long before the changes of the early 20th century. Although during the 20th century the villages began to gain an income from this undertaking, when this function clashed with community interests, village leaders readily exercised their option of passing on the contracts to someone else. The result in both cases was the same: the village government abandoned whatever protective role it might have sought to play at an earlier stage.

For all of these reasons, the state, or more accurately the provincial government, sought to impose stricter formal controls on revenue farmers. In 1925, the provincial government of what was to become Hebei legalized the practice of revenue farming and gave formal sanctions to merchants acting as agents of the government.[71] The Nationalists made an effort to bureaucratize the system in the early 1930s.[72] In 1932, an investigative committee of the provincial finance department proposed the adoption of a fully bureaucratic mode of collecting these taxes that would replace tax farmers and commercial middlemen with specialized salaried officials. But only a few counties implemented the proposal. Apparently, the counties preferred the system of revenue farming because of its greater efficiency over bureaucratic collection in gathering the tax on the small transactions constituting the bulk of the revenues.[73] Whatever the merits of bureaucratization, the abolition of revenue farming would also have significantly affected the nonstatutory income of the county administrators. This must have been a factor behind the lukewarm response.

In most of the *CN* counties, this bureaucratization did not take place until 1941 and 1942, well after the establishment of Japanese rule. As in other spheres of administration, several Nationalist projects that had been considered and tried during the 1930s were implemented by the Japanese. And as in the implementation of land investigation and the establishment of the large township, they were able to do this because they were alien rulers with few qualms about destroying existing social arrangements.

In order to understand the Japanese efforts to control the marketing process in North China, it is necessary to summarize their general plan for the region. Soon after its conquest of North China in 1937, the Japanese army there was beset by desperate shortages of capital and supplies. It embarked on an ambitious plan for a controlled economy, a project that acquired even greater urgency in 1940 when it sought to impose a blockade on communist-held territories. Through its hold over major communication lines, the army gained control over the supply of many essential commodities, such as iron and steel, coal, oil, and salt. At the same time, it sought to develop controls over food supplies to feed its troops and the urban population. Lincoln Li writes of the Japanese army's policy of "kill all, burn all, and take all" that "more than an effort at terrorizing communists, it was a desperate effort to survive by redirecting its drive for requisitioning conquered resources to the rural sector."[74]

Less dramatic but more calculated were its efforts to acquire food supplies through control of the distribution networks between the village and the markets. The principal agency involved here was the New People's Society (Xinminhui), a quasi-governmental, hierarchically organized agency reaching down to the village and designed to promote collaboration with the new rulers and their goals. However, the fact that the villagers were members of the organization did not imply any ideological commitment on their part to its goals. In some areas, membership gave them a few advantages, such as access to small loans provided at low interest rates by the rural cooperatives organized by the society.[75]

A significant function of these cooperatives was to act as channels for the mass purchase of agricultural produce for Japanese consumers. The best account of this role comes from Licheng county in Shandong. The county authorities demanded that certain crops like rice be sold only to the cooperatives. It explained that in this way the peasants could avoid being exploited by merchants. The truth was that the cooperatives bought the produce and sent it to

Japanese distributors in Jinan. The group most seriously affected by this was the Chinese merchants, but the peasants also complained that they could get a better price by selling their produce directly at Jinan than at the cooperative. They were also forced to buy retail items like oil, matches, and tobacco from the cooperatives at prices higher than those charged in Jinan.[76]

Under the aegis of the New People's Society, direct collection by state officials supplanted the revenue-farming system. Partly in order to streamline the collection process, a reorganization of the market system was undertaken in 1941. The number of markets in a county was often reduced, perhaps in an effort to achieve a congruence between markets and wards.[77] Within the market town, the locations at which transactions were permitted were consolidated into a single territory called the *jiaoyichang*, and the system whereby markets were arranged by commodities was eliminated. Collection bureaus, independent of the county and responsible to the provincial financial department, were established in every county. Below them branches were established in every ward to regulate the market in that ward.[78]

The chief personnel at the county level and the supervisor at the ward level were appointed and salaried by provincial authorities. But the crux of the problem lay with the collectors. Although the ward-level collectors also received salaries, their remuneration was small, ranging from 20 to 30 yuan a month.[79] Moreover, the collectors were almost invariably the same revenue farmers who had collected the taxes earlier, and in some places they continued to employ the same petty commercial middlemen. These were the actual collectors, and the state still had no real control over them. In the view of one contemporary, despite these seemingly massive transformations, not much had changed at the lowest levels, and those who levied the taxes still eluded the control of the state.[80]

Even where they were not employed as collectors, commercial middlemen did not disappear. The official collectors went about collecting the excise taxes, and these middlemen continued to charge commissions for services they may or may not have performed.[81] The New People's Society also collected a commission on every transaction in order to defray its own expenses.[82] Thus, every time a peasant made a purchase or a sale, he was effectively saddled with three taxes. Bureaucratization may have ensured the state its share of the pie, but it did little to reduce and much to increase what the taxpayer was already paying.

Conclusions

Before the 20th century, the imperial state in China dealt with rural communities in fiscal and administrative matters through "state brokers." There were two types of state brokers: those who viewed their job in entrepreneurial terms, such as clerks and runners at all levels of the sub-bureaucracy; and community organizations that undertook these roles in order to protect the interests of the community against the demands of the state and the entrepreneurial brokers.

Although the literature abounds with complaints against the state broker throughout the Qing, the brokerage model may even have made for a certain flexibility in state-society relations. Insofar as state brokers were local people, they may have been more approachable than a fully bureaucratic agency. Yet because the paternalistic state was loath to admit that its functions had in practice been brokered out to entrepreneurs, it became impossible to develop a vocabulary and a framework within which these personnel might have acquired a legitimate role in the polity. Consequently, they always tended to appear as the oppressors of the people. This oppressive characteristic became even more pronounced as the state sought to enhance its role in local society. Especially after the idea of modernization began to take hold in the 20th century, they came to be viewed increasingly as so many bottlenecks to the nation-building goals of the state.

The state sought to transform this situation in the 20th century in two ways. One conformed to the explicit goal of the state to bureaucratize subadministrative staff, including those at the ward and township. Success in this venture below the county level was rather limited and did not come until after Japanese rule. Even when this limited bureaucratization did take place, as at the county level, it did not eliminate entrepreneurial brokerage, as we saw in the enforcement of the township and the superimposition of officials on commercial middlemen. Indeed, partial bureaucratization, proliferating personnel, high revenue demands, and the absence of any real enhancement of the abilities of superior authorities to control the extractive power of these agencies transformed the penetration of state power into the replication of entrepreneurial brokerage down to the lowest levels.

The second way in which the state sought to dispense with intermediaries was by assigning certain tax-collecting and other governmental responsibilities to the leadership of village communities, without ever explicitly declaring this to be its goal. This kind of delegation of administrative responsibility resembled the traditional form of protective brokerage—at least initially. In time, however, the pressures and dilemmas introduced by state strengthening often destroyed the protective character of these organizations, and the power that derived from discharging a state function began to be sought by entrepreneurial state brokers. We saw this happening first in the levying and collection of tankuan and the deed tax; in commercial revenue farming, when the village subcontracted its franchise to private entrepreneurs; and finally, in land investigation, the successful implementation of which necessitated the separation of village leaders from the structure of power.

The replication and extension of entrepreneurial brokerage that accompanied state penetration would cost the state dearly in terms of legitimacy. It is perhaps not so ironic that the Japanese imperialist regime, which enjoyed great success in increasing its revenues through a combination of rationalization and state involution, was also the regime least capable of establishing its authority. Until the creation of the enlarged township, the process of the disarticulation of political leadership from the cultural nexus had been gradual. Whether because of inability or disinclination to create a sudden rupture between the old elites and the state, the Chinese regimes had not pushed such a drastic restructuring of the polity as the enlarged township.

But could these regimes have successfully implemented their policies and raised enough revenues to beat the race with involutionary forces, which seemed to spring up everywhere—at their very touch, as it were—without employing such radical measures? Would the Republican regimes have been able to create a new basis of legitimacy if they had implemented these drastic measures? The answer to these hypothetical questions may well lie in the experience of contemporary developing states in their race to nurture new forms of legitimation before they are overwhelmed by the forces of delegitimation that they have themselves unleashed.

Conclusion

In the three parts of this conclusion, I first try to weave the historical arguments of the various chapters into a coherent whole. Next, I consider the implications of this study for understanding the socialist revolution and society in China; and finally, I place the concept of state involution in a cross-cultural and cross-temporal perspective. A Postscript following this Conclusion addresses methodological issues in social history encountered.

The Historical Argument

Around the turn of this century, political authority in rural society was represented within an organizational and symbolic framework that I have called the cultural nexus of power. Although symbolic and institutional materials from a variety of organizational forms went into the ultimate construction of legitimate authority within the nexus, the most direct and exemplary representation of rural authority was to be found in religious and lineage organizations. In villages where there was some congruence between the units of village governance and those of the lineage, or "kinship space," village politics and authority were shaped by councils formed of lineage representatives. Ascriptive temple associations provided the format through which the elite expressed its leadership aspirations and social responsibilities in the community in all villages, albeit in differing degrees.

To be sure, status and prestige were conferred on village patrons who secured favorable terms for villagers in contracts and per-

formed other social functions. But in order to become full community leaders, these patrons needed to transfer the "symbolic
capital" accumulated in interpersonal relationships to the institutionalized domains of lineage and religion and, at higher levels, to
protective-brokerage arrangements. In no small measure, these
domains acquired their special legitimating aura because the imperial order—the state and orthodoxy—was symbolically represented in them, as we have seen, for instance, in lineage ideology. In
fact, in the religious domain, the state actively sought to superscribe
its hegemony on popular symbols; this is most clearly evident in the
historical development of the Guandi cult, particularly from the
Yongzheng reign in the 18th century. The prestige-laden and
emotive power of symbols, such as those of Longwang and Guandi,
which were at the same time sufficiently vague (or multi-vocal) to
accommodate different interests, were the key to the generation of
authority in the cultural nexus. The Guandi cult, in particular,
reveals that the symbols generating legitimacy sometimes did so
precisely because they were pursued by various interests.

Of course, the state was unable to impose its will on all organizations in the nexus. Not only were such obviously heterodox organizations as the White Lotus sectarians able to elude its symbolic
dominance—although not always successfully, as Susan Naquin
has recently shown[1]—but community religious groups, such as the
Red Spears studied by Elizabeth Perry, openly resisted the power of
the state—although not necessarily the power of orthodoxy.[2] Nonetheless, in the villages studied here, the late Qing state appears to
have been quite successful in imposing its prestige and interests on
those symbols that were also patronized by the rural elites.*

Developments in the 20th century, particularly state expansion
and penetration, profoundly eroded these local sources of political
authority. However, that is not to say that the intrusive state went
about systematically destroying the entire nexus; it scarcely had the
capacity to do so. Although it undermined the basis of village
community religion, militant sectarian and other organizations

---

*It is, of course, entirely possible that the state was unable to penetrate the cultural
nexus outside the heart of the North China plain, in the untamed, peripheral regions
studied by Perry. If this is so, it would suggest a future line of enquiry: Do the
organizational and symbolic characteristics of the cultural nexus, measured in terms of
the density of interaction or the degree of state control, differ in the cores and peri-
pheries of the macroregions delineated by Skinner?

mushroomed. Indeed, in this respect, the cultural nexus formulation provides an alternative to prevailing views of how rural communities adapted to the external pressures stemming from state penetration and the general disruption of the times.

G. William Skinner, in his argument about open and shut peasant communities, suggests a pulsating pattern in which communities tend to protect themselves by closing themselves off and reducing their contacts with the outside world in periods of disorder and to open up again with the restoration of order.[3] Philip Huang, however, sees villages as either responding to these pressures through a process of community solidarity and closure or disintegrating in a process of atomization—a view considered in Chapter 7.

Both formulations presume the analytical priority of a settlement—the village—and examine its behavior in rural society. Such an exclusive analytical focus—whether on the village or on the market town—is an arbitrary and abstract procedure. Extra-village relationships organized outside the marketing system, among militant sectarians, affines, irrigation associations, and crop-watching networks to name a few, continued to flourish and enabled villagers to carry on despite the pressures on villages and markets. By focusing attention on concrete relationships within and among particular organizations, the concept of the cultural nexus enables us to avoid slipping into the traps laid by received categories and allows us to see how rural groups were able to react in complex and diverse ways to forces impinging on them.

Thus the erosion of local sources of authority was only partly a result of the attack on the cultural nexus. Just as important, it came about because the modernizing state simply ignored the resources in the cultural nexus and sought to build a political system outside it. In no small measure because of the ideology of modernization that it had embraced, the state sought to diminish its identification with, and representation in, what must now have seemed an unrepentantly traditional and "backward" cultural nexus. Consequently, the capacity of the cultural nexus to articulate local political leadership roles for the rural elite within a national context—where elite leadership aspirations joined with state interests—diminished.*

*Not all modernizing states attack all traditional structures; some, like the Meiji state, actively appeal to traditional identities to build the modern nation-state. Indeed,

The political role of the nexus gradually fell away as the functions of lineage organizations in the polity were replaced by the new numerical systems of administration instituted in 1929 after the Nationalist takeover. The implementation of the enlarged, artificial rural township (daxiang) grievously affected the capacity of village-level lineage organizations to influence the political process as decisionmaking became concentrated in the hands of the township headman. The management of tankuan, the predominant, new type of protective-brokerage service for the community, became much too onerous for prestigious leaders to engage in. Moreover, the establishment of village "territoriality," although advantageous for the state, weakened the efficacy of this kind of village-level protective-brokerage arrangement since village leaders now had to collect taxes from outsiders and absentee landowners.

But nowhere was state penetration more serious than in village religion. Religious properties and institutions were transformed into components of a purely political public sphere. To a great extent, this transformation was made possible by the earlier symbolic identification of the village elite with the imperial state through the common patronage of gods like Guandi and Longwang. The new political arrangements of the nascent nation-state initially provided elites with alternative sources of power and prestige that enabled them to transfer this identification to the new nation-state.

The Republican state was unable to hold on to this identification and build on it. The budding alliance between the modernizing state and the rural elites—which Charles Tilly and others have noted to be a significant stage in European state making—failed to flower. The new ideology of the modernizing state did not succeed in providing a viable alternative to the cultural nexus that had generated legitimacy both for local leaders and for the state. The

---

the Yuan Shikai administration sought a very selective revival of Guandi and other apotheosized martial heroes under a centralized form of control, and even Chiang Kai-shek sought to revive a form of tradition in his New Life Movement. But this self-conscious reconstructing of the past for nationalistic goals took place even as the modernizing state was undermining the very institutional and cultural bases on which this "tradition" rested—witness especially the repeated destruction of temples and the Nationalists' "anti-superstition" campaign (see, for instance, C. K. Yang 1967: 372–77).

reasons for this failure had much to do with the rapidly growing revenue needs of the modernizing state in a traditional agrarian economy that was not growing appreciably. The utilization of traditional entrepreneurial brokerage to generate the needed revenues led to what I have called state involution. The disruption produced by warfare can also hardly be ignored. Wars, however, were like natural disasters, utterly devastating but ultimately temporary. The impact of state penetration in North China was scarcely so spectacular; its effects were on everyday life, subtle but deep-reaching, like the slow erosion of soil.

The heavy taxes levied by all levels of civilian and military state structures made the job of assessment and collection extremely unrewarding for village leaders. But the political disenchantment of the rural elite was caused as much by state-involutionary forces as by the policies of the formalizing agencies of the state and, perhaps most of all, by the indirect effects of the contest for power between the two. The establishment of the subcounty wards and the administrative townships was designed to bring the state closer to the village. For the village, this meant that new extractive agencies—ones, moreover, with a reduced span of control to ensure better compliance—were added to their burdens. Furthermore, state policies regarding the deed tax, the commercial taxes, and land investigation forced village leaders to side either with the state or with the communities they led. No village leader who cared about his status in the community could survive under such circumstances. They began to relinquish village office in increasing numbers and even flee the village. The early identification of village leaders with the nation-building goals of the state gave way to alienation and despair as the goals of aggressive state making assumed priority over all else. This crisis of authority created a political vacuum, and the only figure who cared to step into this vacuum increasingly resembled the "entrepreneurial state broker" of former times.

The study has focused on the transformation of rural leadership and its relations with the state. What of the response of the ordinary rural folk? The transformation of the religious domain was less welcome to the ordinary villagers than to the elite. Resistance to the appropriation of their religious properties and organizations often took violent forms. The destruction of village religion was to have other, less tangible, but equally significant effects on their relations both with their leaders and with the state. Although the elite had shaped the figure of Guandi in the village temples to conform to his imperial image, the rural folk had shared this image. For them, Guandi may have been many different things, but he also exemplified the values of the imperial culture. Indeed, the strength and vigor of the Guandi image derived precisely from the composite character of the cult—a vigor not found in the other gods patronized by the imperial bureaucracy. The cult of Guandi in the villages of North China brought together villagers, their elite leaders, and the state in a shared political universe.

From this perspective, it is likely that the destruction of the temple associations had the effect of sundering the links between the people and the leaders, as well as those between the people and the state. Although the elite leaders had found new routes to power and prestige in the political forms of the incipient nation-state, there was as yet little in these forms for the rural folk. Religion had been a far more vital factor in their lives than administrative offices, police bureaus, and modern-style schools (which were attended mostly by the children of the elite). At the same time, the new leadership functions appeared to most villagers not to work in the interests of the community. If anything, they worked against these interests. They saw little to be gained, and much to be lost, from land investigations, the new commercial and other taxes, and even the redefinition of village boundaries. But what they found most irksome were the tankuan dues levied by all levels of the new political apparatus. These dues appeared all the more unreasonable since they increasingly took more out of the community than the promise of modernization brought in.

The State and the Chinese Revolution

Tankuan, which came to symbolize state penetration, were regarded as oppressive by the peasants and indeed by the state itself, not solely because of the weight of the tax burden;[4] just as significant was the sheer unpredictability of the provisional tankuan, which made production plans extremely uncertain for peasant households.[5] These factors made taxation an important source of rural unrest. Studies of peasant violence in China during the 1920s and 1930s by Lucien Bianco, Tanaka Tadao, and others emphasize that antitax protests, not class violence, was the major cause of peasant protest.[6] But tax protests were just one aspect of the widening rift between state and society.

The involutionary process in the villages became a vicious cycle: the increased demands of the state led to the proliferation of entrepreneurial brokerage, and this proliferation led to yet higher demands. Under these conditions, traditional leaders were increasingly replaced by political entrepreneurs, who, in the vocabulary of the countryside, began to be known simply as "local bullies." The local bully (*tuhao, wulai, eba*) was a ubiquitous character whose notoriety was so great in the 1920s and 1930s that the Nationalists conducted a campaign directed mainly against him. Late-19th-century observers described him as someone with enormous physical power who was frequently tied to the network of county underlings and brokers.[7] Although he often used his powers destructively, in those days he customarily operated on the margins of the political process in the village. With the involutionary expansion of entrepreneurial opportunities that public office provided during the Republic, the local bully came to dominate the mainstream of political life in the village.

What distinguished the bully from other political leaders in the village was his approach to power: he pursued office for entrepreneurial gains and did so at the expense of the interests of the community he supposedly led. In this sense, the local bully is to be defined not as a social category—he could be rich or poor—but as a political type with a distinctive approach to power. And it is this definition that makes him virtually indistinguishable from the state broker, who had operated only out of the county seat in imperial times. Small wonder then that contemporaries, such as the reformer Liang Shuming, spoke of the startling visibility of local bullies among revenue farmers, tax collectors, ward and village headmen, and brokers of every hue. The Republican state ended up creating a stratum of political entrepreneurs who became a dominant form of predatory power in rural society before the Revolution.[8]

But what about landlordism and class relations in the CN villages? What was the role of class in the revolution that was engulfing the countryside at this time? Although economic

differentiation—the difference between the elite and the people—
has been an important category of analysis in this book, class
relations, which derive directly from the relations of production,
were discussed mainly in the context of North Brushwood and, to a
lesser extent, Wu's Shop. In particular, North Brushwood is a
powerful reminder that class antagonisms could be an extremely
potent force in areas where there was extensive production for the
market. However, in most of the villages of North China, the
relations between landlord and tenant did not constitute a major
contradiction.

In this context, it is important to note that even in North
Brushwood and Wu's Shop, where landlordism was becoming a
dominant phenomenon, absentee landlordism was the rule. Powerful merchants operating from the market town had succeeded in
accumulating land and increasing their domination of these villages from the outside since at least the early 1930s. Landlordism
was an issue that was not easily available for purposes of mobilization along class lines *within* the village. Even communist cadres in
Shandong "tended to believe that rent and interest reduction were
not important revolutionary tasks, since they could neither activate
the majority of peasants nor weaken the forces of feudalism in the
countryside. . . . Indeed some cadres had found that alleviating the
tax burden was the most pressing demand of the masses."[9]

When the Communists tried to enter the villages of North China,
they must have found villages where most peasants were not
dependent on the landed elite to any great extent. Thus, the initial
task of penetrating through to the impoverished masses was hardly
as difficult as it may have been in other parts of China or in other
agrarian societies such as that of India. Yet the very conditions that
permitted easy entry into the village implied that the objective
bases of class contradictions within the village were hardly such
that they could light the "prairie fire" of revolution. So what factors
were behind the communist revolution in the north?

It is becoming increasingly clear that there was no single
factor—such as landlordism or imperialism—that brought the
Communists to power in China; if there was one, it was their ability
to mobilize along a range of local grievances: from wife beating to
concealed land. A significant set of local grievances in northern
villages was the product of the state-society relations: heavy taxa-

tion, political arbitrariness, and the pursuit of village office for profit. The prominence of precisely these themes is seen in Suzanne Pepper's study of North China, where taxation, local bullies, and corruption were the most important local issues in the program of revolutionary mobilization. In Junan county, Shandong, local bullies and corruption headed the Communists' list of targets, whereas interest and rent reduction ran a poor fourth. The same was true in Laidong county, also in Shandong. Baba Takeshi's recent work shows the extraordinary importance of the reform of fiscal administration in the establishment of communist power in Shandong.[10]

If research continues to provide evidence for direct causal links between state involution and the Revolution, then we will need to modify several of the arguments that have been offered to explain the communist revolution. For instance, a common assumption is that the state must weaken before a revolutionary condition can develop. Theda Skocpol, who otherwise has a complex understanding of the state, can be said to hold such a view. State involution would suggest a more differentiated perspective on the state in which growth in certain spheres could unleash a process of self-destruction and revolutionary transformation.[11]

In another example, Chalmers Johnson's view that the Japanese invasion of China permitted the Communists to mobilize the peasantry by appealing to their nationalism would have to account for the persistence of bullies, corruption, and heavy taxation as mobilizing issues throughout the Revolution, issues generated to a significant extent by state involution.[12] Certainly, all three were burning local issues during the 1920s and 1930s; Japanese rule often simply intensified these problems by driving the involutionary process even harder. This is not to overlook the monstrous violence that the Japanese army perpetrated in the countryside but to suggest that in certain equally important respects, the effects of the Japanese regime in North China should not be too sharply differentiated from those of its native predecessors. Although the Japanese regime was able to force through rationalizing measures, the draconian nature of these measures ensured that only entrepreneurial brokers would undertake their implementation. In the end, state involution was the common mode of expansion in all Republican-era regimes.

The new communist state marked a radical departure from the involutionary pattern of state expansion. Indeed, the elimination of entrepreneurial state brokers during the early years of communist rule was an important factor behind the Communists' ability to generate critical increases in revenue, as is evident from the work of Baba Takeshi and Vivienne Shue.[13] They were able to do so by building political organizations linked to state structures from the grass-roots level up. But in other respects, the early communist regime was fulfilling the state-making goals of the Republican regimes. This is most apparent with regard to the fiscal problems that plagued every Chinese regime since at least the Ming: tax evasion and engrossment.

Historically the Chinese state had sought to link tax responsibility to a stable and accountable community structure. Although the lijia units of late imperial times developed precisely this responsibility, we have noted how the system became increasingly irrelevant to the structure of this society. The management of tankuan in the 20th century was similarly designed to link tax responsibility to the leadership of the village community. But the modernizing state was forced to address the many irrationalities in the levying and collecting of this tax that affected its own flow of revenue; in response, it implemented the system of village territoriality in rural Hebei. Village territoriality transformed the taxing power of village leaders from control over village residents to control over a bounded territory of privately held land. Since the state could not, at the same time, enhance the ability of village leaders to obtain these taxes from outsiders or absentee landowners, collecting these taxes continued to remain a problem. The problems of evasion and engrossment were finally solved only with the collectivization of the 1950s, which created a perfect congruence between the unit of taxation, the ownership of land, and the structure of authority. Collectivization fulfilled state-making goals just as much as economic and ideological ones.

The liberalization of recent years has reintroduced these historical issues, although in a vastly different context. Some scholars are beginning to see village cadres as entrepreneurs and brokers mediating the relationship between state agencies and villagers. The separation of administrative and collective structures, the gradual privatization of land ownership, and the weakening of local, formal authority structures could well reintroduce the problems of local control for the state. It will be instructive to see how the communist regime's handling of these problems differs from that of other developing states.

State Involution in Comparative Perspective

The modernizing goals of many emergent states in the 20th century have their inception in the international system of nation-states, which has been broadening the scope of state intervention since at least the 1870s. But the state-building process is increasingly being legitimated by the ideology of nationalism and modernization within the domestic order. These states have become bound to a new logic of legitimation in which they must deliver the goods of modernity promised by the progressive extension of citizenship in an era of self-generated rising expectations. This dialectic of "modernizing legitimation" is all the more urgent because the modernizing process has committed it to destroying the traditional bases of legitimation. Thus it is clear that, in part at least, the Chinese experience needs to be understood in a wider perspective.

As in China, it is also clear that the dominance of state-involutionary forces, or something resembling them, is central to the frustration of state-making goals in many new states.[14] The right question to ask about state involution is probably not how and why brokerage forms emerge, because these are historically easy options for a state in a hurry to expand its resources; rather, the more important question is How were traditional states historically transformed into modern ones when the very agencies and channels of transformation were resistant to change and obstructed change by controlling the flow of resources and information?

What answers does the European experience furnish? Tilly and his colleagues focused on European states that had been successfully transformed and had survived into the 20th century. Tilly himself notes that the survivors were only a handful among some 500 state formations in existence in Europe around 1500. He enumerates several historical conditions that distinguish the survivors, but because he focuses on the survivors rather than the failures, he is unable to specify what the failures lacked that prevented them from making the transition.[15]

Immanuel Wallerstein addresses the question more centrally.

Basing himself on the work of Georges Duby on France, he suggests that the process by which European absolutist states became fully bureaucratized involved two stages. In the first stage, the strengthening of the absolutist state over the feudal nobility took place through such typically entrepreneurial-brokerage schemes as tax farming and the sale of office. Even though tax farmers and venal officials may have absorbed a substantial proportion of the resources extracted from society, the absolute increase in state revenues enabled this state to develop a standing army and bureaucracy, in a process we might call "primitive bureaucratic accumulation." In time, the power of these new, formal state structures was able to overwhelm not only the feudal structures but also the class of entrepreneurial brokers standing in its way. Not all absolutist states were successful in this second stage. Presumably, they were among those who never succeeded in state making and thus never made the pages of history.[16] If this is historically accurate, then brokerage forms appear to be a necessary intermediate phase marking the transition from the pre-bureaucratic or patrimonial-bureaucratic state to the rational-legal bureaucratic state, but one that is not always easy to pass through.

The model of state involution suggests that brokerage formations tend to grow rather than to diminish in the new states. Although state involution is unlikely to lead to the Chinese path to revolution elsewhere, it does have a profoundly disintegrative and delegitimating impact. Why then is it so much more difficult for the formalizing interests of these states, compared with, say, the French state, to overcome these formations? Does it have to do with the fact that the state in the contemporary developing world has grown faster than the economy? This doubtless increases the tax burden on the populace, but it does not explain why the formal agencies of the state are not able to bureaucratize the broker-bureaucrats fully. Cultural arguments about the pervasiveness of parochial and traditional attitudes, beloved of modernization theorists, beg the question rather than answer it, especially since all societies were once pervasively "traditional."

At least part of the reason for the tenacity of broker-bureaucrats in the new states has to do with the vastly increased role of the state in the 20th century. The growing expenditures of this state, worldwide and across time, have led to new forms of entrenched brokerage structures that may not even have existed before World War II. Insofar as it involves the provision of adequate salaries orienting bureaucrats and state brokers to state goals, bureaucratizing these structures is much more difficult now. For instance, the large sums of money and political resources passing through the hands of broker-bureaucrats in the disbursement of state expenditures push up the incomes of some among them to levels much higher than the salary increases the state can reasonably offer, especially since much of this expenditure will not bring in returns.

Moreover, although the design of a rule-governed bureaucracy predisposes it toward a certain autonomy from all social classes, the prevalence of a profit-maximizing attitude toward public office necessarily directs public goods toward those who can most afford to "buy" these goods. Thus the involutionary state not only tends to reproduce class relations in that society but also manages to reproduce itself by creating a framework of mutual interest between it and better-off groups in every sector and at every level of society. This last feature reveals, incidentally, not only the depth of its entrenchment but also the manner in which brokerage formations have accommodated themselves to social interests in such a way that there are immediate disincentives for elites at all levels of society to change the system.

My purpose in focusing on the modernizing state to the exclusion of other major historical forces, such as capitalism, is not to suggest that it worked in isolation from these forces, but rather to suggest that there were sufficiently complex processes going on within the state to merit independent study. What we see is a fundamental transformation in state structures throughout the world that appears to be broadly associated with other epochal economic, social, and political changes, but whose precise orchestration with these forces differs significantly from society to society. One conclusion of this study is that the demands of state making in the 20th century in a basically agrarian society—when the role and the people's expectations of the state increase rapidly, certainly more rapidly than the growth rate of per capita income— produce a set of problems that is, perhaps, critically different from that of the earlier era of state building in societies in which state expansion was more organically linked to other social, political, and economic processes.

Postscript

Postscript

The Methodological Limbo of Social History

As the bastard children of historians and social scientists, social historians constantly confront the differences that originally kept the two modes of inquiry intellectually apart. These differences are best expressed in a series of related oppositions: the study of central processes versus local processes, of high culture versus popular culture, agency versus structure, diachrony versus synchrony, and narrative versus analysis. Although it would be hopelessly outdated to suggest that historians are concerned with the former terms and social scientists with the latter, nonetheless, the task of bridging the gap between these oppositions lies at the heart of the vocation of the social historian.

For instance, as historian, the job of the social historian is to identify cause and effect over time, an objective most arrestingly captured in narrative form. But the chosen subjects of the social historian—which cover social life–forms of every ilk—frequently leave little trace of their history, and local and popular institutions (depending on different levels of popularness in different societies) are notoriously insusceptible to narrative representation. Given these intransigencies, the social historian often turns to the domain of the sociologist and the anthropologist: the synchronic study of institutions and culture.

The most promising examples of this type of history still strive to create historical depth by embedding the study of local forms within that of wider processes—by registering the refraction of the general within the particular. But even this is easier said than done. And the problem is not merely one of sources. Even where local institutions are well documented and it is possible to construct "mini-narratives" of each of them, the effects of the broader processes—for example, capitalism or state-building—on them are often not uniform or synchronized. Local institutions have their own time scales—their particular trajectories and cycles—which are affected differently and respond variously to external forces. Under these circumstances, discerning a single or a dominant pattern of social change may well be an impossible task within our present conceptual framework. In other words, placing local social institutions in a time dimension causes a double loss: the loss of the symmetrical elegance characteristic of synchronic social analyses and the loss of the coherence associated with traditional narrative.

What we need to develop are mediating concepts—concepts that negotiate the area between the structural regularities of social systems and the contingency of history, between high culture and popular culture, and between the other oppositions we face; concepts capable of persuading these realms to speak to each other without reducing the one to the other. Antonio Gramsci's concept of "cultural hegemony" and Pierre Bourdieu's notion of the "habitus" come immediately to mind as good examples of such concepts.[1] But although these ideas do indeed mediate some of the oppositions outlined above—most notably those directly related to structure/agency, high culture/popular culture—their universalistic scope makes them too abstract for the social historian who has to deal with the details of a particular culture. What we need are concepts that mediate between the universality of our ideas and the specificities of the culture being studied.

The "cultural nexus of power" is intended precisely as such a mediating concept. It was the product of a constant interplay between the methods of a historian recording the unfolding of events within an institutional context and those of the social analyst, periodically taking stock of my findings to generate hypotheses to guide me through different social-temporal domains. Beginning with the study of village society, I found that in order to understand changes in the power structure there, I had to turn to larger historical transformations—in this case, the state—and then return to the village, equipped with more powerful lenses to gain a deeper perspective. The notion of the cultural nexus came out of this complex interplay, which was repeated over and over again, as

I went back and forth from domain to process to other domains, in the writing and rewriting of this ever-unfolding history.

The cultural nexus addresses the methodological gaps not only within the China field—bringing the imperial state, gentry culture, and local peasant society within a common discourse—but also between the abstract notions of power and domination and the particular cultural complex of Chinese society. It does this by identifying the process of production, and the representation, of authority in local society. And drawn further into the methodological limbo, I faced the most serious opposition of them all: of how a synchronic analysis that emphasized the functioning and reproduction of societies could be reconciled with the record of persistent conflict and change.*

An important way in which this and other related oppositions are mediated is by identifying dualities among social phenomena. Institutions and practices in this study abound in paradoxes, contradictions, and dualities, especially when viewed over time. Not only the cultural nexus, but the concept of state involution also addresses a paradox: growth and disintegration within the same state structure. Additionally, we saw strategies that incorporate cooperation and competition, institutional practices that combine affect and advantage, symbols that generate consensus and promote sectional interests. The observation that social reality has a dualistic character is hardly novel; the Marxist notion of the materialist dialectic made that point a long time ago: But the dialectic was to be the foundation stone of the new science of society. What we find instead is that this dualism is precisely one reason why

---

*For some time now, functionalism has been a pejorative word. It seems to me, however, that there are two senses in which the word is used. One sense is derived from its usage in "structural-functionalism," where it is rooted in the biological metaphor of a system tending toward homeostatic equilibrium. Despite latter-day efforts to qualify and broaden it, this conception of functionalism remains difficult to reconcile with conflict and change in society. The second sense is close to the everyday, commonsensical usage of the word. A social practice may function to reproduce existing relationships, but there is no natural or law-like tendency for such practices to function thus. Claude Lévi-Strauss (1963: 13) has remarked, "To say that a society functions is a truism; but to say that everything in a society functions is an absurdity." Thus, if the cultural nexus functioned in some important ways to reproduce the dominant order (and did not, in some other important ways), it was not because of a tendency toward equilibrium, but because the Qing state and its allies did hard institutional and ideological labor to preserve their domination.

social reality is so *in*susceptible to scientific, law-like understanding.

For instance, this study enables us to entertain the theories of both James C. Scott and Samuel L. Popkin, who adopt divergent views on the basic principles governing peasant behavior.[2] Neither model seems to characterize the behavior of the peasants in North China adequately. The different elements emphasized by the two appeared to coexist quite easily in these villages. One sees redistributive mechanisms in the normative principles governing tankuan allocation in the villages that were not only equitable but sometimes even progressive. For example, in some places, peasants owning under 5 mou of land (who nevertheless had to pay the land tax to the state) were exempted from the tankuan levied by the village.[3] Moreover, particularly in the early part of the period, village patrons often performed various community services. Sometimes the village, and indeed several villages, developed close ties to protect its collective interest. On the other hand, sectional and competing interests in the village were furthered through village rituals, religious groups, fictive kinship terms, the general absence of large scale cooperative economic endeavors, and by fierce conflicts over tax dues between villages.

As an example of specific institutions embodying dualities, consider lineages. The primordial affect bonding kinsmen together was often combined with some practical consideration dividing kinsmen. The fusion of kinship and economic criteria was the basis on which leadership was determined in lineage-community villages, the successors of village leaders were traditionally recruited, and families agreed to enter into cooperative arrangements with each other. In each case, the choice of the representative or preferred partner was based on the affective bond with the agnatic kinsman, but at the same time, the choice reproduced the stratification of the social structure. In lineage communities, the representative of the lineage belonged to the lineage elite. A wealthy son might succeed his father, but a poor son could not. When a family sought to cooperate with another, it often sought a family related by blood. However, it did so only if the resources of the two parties were well matched because otherwise the exchange could well turn out to be an unequal one and of no practical advantage.

Ritual and religion also worked to define communities both inclusively and exclusively. Among irrigation associations, ritual hierarchies had the flexibility to define and redefine communities at different levels to adapt to circumstances of scarcity and plenty and to permit both cooperation and competition for water. In another way, the Guandi myth also incorporated a dualism: the capacity to generate various different and perhaps, even opposing, meanings for different social groups while constructing a consensual framework for the pursuit of sectional goals. In these cases, the duality is not some stray element of an irrational folk culture; it serves an important social purpose by creating an arena in which legitimate authority is represented in society.

If social phenomena exhibit contradictory and paradoxical tendencies that are not necessarily predictable, does this mean that social historians must abandon the hope of formulating falsifiable propositions? If a social practice with one supposed function can produce an opposite function as well, on what leg can we stand on the question of method? Without seeking to delve too deeply into the implications of this question, I believe that in order to avoid the problem of falsifiability, our first task is to record our observations in a sufficiently specific context.

To this end, we need to set a methodological priority that establishes that social relationships be analyzed in their specific organizational context before they are located in settlements such as villages and towns. Within the specific organizational context, we still need to observe and record the many ways in which dualities are expressed in institutions, practices, ideas, and symbols; ways, for example, in which they are predominantly functional, as in authority-creating structures, and dysfunctional, as in state involution; ways in which they do both—holding together the cultural and political machinery of the old empire while allowing for change in the system. And as we begin to understand them, we will need to make use of these paradoxes and deploy them to grasp the oppositions that the social historian faces—especially the most fundamental: the manner in which a culture retains its identity even as it undergoes deep historical transformations.

Reference Matter

Notes

Complete authors' names, titles, and publication data are given in the Bibliography, pp. 296–308. The following abbreviations are used in the Notes:

CN   *Chūgoku nōson kankō chōsa* (Investigation of customs in Chinese villages)

HNK   *Hokushi no nōgyō keizai* (The agricultural economy of North China)

HSZ   *Hokushi shijō zōkan* (A broad look at conditions in North China)

NFWH   *Nongcun Fuxing Weiyuanhui huibao* (Reports of the Committee to Revive the Villages)

Volume and page numbers for *CN* and *NFWH* are cited as follows: *CN*5 247, for vol. 5, p. 247; *NFWH* 1934.3: 6, for vol. 3 (published in 1934), p. 6.

Introduction

1. See e.g., Yoshida 1975; and Grove 1975.
2. Myers, 1970: 207–14; and P. Huang 1985: 121–22.
3. Tilly 1975. See in particular Tilly's introduction.
4. Tilly 1975: 70, 80.
5. Wright 1968. See Wright's introduction. For a sensitive treatment of the different regional and historical dimensions of the reform agenda of various statesmen—what I sweepingly refer to as the "modernizing program"—during the first decade of the 20th century, see Thompson 1985.
6. MacKinnon 1980: 4.
7. Meyer 1980: 121.

8. Thomas and Meyer 1980.

9. The concept of power that has influenced this study at a most basic level is that of Michel Foucault (1979a; 1979b: esp. 93–96). From Foucault, I derive the idea that power relations do not emanate from any one specific source but are "exercised from innumerable points" and the related idea that the relations of power do not operate outside other relations such as economic or sexual ones but are immanent within these. Most significant, perhaps, is the idea that the institutions of an epoch (especially the institutionalized forms of knowledge) work to represent power in a particularly unique way, an idea that can be adapted to historical cultures as well. Finally, I find his idea that power is not always and necessarily repressive but can be a creative force as well to be very suggestive.

However, we can scarcely brush aside the radical critique of Foucault, which attacks the omission in his conception of power of strategy and interests as significant elements. Power not only is an immanent or embedded phenomenon but is so often intertwined with "interests" in the course of history that we can ignore this manifestation of power only at our own peril. A most interesting effort to relate the expression of power as instrumental strategy to other embedded forms of domination is the work of Pierre Bourdieu (1977). His remarkably original work has also influenced this study.

Finally, my notion of power has been shaped by a tradition of political anthropology that includes the writings of Clifford Geertz, Stanley Tambiah, and Victor Turner. For instance, I have translated into my own vocabulary Turner's ideas of "fields" and "arenas." Turner (1974: 139–40) writes that when characterizing a political field "relations of likeness such as class, categories, similar roles and structural positions" are of prior sociological importance. When successive arenas are to be characterized, "systematic interdependencies in local systems of social relations, going from demography to residential distribution, religious affiliation and genealogical and class structure become significant." When I study religion, kinship, and patronage networks and the relations of power within them, I am examining the arenas from which actors bring their normative, symbolic, and material resources to bear on the political field.

10. Ho 1959: 136.

11. Yamamoto 1975: 26–27; Farmer 1976: 95–101, 114–16.

12. Over 95 percent of the oldest villages in this area date from this time (Yamagata 1941: 1–2). Ishida Hiroshi (1982: pt. 1, 107) has collected data on all of Yamagata's surveyed villages into a single table.

13. Yamamoto 1975: 27; Ishida Hiroshi 1982: 106.

14. Smith 1899: 7.

15. Yamagata 1941: 28, 29; Ho 1959: 136; Yamamoto 1975: 22–35.

16. Yamamoto 1975: 26–27, 30; Ishida Hiroshi 1982: 106.

17. Yamagata 1941: 26.   18. Skinner 1977: 283–84.

19. Cressey 1934: 167–69.   20. Cressey 1934: 171.

21. Cressey 1934: 171.

22. Myers 1970: 288. Pers. comm. with Huang.

Chapter 1

1. Kuhn 1980.

2. Skinner 1977: 721n. For his study of the marketing system, see Skinner 1964–65.

3. *CN*5 247.

4. *CN*4 510, 515; see also *CN*5 339.

5. *CN*2 202; *CN*3 329, 351.

6. *CN*3 329. Skinner 1964–65: 33. Skinner puts the average at eighteen villages per standard market.

7. *CN*5 568; see also Myers 1970: 67; and P. Huang 1985: 106–18.

8. *CN*3 325; *CN*4 2; *CN*5 253, 568, 569.

9. *CN*2 270–91; *CN*4 2; *CN*5 568, 571.

10. *CN*5 255. For village population, see *CN*5 preface 5.

11. *CN*2 205; *CN*3 329; *CN*4 235, 399, 505, 510; *CN*5 570.

12. *CN*2 226. For village population, see *CN*1 preface 75.

13. *CN*4 237, 423. A Cold Water Ditch informant said that what loans came from outside the village came from moneyshops in Jinan. After 1928, this source, too, dried up when the moneyshops were converted into banks under the Nationalists. These banks made only large loans of over 1,000 yuan, which automatically excluded the peasantry. Throughout the Republican period, pawnshops were often plundered by wandering armies, leading to the closure of an important source of credit for villagers in the market town. *CN*5 584.

14. *CN*5 564.

15. *CN*2 230–31.

16. For middlemen in land contracts, see Chapter 6.

17. *CN*3 326; *CN*5 570.

18. Skinner 1964–65: 36. Freedman (1966: 101–2) made certain qualifications of this model. Although Freedman basically accepted Skinner's scheme, he felt that it would have to be modified to account for upper-class families and endogamous ethnic minorities who may have sought their brides from outside the standard marketing area.

19. *CN*5 449.

20. *CN*5 501–6.

21. *CN*3 97–100, 114, 116, 118.

22. *CN*3 97–100. The fact that both markets were higher-level market towns does not make this a particularly strong test.

23. *CN*5 449, 501–6.

24. *CN*3 97–100, 114, 116, 118.

25. Ishida Hiroshi 1980: 121. In this interesting piece, Ishida develops the idea of *seikatsu kyōdōtai* or a "communitarianism of everyday life." Groups of peasants cooperate in matters not directly related to production, utilizing the ties formed from kinship and village connections independent of the market.

26. *CN*5 28.

27. For the 15 percent figure, see Murphey 1982: 57. The core of my study is based on the *CN* investigation of Xingtai and its neighbors conducted during the early 1940s. This investigation is a good example of the kinds of materials presented in the *CN* survey, apart from the better-known interview materials. These include descriptions of the environment and whatever written records—registers of gate associations, stelae, and court cases—could be found in the area. All these materials are collected in the sixth volume of *CN*. I have supplemented them with information from the following gazetteers: *Xingtai xianzhi* 1905: *juan* 2; *Mancheng xianzhi* 1757: *juan* 2 and supplement 1–2; *Xingtang xianzhi* 1772: *juan* 2–3; *Ren xianzhi* 1915: *juan* 1.

28. *Xingtai xianzhi* 1905: 1.27–37, 2.55.

29. *CN*6 112, 115. The numbers of managers (*xiaojia*) were fixed and unequal (*CN*6 104).

30. *CN*6 252–57, 358, 359, 365, 366; see also Maeda 1966: 47–48.

31. *CN*6 100.   32. *CN*6 117, 119.

33. *CN*6 372.   34. *CN*6 229.

35. *CN*6 105, 106, 118.

36. Grootaers 1951: 26, 40; Imahori 1963. See also Shinjō 1941: 81–83; Eliassen 1955; Morita 1967: 73; Wang Songxin 1975–76: 49; and Brim 1974.

37. *CN*5 297–98.   38. Grootaers 1951: 41.

39. Shinjō 1941: 85.   40. *CN*6 256, 265.

41. *CN*6 105–7, 268–78.

42. *CN*6 268. For instance, the waters used by Eastern Pond were called *zhengshui* (main waters), whereas those used by others were called *yushui* (surplus waters).

43. *CN*6 265.   44. *CN*6 270, 278.

45. *CN*6 230, 372.   46. Brim 1974; see esp. p. 98.

47. See C. K. Yang 1967; and A. Wolf 1974.

48. C. K. Yang 1967: 67. See also *Daqing luli* 1908: 16.4–5 of the section on sacrifice; and also *Qingchao xu wenxian tongkao* 1935: *juan* 158.

49. *CN6* 100, 105, 115.

50. *CN6* 329.

51. See Duara 1983: 290–92. I found instances of such a pattern outside the Xingtai area as well, in conflicts between villages in two counties engaged not in irrigation but in flood control; see Xiao 1935.

52. *CN6* 109.

53. Kuhn and Mann 1979.

54. Rankin 1986.

Chapter 2

1. Kuhn 1979: 110–12.

2. Li Ling 1938; see also Amano 1936; and Wan 1936.

3. Dennerline 1975: 94.

4. Wan 1936: 132; Hsiao 1967: 85, 589.

5. Wan 1936: 133; Li Ling 1938; Amano 1936: 33; *CN3* 367.

6. *CN6* 1. The Chinese Communists used the concealed land issue as a major campaign strategy to powerful effect in North China even after the War of Resistance; see Pepper 1978: 261, 269, 270.

7. Weber 1968: 55–56.

8. Zelin 1985.

9. Weber 1968: 49–50.

10. Watt 1972: 144; see also Watt 1977: 364.

11. Ch'u 1969: 38, 55; see also Watt 1972: 142.

12. Ch'u 1969: 46.   13. Ch'u 1969: 28, 46.

14. Amano 1936: 34–35.   15. Ch'u 1969: 51.

16. *Shunyi xianzhi* 1933: 2.5–7, 5.29–30, 16.21; *Changli xianzhi* 1933: 4.38–39; *Luancheng xianzhi* 1871: 2.1–2; *Liangxiang xianzhi* 1924: 1.12, 15; *Licheng xianzhi* 1926: 2.1, 3.6–17; *En xianzhi* 1909: 1.26–28, 2.16. See also *CN2* 297, 342; *CN3* 325, 406; *CN4* 290, 369–70, 399; *CN5* 12, 38, 662.

17. Saeki 1964: 92.

18. Hsiao 1967: 12.

19. Hsiao 1967: 12, 546.

20. *Changli xianzhi* 1933: 4.38–39; *Luancheng xianzhi* 1871: 2.2; *Liangxiang xianzhi* 1924: 2.43.

21. *CN5* 43, 350; see also Geissert 1979: 43.

22. *Zhili quansheng caizheng shuomingshu* 1915: land tax section 37.

23. Hsiao 1967: 546.

24. Hsiao 1967: 527. See also *En xianzhi* 1909: 2.16.

25. Zhang Yufa 1982: 2.46; Hsiao 1967: 39.

26. Kuhn 1979: 107.

27. Konuma 1966: 23–24.

28. *CN2* 297, 339, 388, 420; *CN5* 13, 319, 392.

29. Hsiao 1967: 60.

30. *CN*5 622; *CN*2 339; see, e.g., P. Huang 1985: 225–27.

31. Weng 1952: 35–37; Mann 1987: 104, 116.

32. Hsiao 1967: 64–66, 98–99; Ch'u 1969: 3–4; Watt 1972: 190; Saeki 1964: 91–100; P. Huang 1982: 137–38; see also Sweeten 1976: 2–3.

33. Ch'u 1969: 4; Hsiao 1967: 97; Sweeten 1976: 5, 22; Watt 1972: 190; *CN*3 44.

34. Saeki 1964: 91–99.

35. *CN*3 406; *CN*5 333.

36. Kuhn 1979: 109; Mann 1979: 85.

37. P. Huang 1985: 225–27.   38. Allee 1985.

39. *CN*5 12, 43, 320, 350.   40. *CN*5 13, 321.

41. *CN*5 375. Changli county, where Hou Lineage Camp was located, had one of the most dramatic increases in the numbers of markets in the province—from 12 in 1865 to 30 in 1933. The average population per market declined from 22,645 to 13,358 between the two dates. This increased marketing activity was perhaps a result of the injection of wealth from Manchuria. See Ishihara 1973: 248, 249, 251.

42. *CN*5 376.

43. For Shunyi, see *CN*2 337–38, 389; for Licheng, see *CN*4 34.

44. Kuhn 1980: 98–99; Hsiao 1967: 132–39.

45. Allee 1985: 9–12.

Chapter 3

1. Quoted in Thompson 1985: 16.   2. Thompson 1985: 459–60.

3. MacKinnon 1980: 22, 136–79.   4. Weber 1978: 2:968.

5. Lü 1972: 113; see also Ocko 1983: 133.

6. *Qingmo shoubei lixian* 1979: 2:761; see also *Zhili quansheng caizheng shuomingshu* 1915: land tax section 21; *Shunyi xianzhi* 1933: 16.19; and MacKinnon 1980: 22.

7. Kuhn 1979: 116–17; see also Amano 1942: 2:39–47.

8. Li Zonghuang 1954: 340.

9. Wou 1974; see also Zhang Yufa 1982: 325.

10. Wou 1974: 221, 227–29.

11. Zhang Yufa 1982: 325; Kuhn 1979: 119; *Shunyi xianzhi* 1933: 16.19.

12. Peng 1945: 131.

13. Peng 1945: 132; Matsumoto 1977: 529; Zhang Yufa 1982: 325; Li Zonghuang 1954: 340.

14. Kuhn 1975: 286.

15. *Shunyi xianzhi* 1933: 2.7; *Wangdu xianzhi* 1906: 3.10; see also *CN*2 333–34; *CN*3 406; *CN*4 298.

16. *Zhonghua minguo fagui daquan* 1936: 1:638.

17. *CN*2 333–34; *CN*3 416; *CN*4 300; see also Eastman 1975: 181–244.
18. *CN*4 298.
19. See the statistics compiled by Nakamura 1951: 105–6. In Shunyi county, the first ward received only 50 yuan a year for all its expenses (*CN*2 336; Xu Delin 1937: 174; see also *CN*2 336; *CN*3 437; *CN*4 292, 298; *CN*5 11–12).
20. Nakamura 1951: 88–89 and *passim*; *CN*4 325.
21. *CN*1 175, 186–87; *CN*3 50, 414; *CN*5 9, 41, 407, 418.
22. Kuhn 1975: 284.
23. See Chapter 6.
24. *CN*2 372; *CN*3 406; *CN*5 12, 319.
25. Wang Yeh-chien 1973: 113.
26. Wang Yeh-chien 1973: 121, 125–26.
27. Wang Yeh-chien 1973: 81.
28. Wang Yeh-chien 1973: 119, 126.
29. Li Chuan-shih 1922: 70–83.
30. Li Chuan-shih 1922: 83.
31. For 1929, see Gamble 1968: 183; for the mid-1930s, see *NFWH* 1935.14–19: 39.
32. Young 1970: 102.
33. Chang 1934: 234.
34. The provincial-level estimates of income and expenditure taken from Zhang Yifan are in turn derived mainly from the yearbook of the Shanghai-based *Shenbao* newspaper (*Shenbao nianjian* 1935: G–36). The compilers of the yearbook reported that the data for the period before 1925 were based on the annual provincial budgets and those for the period after 1925 were taken principally from the Chief Statistical Office of the Nationalist government. These have been supplemented by the relevant publications of the provincial government as well as materials found in newspaper and journal publications. Although there is no foolproof method of testing the accuracy of these formal estimates, I have found them to be broadly consistent with other Chinese sources for periods for which we have such estimates. See Zhang Sen 1936: esp. 174, 180, 196. Ironically enough, the county-level data are more consistently reliable than the provincial estimates. This is because they are based on an intensive investigation of the records and financial practices of a few counties conducted by researchers from Nankai University in Tianjin, specifically, Feng Huade and Li Ling. As for the qualitative materials, their general tone, which speaks of a growing burden on the rural populace in North China, is certainly consistent with the researches of scholars from other parts of China.
35. Yeh 1979: 105.
36. Sun Zuoji 1935: 155, 238.
37. Mann 1987: 188–89.
38. Zhang Yifan 1935b: 6.

39. Sun Zuoji 1935: 292–95.
40. Zhang Yifan 1935a; see also Zhang Yifan 1935b: 7–8.
41. Sun Shaocun 1936: 36–37.   42. Mann 1987: 188–99.
43. Ding 1931: 419.   44. Braun 1975: 135.
45. Braun 1975: 136.   46. Sun Zuoji 1935: 371.
47. Li Ling 1938: 998–1000.
48. Chen 1934; see also Ding 1931: 409–13; and Zhang 1935a: 3.
49. *HSZ* 126–27.
50. Yeh 1979: 104.
51. Geertz 1963.

52. In a historian's dream world of complete information, the difference between state making (sm) and state involution (si) may be expressed in a precise and quantifiable manner. In both cases, the ratio of the rate of growth of revenue (R) (or the formal income of the state) to the rate of growth of national income (Y) should be rising. If the rate of growth is expressed by the superscripted $\cdot$, then

$$\text{sm and si} \Rightarrow (\dot{R}/Y) > 0$$

The difference between the two is expressed with reference to the total payments extracted from the taxpaying populace, or surplus, where S is composed of revenue (R) and the income of brokers (B).

$$S = R + B$$

Therefore,

$$R/S + B/S = 1 = S/S$$

State making is defined as the situation in which the rate of growth of revenue to national income is rising *and* the ratio of revenue to surplus is growing faster than the ratio of brokerage income to surplus:

$$\text{sm} \Rightarrow (\dot{R}/Y) > 0 \qquad \text{and} \qquad (\dot{R}/S) > (\dot{B}/S)$$

State involution is defined as the situation in which the rate of growth of revenue to national income is rising *and* the ratio of brokerage income to surplus is either growing faster than, or at a rate equal to, the ratio of revenue to surplus:

$$\text{si} \Rightarrow (\dot{R}/Y) > 0 \qquad \text{and} \qquad (\dot{B}/S) \geqslant (\dot{R}/S)$$

The purpose of engaging in this formal exercise lies in the expectation that the model may be rigorously utilized to study state involution in a society where some estimate of brokerage income is available (as in India, where vigorous efforts are being made to estimate the volume of "black money" in circulation in the economy). I thank Sudipto Mundle, Chandra Kant, and Adhip Chaudhuri for helping me construct the model. Note also that state involution should be distinguished from Tambiah's (1985) rather inspiring but different concept of "administrative involution."

53. Peng 1945: 1–2, 131–32; Sun Zuoji 1935: 155.
54. Peng 1945: 3; Feng 1935: 702–3.
55. *HNK* 60; *NFWH* 1934.3: 6, 8; Sun Zuoji 1935: 167.
56. *HNK* 58; Xu Zhengxue 1936: 6.
57. *HSZ* 62.
58. Zhang Yifan 1935a: 12; *NFWH* 1934.5: 163.
59. *NFWH* 1934.7–12: 20, 21.
60. Feng 1935: 712.
61. *NFWH* 1934.7–12: 39; see also Feng 1938e: 1032.
62. Gamble 1968: 183.   63. Sun Shaocun 1936: 37.
64. Feng 1935: 713.   65. Feng 1938b: 1048.
66. Feng 1938b: 1051.   67. Feng 1938b: 1045. *HNK* 58.
68. Feng 1934; see also Feng 1935: 713, 739.
69. Feng 1934: 512; see also Feng 1938b: 1045. Geissert 1979.
70. Kuhn 1979: 121–25.
71. Li Ling 1935; Chen Juren 1934: 13–15; *HNK* 62–63; Sun Zuoji 1935: 355; Xu Zhengxue 1936: 54, 57–60; Feng 1938a: 1119.
72. *NFWH* 1934.5: 164.
73. *NFWH* 1934.5: 167, 168; Xu Zhengxue 1936: 122–27; Duara 1983: 220–26.

Chapter 4

1. Perhaps the most comprehensive treatment of these differences and their causes is Potter 1970. The standard work on southern lineages is that of Freedman 1966.

2. Rawski 1986. Large, complex, and wealthy lineages were not entirely absent in North China. The *CN* surveys mention a lineage in Qingdao county in Shandong that possessed over 100 mou of corporate land. The Sun lineage of Qingdao county was comparable to the great lineages of the south. It once possessed over 3,000 mou of corporate land and, by the 1930s, despite the loss of considerable lands in a protracted legal battle, still retained over 1,000 mou. The lineage was very deep, and its many segments spread over several villages. Since its founding in Ming times, it had also produced many officials. Finally, in the way it used and controlled its property and income, it resembled the southern lineage very closely (*CN*4 65).

The surveys also mention the Yang lineage of Lujiazhuang, which, although it possessed little corporate property, had maintained ties with its agnatic kinsmen in its ancestral village at Yangjiadun, in the same county, for fourteen generations. On the first day of the tenth lunar month (the festival of the Cold Feast), the Yangs of Lujiazhuang sent three or four representatives to the gathering in the ancestral village. However, apart from this ceremonial tie and a written genealogy, there appeared to be no other connection with the main line. In fact, the persistence of the tie over such a long period was surprising. In general, lacking corporate estates or other collective resources, the supra-village ties of the lineage did not survive for long (*CN*4 362–63).

3. Strauch 1983.

4. Sangren 1984.

5. Ebrey 1984: 221–22, 231–32.

6. Bourdieu (1977: 34) writes, for instance, "Marriage provides a good opportunity for observing what in practice separates official kinship, single and immutable, defined once and for all by the norms of genealogical protocol, from practical kinship. . . . It is practical kin who make marriages; it is official kin who celebrate them."

7. Ebrey 1984: 220–221, 223.

8. Shiga 1978: 111–12. For a far more exhaustive treatment of the subject, see Shiga 1967. Ebrey (1984) regards court decisions on inheritance as following a third orientation, a compromise, if you will, between the zong and jia orientations.

9. Wolf and Huang 1980: 58.   10. Wolf and Huang 1980: 62.

11. Cohen 1976: 62.   12. *CN*3 68.

13. *CN*3 67, 68, 71; *CN*5 464. In Sand Well, Shunyi county, even after the partition of the family, only one representative, from either the father's or the son's family, was required to attend village ceremonies (*CN*1 136).

14. *CN*6 87.   15. *CN*5 420.

16. *CN*5 473.   17. *CN*5 458.

18. *CN*5 454–55.   19. Hsu 1967: 116.

20. *CN*6 104, 117, 229, 239, 243, 256, 281, 300, 303.

21. *CN*6 104.

22. *CN*3 85; *CN*4 279, 481, 484; see also Amano 1936: 33.

23. *CN*6 87.

24. See esp. Wang Liu Hui-chen 1975. See also Baker 1979: 107–113, 161; and the suggestions of Watson (1982: 616) that there was more of a symbiotic relationship between the imperial state and lineages than anthropologists have recognized. Most recently, Faure (1986) has shown how the great lineages of the south developed their "classical" form in the past few centuries as a result of official connections, and how this form spread by imitation from richer villages to poorer ones. Unfortunately, this excellent monograph fell into my hands too late for me to consider its arguments in detail.

25. *CN*3 preface 6; *CN*6 61–62. Of course, as Potter (1970) has pointed out, the numerical domination of a village by a lineage does not necessarily mean that the lineage exercised a powerful influence. I use these figures as only one index of the strength of lineages and will back them up with qualitative information on the role of lineages.

26. *CN*3 preface 6, 103.

27. *CN*3 preface 6.

28. *CN*3 156. During Qingming and the Fathers and Sons Gathering, the western segment held its ceremony and banquet separately, while the rest performed their ceremony jointly (*CN*3 136). When the lineage paid its respects to the ancestors at the grave sites, it first paid respects to the common ancestors, and then the individual segments separated off to pay respects to the founder of their particular segment and his successors (*CN*3 91, 150).

29. *CN*3 113, 128.

30. *CN*3 28, 43, 75, 90, 156.

31. *CN*3 140–41.

32. *CN*3 134.

33. *CN*3 72, 76, 92, 95. The lineage head occupied a primary position in ceremonial matters, and this applied to weddings and funerals as well (*CN*3 94, 95). During the New Year celebrations, the entire lineage paid its respects to him (*CN*3 156). Finally, the lineage heads in North Brushwood often mediated disputes within the lineage and even between members of the same family (*CN*3 97, 112, 153, 154, 155, 301). One informant even claimed that in household matters the authority of the lineage head prevailed over that of the father (*CN*3 76). For further details, see Duara 1983.

34. *CN*3 111–12, 311–12.

35. *CN*3 164.

36. *CN*3 322.

37. See Kainō 1944: 105.

38. *CN*3 250, 253.

39. *CN*3 289.

40. *CN*3 97–98.

41. Lee 1970: 103.

42. See *CN*5 preface 5; and *CN*5 5.

43. *CN*5 149. These figures refer to land held only by these lineages and only within the village area. Another calculation raises the average per capita landholding in the village to 30 mou.

44. *CN*5 31.

45. *CN*5 109–10.

46. *CN*5 81, 83, 84.

47. *CN*5 56.

48. Sheridan 1975: 61–64.

49. *CN*5 70, 115.

50. Freedman 1966: 130–40.

51. *CN*5 44, 70, 88, 208. For his being summoned to court, see *CN*5 76.

52. *CN*5 72, 84, 168.

53. *CN*5 217, 218, 219.

54. *CN*5 257.

55. *CN*5 143.

56. *CN*4 preface 10.

57. *CN*4 410.

58. *CN*4 440.

59. *CN*4 444.

60. *CN*4 468, 471, 478.

61. *CN*4 482, 483, 502, 504.

62. Mizuno 1941: 17. Incidentally, Mizuno, who toured the North China plain extensively in the 1930s, believed that lineage consciousness was highly developed in most villages located away from cities.

63. *CN*4 72, 73, 74, 136.

64. *CN*4 74, 75, 82.

65. *CN*1 242, 257, 489, for Sand Well; *CN*5 469–70, 473, for Wu's Shop.

66. Incidentally, North Brushwood suggests an interesting reversal of the commonly held view that the strength of a lineage was a function of its wealth. In the lineages studied here—but especially in the case of the poorest lineage of the poorest village, the Haos of North Brushwood—villagers in need turned most often to their lineage mates for assistance. We could hypothesize that in some poor villages in North China, the lineage, which was not well endowed with collective resources, functioned less as an instrument of advancement and more as a protective organization—as a kind of a floor in a subsistence society. In this role, the strength of the lineage, in a small-scale unit like the village, would have had little to do with great amounts of property. In fact, the cohesiveness of the lineage, in a limited context, may have been a function of its poverty.

67. Wang Liu Hui-chen 1975; Faure 1986; and Ebrey 1984: 231–32, for the propagation of zong ideas in the Song and their incorporation into the "modern" lineage since this time. Certainly, some informants in North Brushwood, in particular, were quite clear about the official rules and practices regulating lineage behavior.

68. Wang Liu Hui-chen 1975: 28–29.

69. Kuhn 1979: 101–2.

70. Hsiao 1967: 28–33, 53–54.

71. Matsumoto 1977: 510.

72. *CN*6 244. In this village, the position of the village headman rotated every year among the four pai, and it was claimed that all the villagers voted for the pai member whose turn it was to become the village headman.

73. Katayama 1982: 27.

74. *CN*5 9, 18, 44.

75. *CN*5 18, 44.

76. Gamble 1963: 143–45.

77. *CN*3 54.

78. *CN*3 66.

79. *CN*3 302.

80. *CN*3 41.

81. *CN*5 9. See the appended residential map for this village in *CN*5.

82. *CN*5 9.

83. *CN*5 22, 23, 43, 304.

84. *CN*4 424–25.

85. Tian (1934), which describes the social structure of Dabeiyin in Anzu county, Hebei, as it was in 1934. M. Yang 1945; Crook and Crook 1959.

86. Johnston 1910: 157–58.

87. Ahern 1973: 250–63.

88. Yamagata 1941.

89. Not all villages began as single-lineage villages, as we saw from the case described by Gamble (1963). Depending on the relations among the lineages, the trajectory could begin at a point between phase one and two, or two and three. More interestingly, Tian Deyi (1934: 109) notes that the

Tian lineage in Dabeiyin, which was the oldest, most numerous, and most powerful lineage, was not the original settler. The pre-existing lineages had either died out or migrated out of the village by the twentieth century. What this suggests is that the trajectory might be arrested at any stage or develop into a cycle if a single lineage among roughly equal competing lineages—phase three—survived beyond the others and averted the destruction of the village.

90. *CN*4 424.

91. *CN*5 652.

92. *CN*5 654.

93. Crook and Crook 1959: 12.

94. *CN*4 409.

95. M. Yang 1945: 134–35.

96. M. Yang 1945: 175.

97. M. Yang 1945: 161–62.

98. *CN*5 38.

99. *CN*5 56–57.

100. *CN*5 57.

101. In Dabeiyin village in central Hebei, four major lineages, with genealogical knowledge, corporate property, and collective ceremonies, each dominated what had apparently been largely autonomous settlements. With the government reforms around the turn of the century, these settlements were consolidated into a single village under a village government that, nonetheless, recognized the principal divisions of the village based on kinship space. The four lineages had traditionally been rivals, especially the Tians and the Wangs, and expressed their rivalry in terms of opposing social identities. The Wangs had been numerically and economically less powerful than the Tians, but had always prided themselves on the classical educations of their members. With the appearance of missionaries in the village, the less-educated but dominant Tians took up Western-style education with a vengeance. This, in turn, had the effect of reinforcing the Wang's perception of themselves as upholders of tradition and patrons of traditional schools. (Incidentally, the rising competition over educational resources in the Republican villages testifies to the succesful communication of the new and "modern" values of the new elites.) The traditional rivalries also became reformulated as competition for political office between two coalitions centered around the dominant Tians and the Wangs. What we see here is the injection of new political resources leading initially to a crystallization of the rivalry along two coalitions. Lineage rivalry had reportedly become less pronounced by the 1930s. It is unclear whether this was a result of the expansion of public tasks necessitating cooperation, such as village defense, or a result of government-sponsored institutional changes that sought to diffuse leadership power among councillors from the different lineages (Tian 1934: 109–14).

102. *CN*4 404–5, 450.

103. *CN*5 13, 18.

104. *CN*3 43, 82.

105. *CN*3 43.

106. *CN*1 242.

107. *CN*5 27, 34.

108. *CN*5 46, 83.

Chapter 5

1. Litzinger 1983: 40.   2. *CN*1 193.
3. Gamble 1963: 163; *Zhaicheng cunzhi* 1925: 45; *CN*5 27, 351.
4. *CN*4 413–15.   5. *CN*3 355; Kuhn 1980: preface.
6. *CN*3 355; Sangren 1983.
7. The most detailed account of this type is found for a village located near Tianjin. According to informants, members of this sect were to be found throughout the county, as well as in the city of Tianjin. The village, called Shanggulin, was located in the seventh ward of the county in an administrative district called Xiaozhan. The village headman maintained that several villagers were members of the sect. The headquarters of the sect was located in Xiaozhan, which was also a large market town of almost 10,000 people. The leadership of the sect was located in a temple called Shengzhongmiao, or alternatively Songbaitang (Pine and Cedar Lodge). Believers from the surrounding twenty or so villages congregated at the temple on four days of the year to eat together and perform certain rituals on the occasions of the birthdays of the gods in the temple. Believers also visited the master of the sect (*dangjiade*) when they were unwell, and he would administer a treatment made of tea. Members paid according to their means when they entered the society, on the occasion of the banquets, and for the healing services (*CN*6 226–27). Another Zailijiao organization in Sand Well had similar connections to the marketing center (*CN*1 104, 194). The third example is the case of North Brushwood discussed in the following paragraph of the text.
8. Feuchtwang 1977: 590.   9. *CN*5 31, 33.
10. *CN*3 51.   11. *CN*1 225.
12. Litzinger 1983.
13. *CN*1 210, 214–16; *CN*3 152; *CN*4 103, 433–34; *CN*5 35, 132, 431–32. See also C. K. Yang 1967; and A. Wolf 1974. For the relationship of territorial cults to the state cult, see Feuchtwang 1977: esp. pp. 588–89.
14. *CN*1 90, 106, 143. In Sand Well, the tutelary deity went by the names Zangwang, Tudi, and Wudao.
15. *CN*1 130, 143, 145, 187.   16. *CN*1 130, 136.
17. *CN*1 136.   18. *CN*1 145.
19. *CN*1 131.
20. During times of drought, the village held a collective supplication to the rain god. During the prayer, the village head made the offerings at the head of a gathering of all the villagers—that is, one male representative from each member-household of the village. The procession carrying the rain god went around to every house in the village, and each household burned incense to the god. Subsequently, the procession visited neighboring villages that possessed an image of the rain god (*CN*1 104, 220).

21. *CN*1 130.

22. *CN*1 130–31.

23. *CN*4 17, 282, 390–91.

24. *CN*4 17, 30–31, 30–34, 60.

25. *CN*4 43.

26. *CN*5 407, 433. The association of temple activities with the notion of the public is particularly clear in this village:

Q. What is the *gong yihui* (public meeting)?

A. When the temple needs repairs, all the villagers get together and discuss the matter. They buy various things. Since these things are for public use, anybody can use them (*CN*5 414, 418).

27. *CN*5 407, 431, 440, 457.

28. *CN*5 34, 36, 297.

29. *CN*5 27, 34–35.

30. *CN*3 31, 55.

31. *CN*3 33, 65, 82.

32. *CN*3 56–57.

33. *CN*4 413, 478.

34. *CN*4 410, 413, 416. For Zhenwu, see C. K. Yang 1967: 152.

35. *CN*4 418.

36. *CN*4 417–18.

37. Gamble 1963: 301–3.

38. *CN*3 3.

39. *CN*3 3.

40. *CN*5 417. Gamble 1963: 301–3.

41. *CN*6 265.

42. *CN*6 256, 266.

43. Litzinger 1983: 20, 124–26, 179.

44. Litzinger 1983: 124.

45. Litzinger 1983: 216.

46. Gamble 1963: 152, 153, 203, 288–89.

47. See, e.g., C. K. Yang 1967: chaps. 10–11; Feutchwang 1977.

48. *Wangdu xianzhi* 1906: 6.85–91. This gazetteer is particularly useful because it also has a detailed study of the villages in the county. See the appended "Wangdu xian xiangtu shuozhi" (Gazetteer of villages and localities in Wangdu county).

49. A. Wolf 1974: introduction; Freedman 1979: 351–69.

50. C. K. Yang 1967: 276.

51. C. K. Yang 1967: 181–83.

52. We get a particularly elaborate picture of the supernatural bureaucracy presided over by the Jade Emperor from informants in Hou Lineage Camp; see *CN*5 297–98. For Taiwan, see A. Wolf 1974.

53. C. K. Yang 1967: 181.

54. C. K. Yang 1967: 182.

55. *CN*5 442. A villager described attitudes toward the rain god: "If it rains, we repaint the image of Longwang and keep it clean. If it does not rain, we let it be. When it does not rain, the villagers say he lacks divine powers [*bu ling*] and vent their anger on him."

56. Seaman 1978: 56.

57. Feuchtwang 1977: 598.

58. *CN*4 30–33, 60.   59. Feuchtwang 1977: 603.
60. Williams 1913: 11–45.   61. *CN*1 172.
62. "In previous times when we talked of the *hui*, it was only the shanhui" (*CN*1 175). Again, "there were no other functions in the village apart from the hui to burn incense. . . . The huishou was the huishou of the religious association. There was no council of village leaders" (*CN*1 187). The shanhui was interchangeable with the xiangtou.
63. *CN*1 187.   64. *CN*1 174.
65. *CN*1 171–72.   66. *CN*1 125, 174.
67. *CN*2 500–502.   68. *CN*5 418.
69. *CN*5 407.   70. *CN*4 31, 43, 56, 57, 390.
71. *CN*5 432.   72. *CN*5 15.
73. Smith 1899: 140.   74. *CN*1 213.
75. *CN*5 431.
76. Chen Shou 1973: 36.939–42; see also Werner 1932: 227–30; and *Sanguozhi tongsu yanyi* 1974: 6.1–4. For his role in popular literature, see Ruhlman: 1960.
77. Ruhlman 1960: 174; see also Inoue 1941.
78. Inoue 1941: pt. 1, 48.   79. Inoue 1941: pt. 2, 248, 250.
80. Huang Huajie 1968: 100, 122, 227–29.
81. Inoue 1941: pt. 1, 49.
82. Inoue 1941: pt. 2, 249, 253, 257.
83. *Qingshi* 1961: 85.1070.
84. *Daqing lichao shilu* 1937: 1725, no. 14, 31.3.
85. Lu 1769: fourth introduction, 1, 4.
86. Lu 1769: fourth introduction, 4.
87. *Daqing lichao shilu* 1937: 1725, no. 14, 31.3a.
88. Lu 1769: second introduction, 5–6.
89. Lu 1769: third introduction.
90. Lu 1769: second introduction.
91. *CN*4 390.
92. *CN*4 391.
93. *CN*4 391; see also *CN*1 192 for a very elegant literary depiction of Guandi. This plaque and numerous others in the *CN* volumes have both gentry and nongentry signatories; see, e.g., *CN*6 251–52.
94. *CN*5 377.
95. Huang Huajie 1968: 229.
96. *CN*3 55.
97. This is particularly apparent in the Fuanpai case discussed by Litzinger (1983).
98. *CN*1 90.
99. *CN*5 433.

100. Li Jinghan 1933: 432; see also *CN6* 84–85.

101. Watson 1985.

102. This last Republican attack on temples is very well documented for North China. See, e.g., *Shina no dōran* 1930: 80–83; *Mantetsu chōsa geppō* Feb. 1941: 251, 254–55, 306–7, 328; and Gamble 1968: 405–7.

103. *CN1* 172; *CN4* 56, 57; *CN5* 15, 34, 407–18.

104. Li Jinghan 1933: 422–23.

105. *Wangdu xian xiangtu tushuo* 1905. Unfortunately, however, the list is still incomplete because three pages, covering about fifteen villages at a rough estimate, are missing from the text.

106. *Shunyi xianzhi* 1933: 6.17, 19.

107. *Changli xianzhi* 1933: 4.38–39.

108. *Liangxiang xianzhi* 1924: 2.35; *CN5* 629.

109. *CN3* 414.   110. *CN4* 56, 264.

111. *CN4* 478.   112. *CN1* 93, 171.

113. Gamble 1963: 149, 155, 165, 181, 184.

114. *CN5* 46.

115. *Zhonghua minguo fagui daquan* 1936: 1166–67. For monks trying to sell temple lands, see *CN1* 195–98; *CN2* 491; *CN3* 414.

116. *CN5* 629.

117. *CN3* 414. In Shunyi county, an officer maintained that in the early years of the Republic many priests had sued village leaders over temple property (*CN2* 491).

118. *CN4* 286.

119. Gamble 1963: See Villages A and C, 149, 181–82, 184.

120. *CN1* 195–96, 199; *CN4* 195.   121. *CN1* 197, 198, 200.

122. *CN1* 202, 203.   123. *CN3* 414.

124. *CN1* 176.   125. Gamble 1963: 163–65.

126. *CN5* 352.

127. *Zhaicheng cunzhi* 1925: 45; for the biography, see *Zhaicheng fukan* 1925.

128. *Zhaicheng fukan* 1925: 18–19.

129. See esp. Kubō 1953, 1956.

130. C. K. Yang 1967: chap. 12.

Chapter 6

1. *CN1* 131, 175; *CN3* 44–45; *CN4* 20, 34, 405, 407, 409; *CN5* 9, 15. For their formal appointments, see *CN1* 175, 186–87; *CN3* 50, 414; *CN5* 9, 41, 407, 418.

2. *CN1* 104, 116, 121, 151–52; *CN3* 44–45; *CN4* 14, 18, 29, 329, 405, 412; *CN5* 10, 37, 301.

3. *CN*1 99–100, 123; *CN*3 30; *CN*4 6, 24; *CN*5 9.

4. *Zhonghua minguo fagui daquan* 1936: 641–45; see also Matsumoto 1977: 546–47; and Gamble 1963: 41. For the establishment of the xiang during Nationalist rule, see *Zhonghua minguo fagui daquan* 1936: 535, 618.

5. *CN*1 76; see also Myers 1970: 43. Myers (p. 44) has a Lorenz curve showing land distribution in Sand Well, Wu's Shop, North Brushwood, and Xia Walled Village. The data on Wu's Shop are not comparable with those for the others because they are based on the amount of land cultivated per family, whereas for the other villages, they are based on land owned. This was brought to my attention by Suetsugu Reiko. Moreover, the curve does not give a complete picture of distribution of wealth because it ignores the landless villagers.

6. *CN*1 174, 187.

7. *CN*1 76; *CN*2 72.

8. *CN*1 124–25.

9. *CN*1 124–25.

10. *CN*1 188.

11. *CN*1 138.

12. *CN*2 40, 195.

13. *CN*1 187, 189, 190; *CN*2 488.

14. *CN*1 107, 189–90; *CN*2 98.

15. *CN*2 92, 93, 193, 195.

16. *CN*5 preface 5.

17. *CN*5 14, 42, 149.

18. *CN*5 20.

19. *CN*5 37–38.

20. *CN*5 39.

21. *CN*5 5, 37, 39, 41, 50, 58, 131, 258.

22. *CN*5 5, 11, 14, 41, 42–43, 152, 258.

23. *CN*5 43, 56–58, 100.

24. *CN*5 18.

25. *CN*5 100.

26. *CN*5 47, 209.

27. *CN*5 48, 209.

28. *CN*4 preface 9; for another estimate, see Myers 1970: 338, *n*11.

29. *CN*4 8.

30. *CN*4 25, 27, 34. Li Xiangling was the councillor in question.

31. *CN*4 50.

32. *CN*4 20, 57.

33. *CN*4 6.

34. *CN*4 6, 24, 31.

35. *CN*4 25.

36. *CN*4 7, 8, 180, 207, 265.

37. *CN*3 preface 5; *Luancheng xianzhi* 1871: 2.23.

38. *CN*3 preface 5–7.

39. *CN*3 preface 5–6.

40. *CN*3 preface 5–6.

41. *CN*3 preface 6–7.

42. *CN*3 163–64, 173–74, 193, 215, 226.

43. *CN*3 preface 6; *CN*3 41, 50.

44. *CN*3 41, 56.

45. *CN*3 50, 59.

46. *CN*3 50, 51, 53, 56, 63, 170.

47. *CN*3 53, 250, 275, 278–79, 348.

48. *CN*3 164, 170, 171–72.

49. *CN*3 263, 269, 277, 281, 282, 300, 304, 353.

50. *CN*5 preface 6; *Liangxiang xianzhi* 1924: 3.6.
51. *CN*5 preface 6. The average family owned under ten mou of land.
52. *CN*5 preface 6, 7.
53. *CN*5 420 (quotation), 426, 427, 532.
54. *CN*5 420, 426, 430; for the wars, see Sheridan 1975: 60–64.
55. *CN*5 430.
56. *CN*5 430, 509, 553, 574.
57. *CN*5 preface 6; *CN*5 412, 431, 445, 520.
58. *CN*5 421, 422.   59. *CN*4 preface 10.
60. *CN*4 preface 10.   61. *CN*4 408.
62. *CN*4 404, 561.   63. *CN*4 404–5.
64. See, e.g., Gamble 1963: 51.
65. *CN*4 401. This particular combination of functions appears to be characteristic of Chinese village leadership in other areas as well. See, e.g., Strauch 1981: 164–65. Strauch emphasizes the role of external connections in shaping village leadership. This is especially important in the context of the multiethnic society of Malaysia that she studied. My own study suggests that even without this context, external connections were an extremely important factor. See also Hayes 1977: 128, 175–76. Incidentally, my study also bears out Hayes's principal thesis that community organizations at the village level were handled quite adequately by nongentry leaders.
66. The relevant villages are B, D, H, 1, K. Gamble 1963. My characterization of the leadership of these communities is not analytically dependent on what was happening to "community bonds," although the question of village dependence on absentee property holders was obviously important. In this way, my analysis is to be distinguished from that of Philip Huang (1985), who speaks of "community closure and solidarity" and "atomization." The two views are not necessarily incompatible since I am referring only to the leadership system and not to behavior of the community as such, but they do suggest different conclusions. Thus, in Huang's analysis, Xia Walled Village and Cold Water Ditch are communities responding to external threats by closing themselves off and falling back on their internal solidarity. But my analysis shows that Cold Water Ditch saw particularly dramatic changes in its leadership pattern and that by the late 1930s, Xia Walled Village had also begun to exhibit a high degree of leadership instability.
67. M. Yang 1945: 167.
68. See, e.g., Eisenstadt and Roniger 1980; see also Gellner and Waterbury 1977; and Schmidt et al. 1977.
69. See Gouldner 1977.
70. *CN*5 258, 260.

71. *CN*5 17, 24, 32, 39, 42, 58, 95, 206, 258. Kong Ziming owned 31 mou of land when he first served as assistant village headman, but at the time of the survey he possessed less than 20 mou (*CN*5 42).

72. *CN*1 124; *CN*2 32, 41, 44, 77, 107, 108, 260, 311.

73. *CN*1 124, 138, 139; *CN*2 238–39.

74. *CN*2 40, 194, 195.

75. *CN*3 13–14; *CN*5 435, 579–80.

76. *CN*4 220–21, 225–26, 262, 479, 506, 511.

77. See, e.g., *CN*3 275; *CN*4 221; *CN*5 578.

78. *CN*5 268.   79. *CN*2 107, 195.

80. *CN*2 20, 169, 211, 229–30.   81. *CN*3 275.

82. *CN*2 56; *CN*5 438.   83. *CN*2 143.

84. *CN*2 40, 44, 46.   85. *CN*3 179, 206.

86. *CN*4 154, 158, 463–64, 470–71; *CN*5 525.

87. *CN*5 206.

88. *CN*3 278–79.

89. *CN*5 204.

90. *CN*2 20; *CN*3 247, 249; *CN*4 26, 479, 502; *CN*5 436.

91. Myers and Chen 1976.

Chapter 7

1. E. Wolf 1957.   2. *CN*1 130–31, 173; *CN*4 34.

3. *CN*1 104; *CN*2 97.   4. *CN*1 142–43, 157; *CN*4 21.

5. *CN*4 424.

6. *CN*1 128; see also Gamble 1963: 201.

7. *Kitō chiku nōson chōsa hōkokusho* 1936: 1:81, 98–100, 115, 116, 129 (for Xiaoxinzhai); 1:137, 138 (for Huzhuang); 1:60, 78, 79 (for Xiaoyingcun); 1:242, 249 (for Lujiazhai).

8. *CN*4 307.

9. *CN*3 508.

10. Amano 1936: 40–41; see also Feng 1938d: 1117.

11. *CN*1 154, 204.

12. *CN*1 174.

13. *CN*3 42; *CN*4 35; Gamble 1963: 85–96, 163.

14. See Hatada 1976: 66–67, for an interesting analysis of this problem. Some of the problems discussed in this section were first clarified by Hatada (see esp. 53–166).

15. *CN*1 187.

16. *CN*5 preface 6.

17. Gamble 1963: 20–25.

18. Indeed, the association may have had no connection with the village government. Cold Water Ditch had precisely this kind of arrange-

ment. The crop watch collected his dues from those cultivating land within the green circle of Cold Water Ditch. But nonresident cultivators did not pay their tankuan dues to Cold Water Ditch. The crop guards of five other villages, all within a range of 2 li, maintained a system of transferring dues, and so, finally, the crop watch received his wages from all the cultivators of land residing in his village (*CN*4 35, 48, 337–38). In the only village in Shandong in Gamble's survey (1963: 294, 300), although the most important public function of the village was crop watching, the collection for crop protection had no connection with the financing of other village activities. A different form of assessment based on the land tax was utilized to assess tankuan rates. In another type of crop watching, the service was performed not for the village as a whole but for smaller groups of families. Thus, there was no need to create a village boundary or to interact with outsiders. There are three examples of this type in my sources, one from Shandong and two from Hebei (*CN*3 42; *CN*4 398; Gamble 1963: 279).

19. *CN*4 354–55.

20. *CN*4 48.

21. The relative absence of village-level crop-watching associations in southern and central Hebei may have had something to do with cotton, the principal crop grown there. The crop guard system was designed primarily to ward off petty thieves, usually the poor, who stole small quantities of grain for personal consumption. The guards could scarcely have taken on large-scale banditry or military attacks. The village self-defense system was available for this.

22. Gamble 1963: 234–35.

23. *CN*1 206–7.

24. *CN*3 515.

25. *CN*1 6, 206–7. It should be noted that corvée labor dues imposed on the village by higher authorities were not based on the crop-watching system. These dues were levied by the village on its residents, no matter where the land they owned was located. In some places at least, the irregular tax (baidi tankuan) was collected in a similar way. Over the Republican period, as these irregular taxes began to increase, the semiannual spring and fall collections through the crop-watching system became an inappropriate means of collection. Thus, they too, came to be levied on the residents of the village.

26. *CN*1 207.

27. *CN*1 181.

28. *CN*1 181.

29. *CN*1 128, 174, 185, 204; *CN*3 515.

30. *CN*6 380.   31. *CN*6 388.

32. *CN*6 382.   33. *CN*6 383.

34. *CN*6 383–86.
35. *CN*5 198, 512.
36. *CN*3 192, 236; *CN*4 187.
37. *CN*3 512–13.
38. *CN*5 55.
39. *CN*6 387.
40. Kuhn 1979: 104.
41. *CN*1 225, 240, 340; *CN*5 416, 418, 654.
42. Fei 1976: 61–62; M. Yang 1945: 78–79.
43. Households with no adult male member could not participate in public affairs. Their public relations were managed by the closest male relative from the husband's family (*CN*3 73).
44. Fei 1976: 22–23.
45. *CN*1 214; *CN*4 19, 400–401; *CN*5 412, 449; *CN*6 87.
46. *CN*1 214.
47. *CN*1 130–32, 173; *CN*4 21.
48. Scott 1976.
49. Popkin 1979.
50. Hatada 1976: 10–15.
51. In the prewar period, the most important efforts to apply the kyōdōtai idea to modern China were made by Hirano Yoshitarō (1944), Shimizu Morimitsu (1941), and Imahori Seiji (1978). Its most vociferous opponent was the legal scholar Kainō Michitaka (1944). In the postwar period, the most articulate critic of the idea has been Uchiyama Masao (1977, 1984), but recently the kyōdōtai argument has been restated by Furushima Kazuo (1982), who applies it more generally to the marketing area as a whole, and by Ishida Hiroshi (1982), who has developed the notion of *seikatsu kyōdōtai*.
52. P. Huang 1985: 249–74.
53. Hatada 1976: 57–174.
54. Hatada 1976: 153, 154.
55. *CN*1 214; *CN*5 422.
56. *CN*1 214.
57. *CN*1 214–15, 219, 259.
58. *CN*1, 31, 136.
59. *CN*1 214–15.
60. *CN*4 22, 23.
61. *CN*4 23.
62. *CN*3 46; *CN*4 355, 401–5.
63. *CN*3 39, 56.
64. *CN*3 35, 46. Faure (1986) has firmly established the importance of membership in lineages with settlement rights as a precondition for claiming superior rights in villages in the New Territories.
65. Hatada 1976: 153–54.
66. *CN*3 5.
67. *CN*3 193, 207, 225–26.
68. *CN*4 4.
69. P. Huang 1985: 260–63, 264–69, 270–74.
70. See *CN*4 418 for Xia Walled Village; and *CN*4 34 for Cold Water Ditch.
71. *CN*4 48.
72. See *CN*2 513, 527–36; Gamble 1963: 169; and Feng 1933.
73. *CN*6 87.
74. Feng 1933; see also Feng 1938d: 1113–19; and the discussion of Hou Lineage Camp in Chapter 4.
75. Yamagata 1941: 26.

Chapter 8

1. See, e.g., Lary 1985: esp. 42–48, 74–78. In a small number of villages, the traditional elite leadership was ousted from power through the system of elections instituted by the Nationalists in 1929. Included in Gamble's survey (1963: 165–66) was a large village of 307 families located near Beijing in Wanping county. The front street of the village was occupied by relatively poor families and the back street by wealthy families, who also controlled the political organization of the village. Relations between the residents of the two streets had long been hostile. In Chapter 5, I mentioned a religious event sponsored by the poor residents of the front street that dramatized the conflict between the two groups. After annual elections were instituted in 1929, the residents of the front street were able to get their candidates on the village council. Spurred by their political success, the residents of the front street demanded a separate school for their children and control over the portion of village income collected from themselves. The village seemed well on its way to dividing into two units.

Village H in Gamble's study was a large village of 375 families located in eastern Hebei. Until 1929, six influential village families controlled the village government. In 1922, some of the other village families joined together in an effort to force this group to broaden its base. They were unable to achieve much and resorted to setting up what was in effect an alternative government in the village and attempting to collect taxes for local expenses. In a counterattack, the village authorities and the county government ordered the abolition of the alternative government. In 1928, in the initial flush of the Nationalist takeover, the "cry of people's rights was heard everywhere," and the opposition group was able to exert enough pressure to force the councillors to accept six new representatives for a while. However, in the elections of 1929, the previous village leaders, who were very influential, were able to manipulate the elections and retain their posts (Gamble 1963: 229–31).

Generally speaking, elections were not the means whereby the bases of leadership power were transformed. In some places, as in Zhaicheng village in Ding county, Hebei, elections were expected to undermine the control of village government by wealthy and influential families. But even in this model village, the administration of the village remained in the hands of the same group (Gamble 1968: 150). I suspect that in most villages elections were immaterial to political life, at least through the 1930s. More often than not, village conditions were such that the older village leaders gave up this control voluntarily. Or, as in Wu's Shop and especially as in North Brushwood, the general impoverishment of the village left no powerful and wealthy figures who could control village government.

2. Duara 1987.
3. Gamble 1944.
4. See Konuma 1966: 29. For other views on the subject, see Duara 1987; Amano 1936; Eastman 1975: 181–244; Gamble 1968: 166–84. See also the comments in *Hebeisheng gexian* 1934; and the collection of articles in *Dizheng yuekan* (Journal of land economics) 4, no. 2/3 (Jan. 1936) which is a special issue on taxation, particularly in the early 1930s; see esp. the articles by Wan Guoding, Zhuang Jianghua, and Weng Zhiyong.

5. *CN*4 6.
6. *CN*3 55, 63.
7. *CN*5 421.
8. *CN*3 59.
9. *CN*4 6.
10. *CN*4 407.
11. *CN*4 407; *CN*5 18.
12. *CN*5 420, 430.
13. *CN*2 345; *CN*3 47.
14. Gamble 1963: 199.
15. *CN*3 512–13.
16. *CN*3 48.

17. *CN*3 48. Of course, opposition to excessive tankuan levies was not confined to North China. Tanaka Tadao (1955: 379, 427) gathered over 100 major cases of popular movements protesting excessive taxation in the three years relatively free from warlord battles, 1932–34, from contemporary newspapers throughout China. For example, in February 1934, over 2,000 villagers in Xingtai county in southern Hebei, staged a violent demonstration in the county capital to protest excessive taxation. In August 1932, over 700 villagers near Beijing demanded the abolition of heavy taxes called *gongyijuan* levied through the crop-watching association. They demonstrated in front of the Nationalist party office in Beijing and finally arrived at a compromise whereby these taxes were to be reduced and a part of the money was to be returned to the villages. Moreover, any change in the land held by the village was to be reported to the government, and the rate would be adjusted accordingly.

18. *CN*3 369. See also Amano 1936: 15–19.
19. *CN*3 161; *CN*5 200, 660; *Kahoku chiken seido* 1935: 158–59.
20. Feng 1933; *CN*2 513, 527–36; *CN*5 362; Gamble 1963: 169.
21. *CN*2 378, 427.
22. *CN*4 369.
23. *CN*4 6; see also Hatada 1976: 249.
24. *CN*5 354–55.
25. *Zhonghua minguo fagui daquan* 1933: 1:644.
26. *CN*5 52, 610.
27. *CN*5 515–16.
28. *CN*5 48, 50–51, 273.
29. *CN*5 52.
30. Wan 1936: 160. For the mixed results of the previous important land survey—conducted in the 1580s—see R. Huang 1974: esp. 300–301, 329–30.
31. Li Ling 1938; see also Amano 1936: 30–33; Konuma 1966: 21.
32. Wan 1936: 133; Li Ling 1938; Amano 1936: 33; *CN*3 367.

33. *CN*4 403.

34. It was said that when a new official was appointed, he was dependent on the registration clerk for all his "settling-in" expenses (*CN*6 23; see also Konuma 1966: 28).

35. Konuma 1966: 23.

36. *CN*5 333, 362, 400, 403; *CN*6 28.

37. *CN*3 387, 404; *CN*4 210, 538.

38. *CN*4 210, 274; *CN*6 23; Gamble 1963: 127; Ishida Bunjirō 1944: 39, 79; Konuma 1966: 25.

39. *CN*3 404; *CN*4 288, 393.

40. *CN*6 23.

41. Zhuang 1936: 304–5; see also *CN*2 518; and *CN*6 1–3.

42. *Zhili quansheng caizheng shuomingshu* 1915: section on land tax, p ?3; *CN*6 1–3; see also Myers 1970: 218.

43. Wan 1936: 161; see also Weng 1936: 318. For the Liangxiang and Changli cases, see Li Ling 1938; Konuma 1966: 33; *CN*5 622–23; and *CN*6 23.

44. Li Ling 1938.   45. Wan 1936: 161.

46. *CN*2 442.   47. *CN*5 57, 362.

48. See, e.g., "Hebeisheng Huoluxian" 1941: 170.

49. *CN*4 290, 294; *CN*6 23.   50. Wan 1936: 162.

51. Wan 1936: 161–62.   52. Feng 1933.

53. *CN*5 353, 362.   54. *CN*3 417.

55. *CN*6 1. The Chinese Communists used the concealed land issue as a major campaign strategy with powerful effects in North China, even after the War of Resistance; see Pepper 1978: 261, 269, 270.

56. Feng (1938c: 1067, 1073) reports that although provincial income from the tax on commercial middlemen (yashui) in the 19th century was around 5,000 taels (approximately 3,600 yuan), by 1931 this had leaped to 3 million yuan.

57. *CN*5 605.

58. Mann 1979: 72; Feng 1938c: 1067–68; *Zhili quansheng caizheng shuomingshu* 1915: section on likin, p. 10.

59. Feng 1938c: 1070–71, 1073.

60. The exceptional success of the Hebei tax-farming system is discussed in Chapter 3. In Shandong, the yashui continued to remain a tax on the licenses of commercial middlemen until the 1930s, when they were transformed into excise taxes collected by the state. Licenses on which taxes were to be paid were granted to commercial middlemen for a period of five years. Shandong did not adopt the system of revenue farming for the yashui, although it did so for other commercial taxes, such as the farm-animal tax, the butcher tax, and taxes on alcohol and tobacco (Konuma 1951: 233).

61. *CN2* 397; *CN3* 399–400; *CN4* 274.

62. Wang Zhixin 1938: 1060, 1062; see also Amano 1936: 47–48; Konuma 1951: 228; and *CN4* 516. In one county the revenue farmer for the farm-animal and butcher taxes paid 1,200 yuan alone in tips at the county yamen (Wang Zhixin 1938: 1063); see also Konuma 1951: 228; and *CN3* 457–58.

63. Weber 1978: 965–66.

64. *CN5* 328–29, 341; Weng Zhixin 1938: 1060.

65. *CN4* 339; Konuma 1951: 222; Wang Zhixin 1938: 1061.

66. *CN3* 458; *CN5* 342.   67. *CN2* 304; *CN5* 632.

68. *CN6* 370.   69. *CN2* 306–7, 418.

70. *CN3* 387; *CN4* 328, 329.   71. Mann 1979: 83–84.

72. Feng 1938c: 1078–79.   73. Wang Zhixin 1938: 1063–64.

74. Lincoln Li 1975: 133, 166–67; quotation from p. 146.

75. *CN3* 309; *CN4* 15, 505–6; *CN5* 269, 419.

76. *CN4* 15, 227–29, 343.

77. *CN6* 14.

78. *CN3* 488; *CN5* 569; *CN6* 14.

79. Konuma 1951: 235; *CN2* 504; *CN5* 382, 593, 598.

80. *CN2* 303; *CN5* 328–29, 336, 337; Konuma 1951: 235.

81. *CN3* 458; *CN5* 336, 384.

82. *CN5* 593; *CN6* 14.

Conclusion

1. Naquin 1985: 289–90.

2. Perry 1980: esp. 254–55.

3. Skinner 1971.

4. See, e.g., *NFWH* 1933.6: 36; 1934.3: 6–8; and 1934.12: 163.

5. Feng 1938a: 1105, 1106.

6. Bianco 1975: 315; Tanaka 1955: 379, 427.

7. Smith 1899: 158–69. Although Smith initially says that the bully is usually poor, he goes on to describe bullies from all sectors of society.

8. Gu 1933: 7; Liang 1971: 198.

9. Pepper 1978: 262.

10. Pepper 1978: 268–69; Baba 1984: 45–48. It may be objected that I cannot assign such a revolution-causing role to the tax burden since I have not estimated the share of the total take of provincial income by these extractive agencies. It may well be that its absolute size was not very great, although I suspect that at certain times and in certain places it was quite substantial. For our purposes, the important thing is not the absolute size or even the burden per se, but rather how the burden was perceived. And here what is more important is the demonstrable increase in the burden, its

role in creating an atmosphere of unpredictability, and its subversion of the authority of local leadership—all of which made it an eminent issue for mobilization.

11. Skocpol 1979: 27–29.

12. C. Johnson 1962.

13. Baba 1984: 45–50; Shue 1980: 17–18, 23, 30, 37–39.

14. Cf. the remarkably similar course of state expansion in Zaire; see Callaghy 1984.

15. Tilly 1975: see esp. the introduction and chap. 8.

16. Wallerstein 1974: 29–30, 138–39.

Postscript

1. It is difficult to quote a definition of habitus from Bourdieu that would be immediately comprehensible without the illustrative materials in his books. As I understand it, habitus refers to an intermediary level of reality regulating everyday practices. It accounts for the gap between, on the one hand, the objective structures and the behavior they may be expected to produce and, on the other hand, the actual behavior of human agents (Bourdieu 1977: 78).

As for Gramsci's concept of "cultural hegemony," its very richness makes it impossible to give a short definition. The most often quoted, but still one-dimensional, characterization of it is: "the 'spontaneous' consent given by the great masses of the population to the general direction imposed on social life by the dominant fundamental group." Its superiority over the notion of "false consciousness," which also seeks to explain why historical groups do not always behave in accordance with their class or other particular interests, lies in its ability to show how subordinate groups develop their own autonomous substrategies within the culture and ultimately shape the cultural hegemony. See Gramsci 1971: 12. Recently, Lears (1985) has done an excellent job of elucidating and developing the concept of "cultural hegemony."

2. Scott 1976; Popkin 1979.

3. *CN3* 513, Document 38.

Bibliography

Ahern, Emily. 1973. *The Cult of the Dead in a Chinese Village*. Stanford, Calif.

Allee, Mark A. 1985. "The Seal of Legitimacy: County Government and Local Leaders in 19th-Century Taiwan." Unpublished paper, University of Pennsylvania.

Amano Motonosuke. 1936. "Kaen zatsuzeika no Kahoku nōson" (Hebei villages under extortionate levies and miscellaneous taxes). *Mantetsu chōsa geppō*, 16, no. 4/5.

———. 1942. *Shina nōgyō keizairon* (Chinese agricultural economy), vol. 2. Tokyo.

Baba Takeshi. 1984. "Santō kōnichi konkyochi ni okeru zaisei mondai" (Problems in financial administration in the Shandong anti-Japanese base areas). *Shikan*, no. 110.

Baker, Hugh D. R. 1979. *Chinese Family and Kinship*. New York.

Bergesen, Albert, ed. 1980. *Studies of the Modern World-System*. London.

Bianco, Lucien. 1975. "Peasants and Revolution." *Journal of Peasant Studies* 3, no. 2.

Bourdieu, Pierre. 1977. *Outline of a Theory of Practice*. Cambridge, Eng.

Braun, Rudolf. 1975. "Taxation, Sociopolitical Structure and State Building: Great Britain and Brandenburg-Prussia." In Charles Tilly, ed., *The Formation of National States in Western Europe*. Princeton, N.J.

Brim, John A. 1974. "Village Alliance Temples in Hongkong." In Arthur Wolf, ed., *Religion and Ritual in Chinese Society*. Stanford, Calif.

Callaghy, Thomas M. 1984. *The State-Society Struggle: Zaire in Comparative Perspective*. New York.

Chang, C. M. 1934. "Local Government Expenditure in China." *Monthly Bulletin of Economic China* 7, no. 6.

Changli xianzhi (Changli county gazetteer, Hebei). 1933.

Chen Juren. 1934. "Dingxian tianfu xianzhuang" (The present condition of the land tax in Ding County). *Minjian yuekan* 1, no. 4.

Chen Shou. 1973. *Sanguozhi* (History of the Three Kingdoms). Beijing.

Ch'en Yung-fa. 1979. "Wartime Bandits and Their Local Rivals: Bandits and Secret Societies." In Susan Mann Jones, ed., *Select Papers from the Center for Far Eastern Studies*, no. 3. University of Chicago.

Ch'u T'ung-tsu. 1969. *Local Government in China Under the Ch'ing*. Stanford, Calif.

Chūgoku nōson kankō chōsa (Investigation of customs in Chinese villages). 1981. 6 vols. Tokyo.

Cohen, Myron. 1976. *House United, House Divided: The Chinese Family in Taiwan*. New York.

Cressey, George B. 1934. *China's Geographical Foundations*. New York.

Crook, David, and Isabel Crook. 1959. *Revolution in a Chinese Village: Ten Mile Inn*. London.

Daqing lichao shilu (Veritable records of successive reigns of the Qing dynasty). 1937. Mukden.

Daqing luli chengxiu tongcuan zhicheng (Collection of the basic and supplementary laws of the Qing dynasty). 1908. Shanghai.

Dennerline, Jerry. 1975. "Fiscal Reform and Local Control: The Gentry Bureaucratic Alliance Survives the Conquest." In Frederic Wakeman, Jr., and Carolyn Grant, eds., *Conflict and Control in Late Imperial China*. Berkeley, Calif.

Ding Da. 1931. *Chūgoku nōson keizai no hōkai* (The disintegration of the Chinese rural economy). Trans. from the Chinese. Dalien.

Duara, Prasenjit. 1983. "Power in Rural Society: North China Villages, 1900–1940." Ph.D. diss., Harvard University.

———. 1987. "State-Involution: A Study of Local Finances in North China, 1911–1935." *Comparative Studies in Society and History* 29, no. 1.

Eastman, Lloyd. 1975. *The Abortive Revolution: China Under Nationalist Rule, 1927–1937*. Cambridge, Mass.

Ebrey, Patricia. 1984. "Conceptions of the Family in the Sung Dynasty." *Journal of Asian Studies* 43, no. 2.

Eisenstadt, S. N., and Louis Roniger. 1980. "Patron-Client Relations as a Model of Structuring Social Exchange." *Comparative Studies in Society and History* 22, no. 1.

Eliassen, Sigurd. 1955. *Dragon Wang's River*. London.

En xianzhi (En county gazetteer, Shandong). 1909.

Fang Xianding, ed. 1938. *Zhongguo jingji yanjiu* (Researches on the Chinese economy). Changsha.

Farmer, Edward L. 1976. *Early Ming Government: The Evolution of Dual Capitals*. Cambridge, Mass.

Faure, David. 1986. *The Structure of Chinese Rural Society: Lineage and Village in the Eastern New Territories, Hong Kong.* Hongkong.

Fei Hsiao-t'ung. 1976. *Peasant Life in China: A Field Study of Country Life in the Yangtze Valley.* New York.

Feng Huade. 1933. "Lu Jo jianwen zaji" (Desultory notes from travels in Jo county). *Dagongbao* (Tianjin), May 24.

———. 1934. "Local Government Expenses in Hopei." *Monthly Bulletin on Economic China* 7, no. 12.

———. 1935. "Xiandifang xinzheng zhi caizheng jichu" (The financial basis of local administration in the county). *Zhengzhi jingji xuebao.* 3, no. 5.

———. 1938a. "Hebeisheng Gaoyangxian de xiangcun caizheng" (Village finances in Gaoyang county, Hebei). In Fang Xianding, ed., *Zhongguo jingji yanjiu.* Changsha. (Written in 1932.)

———. 1938b. "Hebeisheng xiancaizheng zhi chuzhi fenxi" (An analysis of county expenditures in Hebei province). In Fang Xianding, ed., *Zhongguo jingji yanjiu.* Changsha. (Written in 1934.)

———. 1938c. "Hebeisheng yashui xingzhi zhi yanbian" (The evolution of the character of the tax on commercial middlemen in Hebei). In Fang Xianding, ed., *Zhongguo jingji yanjiu.* Changsha.

———. 1938d. "Nongmin tianfu fudan de yige shilie" (An example of the land tax burden of rural people). In Fang Xianding, ed., *Zhongguo jingji yanjiu.* Changsha.

———. 1938e. "Wuguo xianshouru zhidu zhi tezheng" (Special features of the system of county revenues in our country). In Fang Xianding, ed., *Zhongguo jingji yanjiu.* Changsha. (Written in 1935.)

Feng Huade and Li Ling. 1936. "Hebeisheng Dingxianzhi tianfu" (The land tax of Ding county). *Zhengzhi jingji xuebao* 4, no. 3.

Feutchwang, Stephan. 1977. "School Temple and City God." In G. William Skinner, ed., *The City in Late Imperial China.* Stanford, Calif.

Foucault, Michel. 1979a. *Discipline and Punish: The Birth of the Prison.* New York.

———. 1979b. *The History of Sexuality,* vol. 1, *An Introduction.* London.

Freedman, Maurice. 1966. *Chinese Lineage and Society: Fukien and Kwangtung.* London.

———. 1979. *The Study of Chinese Society.* Stanford, Calif.

Furushima Kazuo. 1982. *Chūgoku kindai shakaishi kenkyū* (Researches in modern Chinese social history). Tokyo.

Gallin, Bernard. 1966. *Hsin Hsing, Taiwan: A Chinese Village in Change.* Berkeley, Calif.

Gamble, Sidney D. 1944. "Hsin Chuang: A Study of Chinese Village Finance." *Harvard Journal of Asiatic Studies* 8, no. 1.

————. 1963. *North China Villages: Social, Political and Economic Activities Before 1933*. Berkeley, Calif.

————. 1968. *Ting Hsien: A North China Rural Community*. Stanford, Calif.

Geertz, Clifford. 1963. *Agricultural Involution: The Process of Ecological Change in Indonesia*. Berkeley, Calif.

Geissert, Bradley Kent. 1979. "Power and Society: The Kuomintang and Local Elites in Kiangsu Province, China, 1924–1937." Ph.D. diss., University of Virginia.

Gellner, Ernest., and J. Waterbury, eds. 1977. *Patrons and Clients in Mediterranean Societies*. London.

Gouldner, Alvin. 1977. "The Norm of Reciprocity: A Preliminary Statement." In S. W. Schmidt et al., eds., *Friends, Followers and Factions*. Berkeley, Calif.

Gramsci, Antonio. 1971. *Selections from the Prison Notebooks*. Ed. and trans. Quentin Hoare and Geoffrey Nowell Smith. New York.

Grootaers, Willem A. 1951. "Rural Temples Around Hsuan-hua (South Chahar): Their Iconography and Their History." *Folklore Studies* 10, no. 1.

Grove, Linda. 1975. "Rural Society in Revolution: The Gaoyang District, 1910–1947." Ph.D diss., University of California, Berkeley.

Gu Meng. 1933. "Benggui guozhengzhong zhi Hebei nongcun" (Hebei villages in disintegration). *Zhongguo jingji* 1, no. 4/5.

Hartford, Kathleen J. 1980. "Step by Step: Reform, Resistance and Revolution in Chin-ch'a-chi Border Region, 1937–1945." Ph.D diss., Stanford University.

Hatada Takashi. 1976. *Chūgoku sonraku to kyōdōtai riron* (Chinese villages and the theory of the village community). Tokyo.

Hayes, James. 1977. *The Hongkong Region, 1850–1911*. Kent, Eng.

Hebeisheng gexian gaikuang yijian (Yearbook of conditions in the counties of Hebei province). 1934. N.p.

"Hebeisheng Huoluxian tianfu jisuan shuomingshu" (An explanation of the calculation of the land tax in Huolu county in Hebei province). 1941. *Mantetsu chōsa geppō* 21, no. 3.

Hirano Yoshitarō. 1944. "Kai, kaishū, sonchō" (Village council, councillors, and the village headman). *Shina kankō chōsa tankō*, nos. 1–2. Tokyo.

Ho Ping-ti. 1959. *Studies in the Population of China, 1368–1953*. Cambridge, Mass.

Hokushi no nōgyō keizai (The agricultural economy of North China). 1939. Tokyo.

Hokushi shijō zōkan (A broad look at conditions in North China). 1936. Comp. Nan Manshu Tetsudō Kabushiki Gaisha. Dalien.

Hsiao Kung-ch'uan. 1967. *Rural China: Imperial Control in the Nineteenth Century*. Seattle.

Hsu, Francis L. K. 1967. *Under the Ancestor's Shadow: Kinship, Personality and Social Mobility in Village China.* New York.

Huang Huajie. 1968. *Guangong de renge yu shenge* (The human and divine characteristics of Lord Guan). Taibei.

Huang, Philip C. C. 1982. "County Archives and Study of Local Social History." *Modern China* 8, no. 1.

———. 1985. *The Peasant Economy and Social Change in North China.* Stanford, Calif.

Huang, Ray. 1974. *Taxation and Governmental Finance in Sixteenth Century Ming China.* Cambridge, Eng.

Imahori Seiji. 1963. "Shindai no suiri dantai to seiji kenryoku" (Water-control communities and political power in the Qing). *Ajia kenkyū* 10, no. 3.

———. 1978. *Chūgoku hōken shakai no kōsei* (The structure of Chinese feudal society). Tokyo.

"Index Numbers of Commodity Prices at Wholesale in North China Classified by Industries (1926 = 100)." 1937. *Nankai Social and Economic Quarterly* 9, no. 4.

Inoue Ichii. 1941. "Kan'u shibyō no yurai narabi ni hensen" (Origins and development of Guan Yu temples). *Shirin* 26, nos. 1–2.

Ishida Bunjirō. 1944. *Tochi kōzō kōka* (Land taxes). Tokyo.

Ishida Hiroshi. 1977. "Kahoku ni okeru suiri kyōdōtai ni tsuite" (Concerning cooperation in water control in North China). *Ajia keizai* 18, no. 12.

———. 1979. "Kahoku ni okeru suiri kyōdōtai ronsō no seiri" (A summing up of debates on community control of water in North China). *Nōringyō mondai kenkyū,* no. 54.

———. 1980. "Kyū Chūgoku nōson ni okeru shijōkan tsūkon kan" (Marketing spheres and marriage spheres in old China). *Shirin* 63, no. 5.

———. 1982. "Kaihōzen no Kahoku nōson shakai no ichiseikaku: Tokuni sonraku to byō no kanren ni oite" (A characteristic of pre-Liberation North Chinese village society: Especially regarding the relations between village and temple). *Kansai Daigaku* [*keizai ronshū*] 32, nos. 2–3.

Ishihara Jun. 1973. "Kahokushō ni okeru Min Shin Minkoku jidai no deikishi" (Periodic markets in Hebei province during the Ming, Qing, and Republican periods). *Chirigaku hyōron* 46, no. 4.

Johnson, Chalmers A. 1962. *Peasant Nationalism and Communist Power: The Emergence of Revolutionary China, 1937–1945.* Stanford, Calif.

Johnson, David, A. Nathan, and E. Rawski, eds. 1985. *Popular Culture in Late Imperial China.* Berkeley, Calif.

Johnston, R. F. 1910. *Lion and Dragon in Northern China.* New York.

Kahoku chiken seido no kenkyū (Researches on the land contract system of North China). 1935. Dalien.

Kainō Michitaka. 1944. *Hokushi nōson ni okeru kankō gaisetsu* (Outline of customs and practices in the villages of North China). Tokyo.

Katayama Tsuyoshi. 1982. "Shindai Kantonshō Shukō deruta no zukōsei ni tsuite: Zeiryō, koseki, duzoku" (The *tujia* system in the Pearl River Delta of Guangdong in the Qing: Land tax, household registers, and lineages). *Tōyō gakuhō* 63, nos. 3–4.

Kitō chiku nōson chōsa hōkokusho (Report of the investigation of villages in the eastern Hebei region). 1936. Vol. 1. Tianjin.

Konuma Tadashi. 1951. "Kahoku nōson shishū no "gakō" ni tsuite; Tokuni chōzei kikō to shite" (Concerning the "yahang" in North Chinese rural markets: Particularly as a tax-collecting structure). In *Tōyōshi ronsō: Wada Hakushi kanreki kinen*. Tokyo.

————. 1966. "Kahoku nōson ni okeru dempu chōshū kikō ni tsuite no ikkōsatsu" (An examination of tax-collecting organizations in North Chinese villages). In *Gendai Ajia no kakumei to hō*. Tokyo.

Kubō Noritada. 1953. "Ikkandō ni tsuite" (Regarding the *Yi Guandao*). *Tōyō Bunka Kenkyūjo kiyō*, no. 4.

————. 1956. "Ikkandō fukō: 'Yi Guandao shi shenma dongxi' no kaishaku" (An introduction to the supplement on the *Yi Guandao*: "What is the *Yi Guandao*?"). *Tōyō Bunka Kenkyūjo kiyō*, no. 11 (1956).

Kuhn, Philip A. 1975. "Local Self-government Under the Republic: Problems of Control, Autonomy, and Mobilization." In Frederic Wakeman, Jr., and Carolyn Grant, eds., *Conflict and Control in Late Imperial China*. Berkeley, Calif.

————. 1979. "Local Taxation and Finance in Republican China." In Susan Mann Jones, ed., *Select Papers from the Center for Far Eastern Studies*, no. 3. Chicago.

————. 1980. *Rebellion and Its Enemies in Late Imperial China: Militarization and Social Structure, 1796–1864*. Cambridge, Mass.

Kuhn, Philip A., and Susan Mann Jones. 1979. "Introduction." In Susan Mann Jones, ed., *Select Papers from the Center for Far Eastern Studies*, no. 3. Chicago.

Lary, Diana. 1985. *Warlord Soldiers: Chinese Common Soldiers, 1911–1937*. Cambridge, Eng.

Lears, Jackson T. J. 1985. "The Concept of Cultural Hegemony: Problems and Possibilities." *American Historical Review* 90, no. 3.

Lee, Robert H. G. 1970. *The Manchurian Frontier in Ch'ing History*. Cambridge, Mass.

Lévi-Strauss, Claude. 1963. *Structural Anthropology*. New York.

Li Chuan-shih. 1922. *Central and Local Finance in China*. New York.

Li Jinghan. 1933. *Dingxian shehui gaikuang diaocha* (Investigation of social conditions in Ding county, Hebei). Beijing.

Li, Lincoln. 1975. *The Japanese Army in North China, 1937–1941*. Oxford.

Li Ling. 1938. "Hebeisheng Qinghaixian zhi tianfu ji chi zhengshou zhidu" (The land tax and its system of collection in Qinghai county, Hebei). In Fang Xianding, ed., *Zhongguo jingji yanjiu*. Changsha. (Reprinted from *Dagongbao* [Tianjin], Mar. 27, 1935.)

Li Zonghuang. 1954. *Zhongguo difang zizhi zonglun* (A general discussion of local self-government in China). Taibei.

Liang Shuming. 1971. "Gangao jinzhiyan difang zizhizhe" (Warning to people who talk of self-government today). In *Zhongguo minzu ziqiu yundong zhi zuihou juewu* (The final awakening of the Chinese people's movement of self-salvation). Taibei.

Liangxiang xianzhi (Liangxiang county gazetteer, Hebei). 1924.

Licheng xianzhi (Licheng county gazetteer, Hebei). 1926.

Litzinger, Charles A. 1983. "Temple Community and Village Cultural Integration in North China: Evidence from "Sectarian Cases" (Chiao-an) in Chihli, 1860–1895." Ph.D diss., University of California, Davis.

Lu Zhan, ed. 1769. *Guanshengdijun shengji tuzhi quanji* (A complete collection of writings and illustrations concerning the holy deeds of the saintly sovereign Guan).

Lü Shiqiang. 1972. *Ding Richang yu ziqiang yundong* (Ding Richang and China's self-strengthening). Taibei.

Luancheng xianzhi (Luancheng county gazetteer, Hebei). 1871.

MacKinnon, Stephen R. 1980. *Power and Politics in Late Imperial China*. Berkeley, Calif.

Maeda Shōtarō. 1966. "Kahoku nōson ni okeru suiri kikō" (The organization of water control in North China). In *Gendai Ajia no kakumei to hō*. Tokyo.

Mancheng xianzhi (Mancheng county gazetteer, Hebei). 1757.

Mann [Jones], Susan. 1979. "The Organization of Trade at the County Level: Brokerage and Tax Farming in the Republican Period." In idem, ed., *Select Papers from the Center for Far Eastern Studies*, no. 3. Chicago.

———. 1987. *Local Merchants and the Chinese Bureaucracy, 1750–1900*. Stanford, Calif.

Matsumoto, Yoshimi. 1977. *Chūgoku sonraku seido no shiteki kenkyū* (Historical research on the Chinese village system). Tokyo.

Meyer, John W. 1980. "The World Polity and the Authority of the Nation State." In Albert Bergesen, ed., *Studies of the Modern World-System*. London.

Mizuno Kaoru. 1941. *Hokushi no nōson* (North China villages). Beijing.

Morita Akira, comp. 1967. "Minsho ni okeru Kananshō Koshiken no suiri kikō" (The structure of water control in Gushi county, Honan, in the Republic). In *Chūgoku suirishi kenkyū*, vol 3.

Murphey, Rhoads. 1982. "Natural Resources and Factor Endowments."

In Randolph Barker and Radha Sinha with Beth Rose, eds., *The Chinese Agricultural Economy*. London.

Myers, Ramon. 1970. *The Chinese Peasant Economy: Agricultural Development in Hopei and Shantung, 1840–1940*. Cambridge, Mass.

Myers, Ramon H., and Fu-mei Chang Chen. 1976. "Customary Law and Economic Growth in China During the Ch'ing Period." *Ch'ing-shih Wen-t'i* 3. no. 5.

Nakamura Jihei. 1951. "Kahoku nōson no sonhi: Gendai Chūgoku no chihō zaisei no kenkyū" (Village expenditure in North China: Research on local financial administration in contemporary China). In Niida Noboru, ed., *Kindai Chūgoku no shakai to keizai* (The society and economy of modern China). Tokyo.

Naquin, Susan. 1985. "Transmission of White Lotus Sectarianism." In David Johnson, A. Nathan, and E. Rawski, eds. *Popular Culture in Late Imperial China*. Berkeley, Calif.

Nongcun Fuxing Weiyanhui huibao. (Reports of the Committee to Revive the Villages). 1934–35. Ed. Administrative Yuan, Nongcun Fuxing Wei-yuanhui. Nanjing.

Ocko, Jonathan K. 1983. *Bureaucratic Reform in Provincial China: Ting Jih-ch'ang in Restoration Kiangsu, 1867–1870*. Cambridge, Mass.

Peng Yuxin. 1945. *Xian difang caizheng* (Local finances at the county). Zhongjing.

Pepper, Suzanne. 1978. *Civil War in China: The Political Struggle, 1945–1949*. Berkeley, Calif.

Perry, Elizabeth J. 1980. *Rebels and Revolutionaries in North China, 1845–1945*. Stanford, Calif.

Popkin, Samuel L. 1979. *The Rational Peasant: The Political Economy of Rural Society in Vietnam*. Berkeley, Calif.

Potter, Jack. 1970. "Land and Lineage in Traditional China." In Maurice Freedman, ed., *Family and Kinship in Chinese Society*. Stanford, Calif.

Qingchao xu wenxian tongkao (Classified collection of official Qing documents, supplement). 1935. Shanghai.

Qingmo shoubei lixian dang'an shiliao (Archival cases and historical materials on preparations for the establishment of the constitution in the late Qing). 1979. 2 vols. Beijing.

Qingshi (History of the Qing dynasty). 1961. Taipei.

Rankin, Mary B. 1986. *Elite Activism and Political Transformation in China: Zhejiang Province, 1865–1911*. Stanford, Calif.

Rawski, Evelyn S. 1986. "The Ma Landlords of Yang-chia-kou in Late Ch'ing and Republican China." In Patricia B. Ebrey and James Watson, eds., *Kinship Organization in Late Imperial China*. Berkeley, Calif.

Ren xianzhi (Ren county gazetteer, Hebei). 1915.

Rowe, William T. 1983. "Hu Lin-i's Reform of the Grain Tribute System in Hupeh, 1855–1858." *Ch'ing-shih Wen-t'i* 4, no. 10.

Ruhlman, Robert. 1960. "Traditional Heroes in Chinese Popular Fiction." In Arthur F. Wright, ed., *The Confucian Persuasion*. Stanford, Calif.

Saeki Tomi. 1964. "Shindai no kyōyaku jihō ni tsuite: Shindai chihō seikō no shaku" (Concerning the *xiangyue* and the *dibao* in the Qing dynasty: An aspect of the local administration of the Qing dynasty) *Dōhōgaku*, no. 28.

Sangren, P. Steven. 1983. "Female Gender in Chinese Religious Symbols: Kuan Yin, Ma-tsu, and the Eternal Mother." *Signs: A Journal of Women in Culture and Society*, 9, no. 1.

———. 1984. "Traditional Chinese Corporations: Beyond Kinship." *Journal of Asian Studies* 43, no. 3.

Sanguozhi tongsu yanyi (The popular romance of the Three Kingdoms). 1974. Shanghai.

Schmidt, S. W., L. Guasti, C. H. Lande, and J. C. Scott, eds. 1977. *Friends, Followers and Factions*. Berkeley, Calif.

Scott, James C. 1976. *The Moral Economy of the Peasant: Rebellion and Subsistence in Southeast Asia*. New Haven, Conn.

Seaman, Gary. 1978. *Temple Organization in a Chinese Village*. Asian Folklore and Social Life Monographs, vol. 101. Taibei.

Shenbao nianjian (Shenbao yearbook). 1935. Shanghai. (Reprinted: Taibei, 1966.)

Sheridan, James E. 1975. *China in Disintegration: The Republican Era in Chinese History*. New York.

Shiga Shūzō. 1967. *Chūgoku kazokuhō no genri* (The principles of Chinese family law). Tokyo.

———. 1978. "Family Property and the Law of Inheritance in Traditional China." In D. C. Buxbaum, ed., *Chinese Family Law and Social Change in Historical and Comparative Perspective*. Seattle.

Shimizu Morimitsu. 1941. *Shina shakai no kenkyū* (Studies of Chinese society). Tokyo.

Shina no dōran to Santō nōmin (Chinese rebellions and Shandong peasants). 1930. Dalien.

Shinjō Morimitsu. 1941. "Hōtō no sosaiengei nōgyō ni okeru kangai: Hōtō Tōkason jittai chōsa hōkoku" (Irrigation in vegetable farming in Baotou: Report of an investigation of conditions in Baotou's Donghe village). *Mantetsu chōsa geppō* 21, no. 10.

Shue, Vivienne. 1980. *Peasant China in Transition: The Dynamics of Development Toward Socialism, 1949–1956*. Berkeley, Calif.

Shunyi xianzhi (Shunyi county gazetteer, Hebei). 1933.

Sih, Paul T. K., ed. 1970. *The Strenuous Decade: China's Nation-Building Efforts, 1927–1937*. New York.

Silver and Prices in China. 1935. Comp. Committee for the Study of Silver Values and Commodity Prices, Ministry of Industries. Shanghai.

Skinner, G. William. 1964–65. "Marketing and Social Structure in Rural China." *Journal of Asian Studies* 24, nos. 1–2.

———. 1971. "Chinese Peasants and the Closed Community: An Open and Shut Case." *Comparative Studies in Society and History*, 13, no. 3.

———, ed. 1977. *The City in Late Imperial China*. Stanford, Calif.

Skocpol, Theda. 1979. *States and Social Revolution: A Comparative Analysis of France, Russia and China.* Cambridge, Eng.

Smith, Arthur H. 1899. *Village Life in China.* New York. (Reprinted: 1970.)

Strauch, Judith V. 1981. *Chinese Village Politics in the Malaysian State.* Cambridge, Mass.

———. 1983. "Community and Kinship in Southeastern China: The View of the Multilineage Villages of Hongkong." *Journal of Asian Studies* 43, no. 1.

Sun Shaocun. 1936. "Difang caizheng duiyu nongcun jingji de yinxiang" (The influence of local financial administration on village economics). *Zhongguo nongcun* 2, no. 9.

Sun Zuoji. 1935. *Zhongguo tianfu wenti* (Problems of land taxes in China). Shanghai.

Sweeten, Alan Richard. 1976. "The Ti-pao's Role in Local Government as Seen in the Fukien Christian Case, 1863–1869." *Ch'ing-shih Wen-t'i*, 3, no. 6.

Tambiah, Stanley Jeyaraja. 1985. *Culture, Thought and Social Action: An Anthropological Perspective.* Cambridge, Mass.

Tanaka Tadao. 1955. *Kindai Shina nōson no hōkai to nōmin tōsō* (The disintegration of the village and peasant struggles in modern China). Tokyo.

Thomas, George M., and John W. Meyer. 1980. "Regime Change and State Power in an Intensifying World-State-System." In Albert Bergesen, ed., *Studies of the Modern World-System.* London.

Thompson, Roger Roy. 1985. "Visions of the Future, Realities of the Day: Local Administrative Reform, Electoral Politics, and Traditional Chinese Society on the Eve of the 1911 Revolution." Ph.D. diss., Yale University.

Tian Deyi. 1934. "Yige nongcun zuzhi zhi yanjiu: Jiazu ji cunzhi" (Research on the organizations of a village: Family and village politics). *Shehui xuejie*, no. 8.

Tilly, Charles, ed. 1975. *The Formation of National States in Western Europe.* Princeton, N.J.

Tongji yuebao (Monthly statistical report). 1932. Comp. Statistical Office of the National Government. Nanjing, Jan., Feb.

Turner, Victor. 1974. *Dramas, Fields and Metaphors.* Ithaca, N.Y.

Uchiyama Masao. 1977. "Kahoku nōson shakai kenkyū no seika to kadai"

(Themes and results of research into the village society of North China). *Shundai shigaku*, no. 40.

————. 1984. "Kindai Chūgoku ni okeru 'kyōdōtai,' sono kō to kei" ("Kyōdōtai" in modern China: Highlights and Shadows). *Kanazawa Daigaku keizai ronshū*, no. 21.

Wada Sei. 1975. *Shina chihō jichi hatatsu shi* (History of the development of local autonomy in China). Tokyo.

Wakeman, Frederic. 1975. *The Fall of Imperial China*. New York.

Wallerstein, Immanuel. 1974. *The Modern World System*. New York.

Wan Guoding. 1936. "Zhongguo tianfu niaokan ji chi gaige qiantu" (A bird's-eye view of Chinese land tax and the future of its reform). *Dizheng yuekan* 4, no. 2/3.

Wang Liu Hui-chen. 1975. "An Analysis of Clan Rules: Confucian Theories in Action." In Arthur F. Wright, ed., *Confucianism and Chinese Civilization*. Stanford, Calif.

Wang Songxin. 1975–76. "Babaojun yu Taiwan zhongbu de kaifa" (Babao Canal and the development of central Taiwan). *Taiwan wenxian* 26, no. 4; 27, no. 1.

Wang Yeh-chien. 1973. *Land Taxation in Imperial China, 1750–1911*. Cambridge, Mass.

Wang Zhixin. 1938. "Hebeisheng zhi baoshui zhidu" (The tax-farming system in Hebei province). In Fang Xianding, ed., *Zhongguo jingji yanjiu*. Changsha.

Wangdu xian xiangtu tushuo (Gazetteer of villages and localities in Wangdu county, Hebei). 1905.

Wangdu xianzhi (Gazetteer of Wangdu county, Hebei). 1906.

Watson, James. 1982. "Chinese Kinship Reconsidered: Anthropological Perspectives on Historical Research." *China Quarterly*, no. 92.

————. 1985. "Standardizing the Gods: The Promotion of T'ien Hou ("Empress of Heaven") Along The South China Coast, 960–1960." In David Johnson, A. Nathan, and E. Rawski, eds., *Popular Culture in Late Imperial China*. Berkeley, Calif.

Watt, John R. 1972. *The District Magistrate in Late Imperial China*. New York.

————. 1977. "The Yamen and Urban Administration." In G. William Skinner, ed., *The City in Late Imperial China*. Stanford, Calif.

Weber, Max. 1968. *The Religion of China*. Trans. and ed. Hans H. Gerth. New York.

————. 1978. *Economy and Society*. Vol. 2. Berkeley, Calif.

Weng Zhiyong. 1936. "Tianfu zhengli wenti" (Problems in land tax reforms). *Dizheng yuekan* 4, no. 2/3.

————. 1952. *Minguo caizheng jianlun* (A discussion of Republican finances). Taibei.

Werner, E.T.C. 1932. *Dictionary of Chinese Mythology*. Shanghai.

Williams, E. T. 1913. "The State Religion of China During the Manchu Dynasty." *Journal of North China Branch, Royal Asiatic Society* 44.

Wolf, Arthur P. 1974. "Gods, Ghosts, and Ancestors." In idem, ed., *Religion and Ritual in Chinese Society*. Stanford, Calif.

Wolf, Arthur, and Huang Chieh-shan. 1980. *Marriage and Adoption in China, 1845–1945*. Stanford, Calif.

Wolf, Eric R. 1957. "Closed Corporate Peasant Communities in Mesoamerica and Central Java." *Southwestern Journal of Anthropology* 13, no. 1.

Wou, Odoric Y. K. 1974. "The District Magistrate Profession in the Early Republican Period: Occupational Recruitment, Training and Mobility." *Modern Asian Studies* 8, no. 2.

Wright, Arthur F., ed. 1975. *Confucianism and Chinese Civilization*. Stanford, Calif.

Wright, Mary C., ed. 1968. *China in Revolution: The First Phase, 1900–1913*. New Haven, Conn.

Xiao Fan. 1935. "Hejian Nanbei Wotoucun ji Suning Shaozhuangcun chupei jiufen" (A dispute over embankment construction between Nanbei Wotou Villages in Hejian county and Shaozhuang Village in Suning county). *Hebei yuekan* 2, no. 1.

Xingtai xianzhi (Xingtai county gazetteer, Hebei). 1905.

Xingtang xianzhi (Xingtang county gazetteer, Hebei). 1772.

Xu Delin. 1937. *Difang zizhi zhi lilun yu shishi* (The theory and practice of local self-government). Shanghai.

Xu Zhengxue. 1936. *Nongcun wenti: Zhongguo nongcun benggui yuanyin de yanjiu* (Village problems: Research into the causes of the collapse of the Chinese village). Nanjing.

Yamagata Kanki. 1941. *Kahoku ni okeru gensonshu buraku (shizenmura) no hassei* (The origins of various rural settlements [the natural village]). Guoli Beijing Daxue Nongcun Jingji Yanjiusuo (Agricultural Economy Research Bureau of National Beijing University) Research Materials, no. 5. Beijing.

Yamamoto Bin. 1975. *Chūgoku no minkan denshō* (Folk legends of China). Tokyo.

Yang, C. K. 1967. *Religion in Chinese Society*. Berkeley, Calif.

Yang, Martin. 1945. *A Chinese Village: Taitou, Shantung Province*. New York.

Yeh, K. C. 1979. "China's National Income, 1931–1936." In Chi-ming Hou and Tzong-shian Yu, eds., *Modern Chinese Economic History*. Taibei.

Yoshida Kōichi. 1975. "Nijū seiki Chūgoku no ichimensaku nōson ni okeru nōminzō bunkai ni tsuite" (Class differentiation among the peasantry in a twentieth-century cotton-growing village in China). *Tōyōshi kenkyū* 33, no. 4.

Young, Arthur. 1970. "China's Fiscal Transformation, 1927–1937." In Paul T. K. Sih, ed., *The Strenuous Decade: China's Nation-Building Efforts, 1927–1937*. New York.

Zelin, Madeleine. 1985. *The Magistrate's Tael: Rationalizing Fiscal Administration in Eighteenth Century Ch'ing China*. Berkeley, Calif.

Zhaicheng cunzhi (Gazetteer of Zhaicheng village [Ding county, Hebei]). 1925.

Zhaicheng fukan (Appendix to Zhaicheng gazetteer). 1925.

Zhang Sen. 1936. "Tianfu yu difang caizheng" (Land taxes and local finances). *Dizheng yuekan* 4, no. 2/3.

Zhang Yifan. 1935a. "Hebeisheng difang caizheng zhi jiantao" (An investigation of local finances in Hebei province). *Fuxing yuekan* 4, no. 4.

———. 1935b. "Shandongsheng difang caizheng zhi jiantao" (An investigation of local finances in Shandong province). *Fuxing yuekan* 4, no. 4.

Zhang Yufa. 1982. *Zhongguo xiandaihua de quyu yanjiu: Shandongsheng, 1860–1916* (Regional research on China's modernization: Shandong province, 1860–1916). Vols. 1–2. Taibei.

Zhili quansheng caizheng shuomingshu (Explanation of financial administration in Zhili province). 1915. Beijing.

Zhonghua minguo fagui daquan (Complete edition of the laws and regulations of the Chinese Republic). 1936. Vol. 1. Shanghai.

Zhuang Jianghua. 1936. "Yinianlai gesheng dianfu zhi xingge" (Reforms in land taxation in every province in 1935). *Dizheng yuekan* 4, no. 2/3.

Glossary of Chinese Terms

baidi tankuan　白地攤款　provisional tankuan levies
baiqi　白契　unstamped deeds
ban　班　subcounty unit
bang　幫　merchants, brokers association
bao　堡，保　subcounty unit
baojia　保甲　decimal system of surveillance
baolan　包攬　tax engrossment by the gentry
baozheng　堡正　head of a bao
bencundi　本村地　green circle
bencunren　本村人　native of a village
bu ling　不靈　to lack divine powers
caoqi　草契　official forms for reporting land transactions
Changli xian　昌黎縣　Changli county
chaiyao　差徭　levy
cundajia gonggong　村大家公共　village collectivity
cungongsuo　村共所　village council offices
dangjiade　當家的　master of a sect
daxiang　大鄉　large township
dayi　大義　righteousness
di　帝　emperor
dibao　地保　subcounty unit
difang　地方　subcounty unit; the rural agent
dongshi　董事　village councillor
duan　段　neighborhood
eba　惡霸　local bully
En xian　恩縣　En county
erjie buqu yiming bugou　二介不取一名不苟　to be loyal and act appropriately to one's station

er zu shashen cheng ren 而卒殺身成仁 to die a martyr's death

fengshui 風水 geomancy

fenxiang 分香 division of incense

fuhu 附戶 supplementary households

fuzhu 浮住 floating residents

fuzihui 父子會 Gathering of Fathers and Sons

gang 綱 institutions of the empire

gangji 綱紀 proper principles

ganqing 感情 good feelings, good relations

gong 功 merit

gong'anfei 公按費 tax for local security forces

gonghui 公會 public association

gong yihui 公議會 public meeting

gongyi juan 公議捐 a tax

gongzheng 公正 village councillor

guanli neizhangfang 管理內賬房 accounts committee

guanzhongren 官中人 overseer of the deed tax

hanshihui 寒食會 Day of the Cold Feast

haoxian 耗羨 local tax surcharge for local projects

heidi 黑地 unregistered taxable land

hongqi 紅契 a contract with a deed stamp

Houjiaying 侯家營 Hou Lineage Camp

Houxiazhai 後夏寨 Xia Walled Village

hu 戶 taxpaying household

huangce 黃冊 yellow registers

hui 會 associations

huishou 會首 managers of religious associations; village council or village councillors

huitou 會頭 village councillors

huoquan 活圈 live sphere

jia 家 household

jia 甲 unit in the decimal system of surveillance

jianzhengren 監證人 official witness

jiaoyichang 交易場 a location at which commercial transactions were permitted

jiaoyou 交友 camaraderie

jiazhang 甲長 decimal headman

jie 潔 pure

jiju 寄居 temporary dwellers

jingji 經紀 licensed middleman

Jingjieju 經界局 Bureau of Land Investigation

jinshi 進士 the highest degree in the Qing examination system

jizhuanghu 寄莊戶 temporary dwellers
juanshui 捐稅 indirect taxes
kyōdōtai 共同體 the corporate village community (Japanese)
laohu 老戶 village residents
laoren 老人 elders
Lengshuigou 冷水溝 Cold Water Ditch
li 理 principle
li 里 subcounty unit
Liangxiang xian 良鄉縣 Liangxiang county
lianquan 連圈 linked circle
lianzhuanghui 聯莊會 linked-village militia organization
Licheng xian 歷城縣 Licheng county
lijia 里甲 the decimal system of surveillance for taxes and corvée
lijin 釐金 transit taxes
lin 鄰 5-household unit
ling 靈 divine powers
lishu 里書 tax clerk
lohu 落戶 outsider residents
lougui 陋規 customary fees
lu 路 subcounty unit
Luancheng xian 欒城縣 Luancheng county
lü 閭 25-household unit
lülin 閭鄰 system of 5- and 25-household units
lüzhang 閭長 head of a lü
maihui 埋會 Gathering at the Graves
men 門 a corporate agnatic unit
mingjie 名節 honor and integrity
moujuan 畝捐 same as tankuan
ni ye laile 你也來了 So you, too, have come
pai 牌 village subunit
qingquan 青圈 green circle
qu 區 subcounty unit
renqing 人情 close ties, fellow feelings
rexin gongyi 熱心公益 ardent in public service
seikatsu kyōdōtai 生活共同體 communitarianism in everyday life
　(Japanese)
Shajing cun 沙井村 Sand Well village
shanhui 善會 village temple council
shanhui 山會 mountain (religious) association
she 社 subcounty unit
shenzhahui 神柵會 Lantern Festival
shendao 神道 godly way

sheng biao 升表 to offer a petition

shengyuan 生員 a holder of the lowest-level degree in the Qing examination system

shen-min 紳民 gentry and people

sheshu 社書 tax clerk

shijia 十家 a 10-household unit

shiju 世居 village residents

shoujing daquan 守經達權 to protect principles and perfect the exercise of power

shoushiren 首事人 village councillor

shudi zhuyi 屬地主義 principle of village territoriality

Shunyi xian 順義縣 Shunyi county

shunzhuang 順莊 tax collection based on residence

Sibeichai cun 寺北柴村 North Brushwood

sidian 祀典 official sacrifices

siquan 死圈 dead sphere

tang 堂 corporate agnatic unit

tankuan 攤款 tax levies

tu 圖 subcounty unit

tuhao 土豪 local bully

tujia 圖甲 same as lijia

waicunren 外村人 outsiders

weigong 為公 public good

Wudian cun 吳店村 Wu's Shop Village

wulai 無賴 local bullies

xiang 鄉 subcounty unit; township

xiangbao 鄉保，鄉堡 subcounty unit; rural agent

xianggongsuo 鄉公所 office of the administrative village council

xianghuohui 香火會 incense associations, religious associations

xiangshou 香首 managers of religious associations

xiangtou 香頭 village temple councillors

xiangzhen 鄉鎮 system of townships and municipalities

xiaogu 小股 subsegments of lineages

xiaojia 小甲 managers of irrigation associations

xietu 協圖 cooperative *tu* (self-taxing *tu*)

Xinminhui 新民會 New People's Society

xinzheng 新政 late Qing political reforms

yahang 牙行 licensed middleman

yashui 牙稅 commercial taxes

yi 義 righteousness

yiji 義集 voluntarist markets

yin 陰 shadow

yitu 義圖 self-taxing *tu*

yuanzi 院子 courtyard
yulince 魚鱗册 fish-scale registers
yushui 餘水 surplus water
zha 閘 sluice gate; irrigation association
zhen 鎮 municipality
zhengshouyuan 征收員 tax collection officer
zhengshui 正水 main waters
zhuangtou 莊頭 manager of banner lands
zong 宗 patrilineal descent group
zongfang 總房 tax collection officer
zongzuhui 宗祖會 Gathering to Worship the Ancestors
zu 組 lineage segment
zu 租 rent
zushenye 祖神爺 founding spirit of an organization

Index

In this index an "f" after a number indicates a separate reference on the next page, and an "ff" indicates separate references on the next two pages. A continuous discussion over two or more pages is indicated by a span of page numbers, e.g., "pp. 57–58." *Passim* is used for a cluster of references in close but not consecutive sequence.

Library of Congress Cataloging-in-Publication Data

Duara, Prasenjit.
   Culture, power, and the state: rural North China, 1900–1942 /
Prasenjit Duara.
      p.   cm.
   Bibliography: p.
   Includes index.
   ISBN 0-8047-1445-2 (alk. paper) / ISBN 0-8047-1888-1 (pbk.)
   1. Rural development—China. North—History—20th century.
   2. Power (Social sciences)—China. North—History—20th century.
   3. Local government—China, North—History—20th century.
   4. China—Social conditions—1912–1949.   I. Title.
HN740.Z9C633 1988   87-18173
307. 7'2'09514—dc19   CIP